History
for the IB Diploma

The Arab–Israeli Conflict 1945–79

Jean Bottaro
Series editor: Allan Todd

Cambridge University Press's mission is to advance learning, knowledge and research worldwide.

Our IB Diploma resources aim to:
- encourage learners to explore concepts, ideas and topics that have local and global significance
- help students develop a positive attitude to learning in preparation for higher education
- assist students in approaching complex questions, applying critical-thinking skills and forming reasoned answers.

CAMBRIDGE
UNIVERSITY PRESS

CAMBRIDGE UNIVERSITY PRESS
Cambridge, New York, Melbourne, Madrid, Cape Town,
Singapore, São Paulo, Delhi, Mexico City

Cambridge University Press
The Edinburgh Building, Cambridge CB2 8RU, UK

www.cambridge.org
Information on this title: www.cambridge.org/9781107662056

First published 2012

Printed in the United Kingdom at the University Press, Cambridge

A catalogue record for this publication is available from the British Library

ISBN 978-1-107-66205-6 Paperback

Cambridge University Press has no responsibility for the persistence or
accuracy of URLs for external or third-party internet websites referred to in
this publication, and does not guarantee that any content on such websites is,
or will remain, accurate or appropriate.

This material has been developed independently by the publisher and the
content is in no way connected with nor endorsed by the International
Baccalaureate Organization.

Contents

1 Introduction

This book is designed to prepare students taking the Paper 1 topic *The Arab–Israeli Conflict 1945–79* (Prescribed Subject 2) in the IB History examination. It will examine the political, economic and social issues behind the conflict, as well as the specific causes and consequences of the wars between Israel and the Arab states between 1948 and 1973. It will also examine the role of outside powers in the conflict, either as promoters of conflict or as mediators in attempts to lessen tensions in the region. In addition, it will show how political, social and economic developments in the disputed territory of Israel/Palestine affected the populations living there. The study ends with the signing of a peace agreement between Israel and Egypt in 1979, which effectively brought the Arab–Israeli conflict to an end, but did not resolve the ongoing conflict between Israel and the Palestinian people.

An Israeli soldier arrests a Palestinian demonstrator in Hebron, a Palestinian-majority city in the Israeli-occupied West Bank, in 1997

Themes

To help you prepare for your IB History exams, this book will cover the main themes and aspects relating to *The Arab–Israeli Conflict* as set out in the IB *History Guide*. It will focus on the following areas:

- the last years of the British mandate; the United Nations Partition Plan; the outbreak of civil war in Palestine
- the British withdrawal; the establishment of Israel; the Arab response and the 1948–49 War
- demographic shifts: the Palestinian diaspora from 1947 onwards; Jewish immigration; the economic development of the Israeli state
- the Suez Crisis of 1956: the roles of Britain, France, the USA, the USSR, Israel and the UN
- Arabism, Zionism and Palestinian nationalism (including the emergence of the Palestine Liberation Organisation)
- the 1967 War (Six Day War) and the 1973 War (Yom Kippur War or October War): the causes, events and consequences
- the roles of the USA, the USSR and the UN in the conflict
- the Camp David Accords and the Egyptian–Israeli Peace Agreement

Each chapter will help you to understand the development of the Arab–Israeli conflict between 1945 and 1979. You will study the political developments, and the impact that they had on social and economic conditions for the people living in the region. You will also focus on the roles of individual leaders, as well as the effect of the policies and actions of outside powers.

Theory of knowledge

In addition to the broad key themes, the chapters contain Theory of knowledge (ToK) links to get you thinking about aspects that relate to history, which is a Group 3 subject in the IB Diploma. *The Arab–Israeli Conflict* topic has several clear links to ideas about knowledge and history. At times, the highly political issues that it covers have influenced the historians writing about these states, the leaders involved, and the policies and actions taken. Thus, questions relating to the selection of sources, and to interpretations of them by historians, are extremely relevant to the IB Theory of knowledge course.

For example, when trying to explain aspects of the policies implemented by leaders, their motives, and their success or failure, historians must decide which evidence to select and use to make their case – and which evidence to leave out. But to what extent do the historians' personal political views influence their decisions when selecting what they consider to be the most important or relevant sources? Or when they make judgements about the value and limitations of specific sources or sets of sources? Is there such a thing as objective 'historical truth'? Or is there just a range of subjective historical opinions and interpretations about the past, which vary according to the political interests and leanings of individual historians?

You are therefore encouraged to read a range of books giving different interpretations of the events covered in this book, in order to gain a clear understanding of the relevant historiographies. It is important to be aware that there are conflicting views on the topic, and that the historiography of the Arab–Israeli conflict is hotly debated by historians.

IB History and Paper 1 questions

Paper 1 and sources

Unlike Papers 2 and 3, which require you to write essays using only your own knowledge, Paper 1 questions are source-based. Whether you are taking Standard or Higher Level, the sources and the questions, and the markschemes applied by your examiners, are the same.

To answer these questions successfully, you need to be able to combine your own knowledge with the ability to assess and *use* a range of sources in a variety of ways. Each Paper 1 examination question is based on five sources – usually four written and one visual. The visual source might be a photograph, a cartoon, a poster, a map, a painting or a table of statistics.

Captions and attributions

Before looking at the types of sources you will need to assess, it is important to establish one principle from the beginning. This is the issue of *captions and attributions* – the pieces of information about each source that are provided by the Chief Examiner. They are there for very good reasons, as they give you vital information about the source. For instance, they tell you who wrote it and when, or what it was intended to do. Chief Examiners spend a lot of time deciding what information to give you about each source, because they know it will help you give a full answer, so they expect you to make good use of it! Yet, every year, candidates throw away easy marks because they do not read – or do not use – this valuable information.

Essentially, you are being asked to approach the various sources in the same way as a historian. This means not just looking carefully at what a source says or shows, but also asking yourself questions about how reliable, useful and/or typical it might be. Many of the answers to these questions will come from the information provided in the captions and attributions.

Types of source

Most of the sources you will have to assess are written ones, and these are sometimes referred to as 'textual' sources. These might be extracts from books, official documents, speeches, newspapers, diaries or letters. Whatever type of source you are reading, the general questions you need to ask about it are the same. These questions concern its content (the information the source provides), its origin (who wrote or produced the source, when and why), and its possible limitations and value as a result of the answers to those questions. For example, is a recent history book *more* valuable than a speech for finding out about a particular event or period?

Although visual (or non-textual) sources are clearly different from written sources in some respects, the same questions and considerations are relevant when looking at them.

Approaching sources as a set

As well as developing the ability to analyse individual sources, it is important to look at the five sources provided *as a set*. This means looking at them *all* and asking yourself to what extent they agree or disagree with each other.

This ability to look at the five sources together is particularly important when it comes to the last question in the exam paper. This is the question where you need to use the sources *and* your own knowledge to assess the validity of a statement or assertion, or to analyse the significance of a particular factor. Here you need to build an answer (a 'mini-essay') that combines precise knowledge with specific comments about the sources. Try to avoid dealing with all the sources first, and then giving some own knowledge (as an afterthought) that is not linked to the sources.

Exam skills

If all this sounds a bit daunting, don't worry! Throughout the main chapters of this book, there are activities and questions to help you develop the understanding and the exam skills necessary for success. Before attempting the specific exam practice questions at the end of each main chapter, you might find it useful to refer *first* to Chapter 10, the final exam practice chapter. This suggestion is based on the idea that if you know where you are supposed to be going (in this instance, gaining a good grade), and how to get there, you stand a better chance of reaching your destination!

Questions and markschemes

To ensure that you develop the necessary understanding and skills, each chapter contains questions in the margins. In addition, Chapter 10 is devoted to exam practice – it provides help and advice for all Paper 1 questions and for Paper 2 essay questions, and sets out worked examples for Paper 1 judgement questions and for Paper 2 essays. Worked examples for the remaining three Paper 1-type questions (comprehension, value/limitations and cross-referencing) can be found at the end of Chapters 2 to 8.

Simplified markschemes have been provided to make it easier for you to understand what examiners are looking for in your answers. The actual IB History markschemes can be found on the IB website.

Finally, you will find activities, along with examiners' tips and comments, to help you focus on the important aspects of the questions. These examples will also help you to avoid simple mistakes and oversights that, every year, result in some otherwise good students failing to gain the highest marks.

Background to the Arab–Israeli conflict

The Arab–Israeli conflict refers to the situation that developed between Israelis and Arabs in the Middle East from 1948. Although the warfare between Israel and the Arab states ended in 1979, the conflict between Israel and the Palestinian Arabs continues.

The Middle East

To understand the Arab–Israeli conflict, you need to see it in the context of the Middle East. The Middle East is often shown in the news as an area of instability and violence. The Arab–Israeli conflict, one of the longest and most bitter struggles of the 20th century, is the cause of much – but certainly not all – of this tension. There is a strong link between current events in the Middle East and the history that you will read about in this book. A knowledge of the Arab–Israeli conflict will help you to understand the complexities of the issues in the modern Middle East.

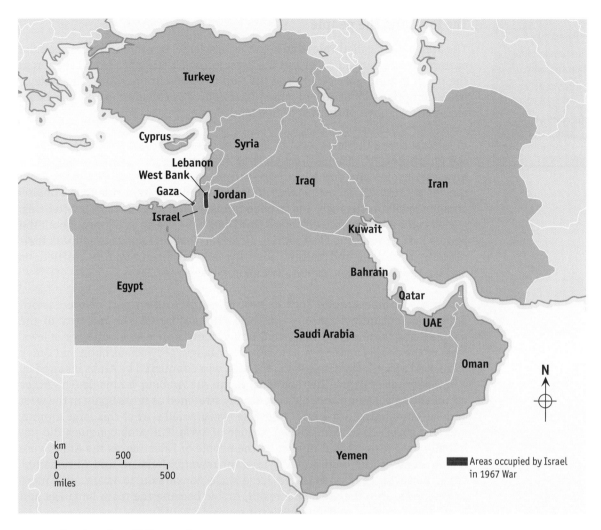

A *map showing the Middle East in 2012*

The Middle East has been an area of considerable importance in history. It lies at the meeting point of three continents (Europe, Asia and Africa), and as a result has been at the crossroads of trade and contact for thousands of years. It was the site of two of the world's earliest civilisations – in the Nile valley in Egypt, and between the Tigris and Euphrates rivers in Mesopotamia (modern Iraq). It is also the source of three of the world's major religions – Judaism, Christianity and Islam – and the city of Jerusalem has significance for all three of these faiths. Most of the people in the Middle East are Muslim, but there are also significant Jewish and Christian minorities. The strategic position of the Middle East has drawn outside interests into the area – European colonial powers before 1945, and then the rival superpowers of the USA and the USSR during the Cold War. The existence of vast oil deposits has had, and continues to have, a significant influence on the politics of the region.

The essence of the conflict

The Arab–Israeli conflict is essentially a struggle between the Palestinian Arabs and the Israelis over a small area of land in the Middle East. The two groups disagree over which of them has the right to live in and control this area. This conflict has its roots in the rise of two forces of nationalism, one Arab and the other Jewish, in the late 19th and early 20th centuries.

Fact
Jerusalem has shrines that are sacred to Islam, Judaism and Christianity. The Dome of the Rock is a Muslim shrine built over a sacred stone, which is believed to be the place from which the Prophet Muhammed ascended to heaven. Also in Jerusalem is the Al-Aqsa Mosque, the third holiest site in Islam after Mecca and Medina. The Wailing Wall is the only surviving part of the Jewish temple destroyed by the Romans in 70 CE, and is an important Jewish religious site. The Church of the Holy Sepulchre was built on the site of Christ's crucifixion, and is a place of pilgrimage for Christians.

Palestine The name 'Palestine' comes from Philistia, the Greek name for the land of the Philistines, who lived in the area in the 12th century BCE. The Romans revived the name in the 2nd century CE, calling it Syria-Paleastina. The Arab name for the area is Filastin.

The land and the people

The area of land called **Palestine** by some, and Israel by others, lies between the eastern Mediterranean coast and the River Jordan. It stretches from Lebanon in the north to the Negev desert and the Gulf of Aqaba in the south. The state of Israel comprises about 80% of what historically was called Palestine, and Israel also controls much of the rest of this land.

In biblical times the Jews lived in Palestine, along with other peoples such as the Philistines. At various times in their history, the Jews were conquered by invading armies and some of the Jewish people were forced into exile. From the 1st century CE, Palestine was effectively under Roman rule. The Romans crushed Jewish resistance, and expelled most of the Jews in 135 CE. After this, Jewish communities were dispersed (the Diaspora – see page 17) throughout the Middle East, Europe and North Africa. However, they managed to maintain their religious traditions and cultural identity, despite discriminatory restrictions and hostile persecution, especially in Europe (see page 23).

When the Roman Empire split in two, Palestine formed part of the eastern Roman (or Byzantine) Empire. Until the 7th century CE, the majority of the people living there were Christian, although there were a small number of Jews. Most of the people spoke Aramaic, but other languages such as Latin and Greek were used as well. Then, in 636 CE, the area was conquered by Arabs inspired by a new religion – Islam – that had emerged in the Arabian Peninsula. The Arabs established a vast empire, which eventually stretched as far as Spain in the west and the Himalayas in the east. Palestine was a small part of this large empire, and was governed as part of the province of Syria. The Arab conquest did not initially have a significant impact on the people of Palestine, as the Arabs were few in number and were initially tolerant towards Judaism and Christianity. Later, however, they encouraged large-scale conversion to Islam, and more Arabs moved into the area. As a result, Arabic became the main language and Islam the dominant religion in Palestine.

A map showing the extent of the Arab Empire in the 9th century CE

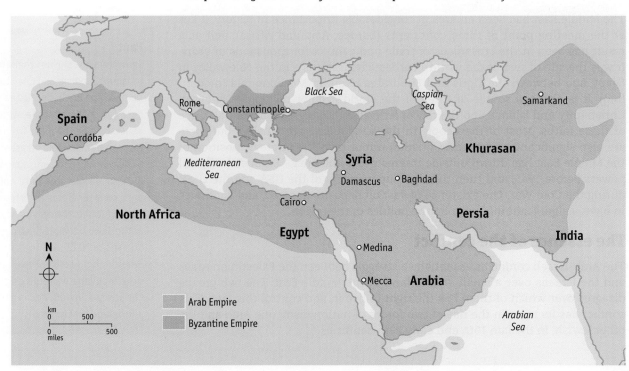

In 1516 CE – almost 900 years later – Palestine became part of the Ottoman Empire, when the Ottoman Turks conquered a large part of the Arab Empire in the Middle East and North Africa. Palestine remained part of the Ottoman Empire for the next 400 years. Most of the population were Arabic-speaking Muslims, although small Jewish and Christian communities continued to live there.

Conflicting nationalisms

The rise of two forces of nationalism in the late 19th and early 20th centuries, one Arab and the other Jewish, led to conflict in Palestine. Although nationalism can be a positive force that encourages a sense of pride, identity and unity, it can also be destructive. It can result in discrimination and violence against outsiders, or in conflict and warfare between rival nationalist groups and countries. The strong rivalry and conflict that developed between Zionism and Israeli nationalism on the one hand, and Arab and Palestinian nationalism on the other, was centred upon the struggle to control Palestine. Zionism was a political movement that sought to establish a permanent 'national home' for Jewish people in Palestine. Palestinian nationalism arose from the displacement of the Palestinian people as a result of the establishment of this 'national home'.

See page 16 for explanations of Zionism, Arab nationalism and Palestinian nationalism.

SOURCE A

Historian James Gelvin explains the significance of nationalism in the struggle for Palestine.

The struggle for control over some or all of the territory of Palestine pits two nationalist movements against each other. In spite of their claims to uniqueness, all nationalist movements bear a remarkable resemblance to one another. Each constructs a historical narrative that traces the unbroken lineage of a group – a nation – over time. Each endows the site of the nation's birth or greatest cultural or political moment with special meaning. Each uses its purported 'special relationship' to some territory to justify its right to establish a sovereign state in that territory. This is where nationalism differs from mere nostalgia or collective memory: Whereas all sorts of religious and ethnic groups feel sentimental attachment to places, nationalism converts sentiment into politics. The adherents of a nationalist movement demand exclusive sovereignty over the designated territory and, for their nation, membership in the global order of nation-states. When it comes to connecting history and geography to political rights, neither Zionism nor Palestinian nationalism is a slacker.

Gelvin J. 2005. The Israel–Palestine Conflict: One Hundred Years of War. New York, USA. Cambridge University Press. pp. 5–6.

The nature of the conflict

The conflict in Palestine has always been more than a straightforward struggle between two rival peoples or forces of nationalism. It has been complicated and aggravated by the involvement of other countries. It is important to understand the wider context of the conflict – the impact of colonialism, the involvement of other Arab states, and the backdrop of the Cold War.

The colonial context

From its very beginning, the Arab–Israeli conflict was complicated by the imperial ambitions of Britain. British interests in the region were determined by strategic and economic factors. In particular, there was concern over the need for stability and control in a region that was a major source of oil supplies, and so near to the Suez Canal – a crucial international trade route.

Contradictory assurances of British support to both the Arabs and the Jews during the First World War were a significant factor in the conflict that developed in Palestine. The British government was given authority by the League of Nations to administer Palestine between 1920 and 1948, but struggled to maintain order in the face of rising nationalist demands and growing conflict between the Arab and Jewish communities. As a result, Britain withdrew from Palestine in 1948, and the Jews established the state of Israel. Britain attempted unsuccessfully to uphold British interests in the region by joining forces with Israel and invading Egypt in 1956, creating an international crisis.

The Middle Eastern context

The Arab–Israeli conflict was initially a regional dispute. On one side were the Palestinian Arabs, supported by the governments of neighbouring Arab states. On the other side was Israel, the Jewish state in Palestine. Between 1948 and 1973, the two sides fought four major wars – in 1948–49, 1956, 1967 and 1973. In the first confrontation in 1948–49, the Jews established the state of Israel and occupied much of Palestine.

During this process, most of the Palestinian Arab population fled – or were forced to leave by acts of violence – and settled in the neighbouring Arab states. This had a significant impact on subsequent developments, both within these nearby countries and in the Middle Eastern region as a whole. The Arab states of Egypt, Syria, Jordan and Lebanon were the most directly affected by these events. In 1979, Egypt – the strongest Arab military power – signed a peace treaty with Israel, effectively ending the series of wars between Israel and the Arab states.

The conflict between Israel and the Palestinians, however, was not resolved by this peace treaty. The anger and bitterness of the Palestinian refugees resulted in acts of violence by the Palestinians, and harsh reprisals by the Israelis. This fighting destabilised the region. When Israel subsequently occupied – and continued to occupy – the rest of Palestine, achieving a peaceful solution became increasingly difficult.

It is worth noting that not all the violence and warfare in the Middle East is a direct result of the Arab–Israeli conflict. Other conflicts in the region have included a civil war in Yemen (1962–70) and recurring civil wars in Lebanon. The hostilities in Lebanon were partly – but not wholly – caused by the presence of a substantial Palestinian refugee population within the country, and by Israeli and Syrian interference in Lebanese affairs. Perhaps the most deadly Middle Eastern war was fought between Iran and Iraq from 1980 to 1988. Other wars have included the Iraqi invasion of Kuwait (1990), the Gulf War (1991) and the US-led invasion of Iraq (2003). More recent conflict in the Middle East in Tunisia, Egypt, Yemen, Bahrain, Libya and Syria has been the result of civil struggles between pro-democracy campaigners and autocratic governments reluctant to accept the need for reform.

The context of the Cold War

From the 1950s to the 1970s, conflict in the Middle Eastern region was complicated by intervention by outside powers during the **Cold War**. The USA and the USSR competed for influence and control in other parts of the world, meaning that their rivalry had global significance. A key reason for the seemingly unconditional American support for Israel was the view that it was a stronghold against the extension of Soviet influence in the region. While the USA backed Israel with aid and arms supplies, the USSR supported several of the Arab states. However, the USA also provided military aid to Arab states that it perceived to be 'moderate' and supportive of American interests, such as Jordan and Saudi Arabia.

In the 1970s, the Arab–Israeli conflict provided the context for a world economic crisis when the Arab states cut oil production, demonstrating the dependence of Western economies on oil from the region. This had far-reaching global economic and political implications.

Over the course of the conflict in the Middle East, there have been changes in Western attitudes towards Israel. There was international sympathy for the Jews at the end of the Second World War because of the **Holocaust**. However, this view later changed when Israeli actions during and after the 1967 War brought widespread criticism. Western attitudes towards the Arab states also changed, especially when the 1973 War forced Western powers to acknowledge their dependence on Arab oil and Arab goodwill. Israel also lost much international sympathy and support as a result of its military intervention in Lebanon in 1978, 1982 and 2006, and its military operation in Gaza in 2008–09.

Western attitudes towards affairs in the Middle East were also affected by the **9/11 attacks** in the USA in 2001. After this, the West increasingly feared the spread of radical Islam in the Arab world, and this influenced its policies towards the region.

Views of the conflict

The Arab–Israeli conflict is a controversial topic about which many people hold fixed opinions and emotive views. It is an issue that evokes strong feelings, and is the subject of passionate and sometimes irrational arguments. So, with this topic perhaps more than many others, it is important to remain as objective and open-minded as possible, and to review the historical evidence carefully before reaching conclusions.

Perspective and terminology

The terminology used in describing the Arab–Israeli conflict can be controversial. To Israelis, the first Arab–Israeli war of 1948–49 is the 'War of Independence'; to Palestinian Arabs it is part of *Al-Nakba* ('the catastrophe'). Other wars are also referred to by different names: for example, some people avoid using terms such as the Six Day War and the Yom Kippur War. This book refers to the Arab–Israeli wars by the year in which they occurred, which is the convention adopted by many historians. Depending on perspective, Palestinian guerrillas are either 'terrorists' or 'freedom fighters'; the areas taken over by Israel during the 1967 War are either the 'Occupied Territories' or the biblical lands of Judea and Samaria. To some, the whole area is the 'Holy Land' or the 'Promised Land', and even the names 'Palestine' and 'Israel' can be controversial.

Cold War This was the period of tension, rivalry and hostility between the USA and its allies (the 'West') and the USSR and its allies (the 'Soviet bloc'), which lasted from 1946 until 1990. It was a clash between competing social and economic systems, and political ideologies. The USA stood for capitalism, and the USSR for communism. This opposition resulted in the formation of rival political and military alliances, a race to develop increasingly powerful weapons, and political crises and military conflicts around the world.

Holocaust The systematic killing of 6 million Jews in Europe by the Nazis during the Second World War, as well as the murder of another 10 million people in the Nazi death and concentration camps. Other victims included Roma, Sinti, gay men, and Russian, Polish and Ukrainian civilians and prisoners of war.

9/11 attacks On 11 September 2001, hijackers seized four American passenger planes and crashed two of them into the World Trade Center in New York, killing nearly 3000 people when the twin towers collapsed. A third plane attacked the Pentagon, the US military headquarters in Washington, DC. In a fourth plane, whose target is believed to have been the White House, passengers overpowered the hijackers and crashed the plane, killing everyone on board. Osama bin Laden, the leader of an Islamist militant group, Al Qaeda, claimed responsibility for the attacks. In response, the US launched a 'War on Terror' and invaded Afghanistan, in an unsuccessful attempt to crush Al Qaeda. Bin Laden was subsequently located in Pakistan and killed by US forces in 2011.

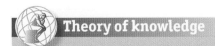

Language and bias
The choice of terminology and use of language is an important element in Theory of knowledge. How can terminology be linked to bias? How can historians avoid using biased language?

SOURCE B

The historian Ilan Pappe explains how the issue of the region's name reflected the rise of conflicting forces of nationalism in the 20th century.

Naming the land was a political act in Ottoman Palestine at the end of the nineteenth century. Before that, there had been no dispute over a name, and whatever the land was called by its rulers, inhabitants or visitors was apparently accepted as one option of many used for religious or administrative purposes. What the land was called did not play an important role in the lives of those who lived there.

It was only with the arrival of Zionism and European colonialism on the one hand, and the emergence of Palestinian nationalism on the other, that the name assumed importance and meaning. Instead of merely describing an area, the name came to represent a claim over it. And so, from the end of the nineteenth century, different groups of people at different historical junctures, when they had the will and the power to do so, named the land in a forceful act aimed at creating a new reality. Such is the power of nationalism.

Pappe, I. 2006. A History of Modern Palestine (Second Edition). Cambridge, UK. Cambridge University Press. p. 11.

Orthodox This is a term used to distinguish religious movements that follow traditional practices, as distinct from more liberal movements. It is used here to describe conservative sections in the Jewish faith. Orthodox Jews follow the traditional interpretation and application of the practices and ethics of the 'Torah'. This is found in the Five Books of Moses (the first five books of the Old Testament).

Bias and stereotypes

While the conflict is essentially one between Jews and Arabs, it is important to remember that each of these groups has its own divisions and conflicts. Within Israeli society, there are contradictions between the demands of a modern secular state and the beliefs of the **Orthodox** religious tradition. There are also tensions between ultra-nationalists who refuse to compromise Israel's position, and those who are willing to negotiate solutions. Not all Jews are Zionists, and from the late 1970s a 'Peace Now' movement (see page 192) developed within Israel to put pressure on the government to negotiate a settlement with the Palestinians.

Amongst the Arab nations, there are marked differences between conservative and more democratic states, between reactionary rulers and the demands of their people, and between political Islamists and those who support a secular form of government. Among the Palestinians themselves there are differences between moderates and radicals, their attitudes towards negotiating with Israel and their views about a future Palestinian state.

Historiography

As may be expected, there are fierce debates among historians about the Arab–Israeli conflict. For example, many differ sharply in their views on topics such as Zionism, Palestinian resistance and the nature of the Israeli state. There is also strong disagreement on questions such as why the Palestinians were not assimilated into the populations of the Arab countries to which they fled. While many Palestinian historians viewed the establishment of the state of Israel as an act of aggression and land theft, many Israeli historians saw it as a heroic victory over huge odds and a noble achievement after years of suffering by the Jewish people. There are many other examples of opposing perspectives such as these.

14

It is important to know that there are differing viewpoints among Israeli historians as well. In 1988, the year of the 40th anniversary of the establishment of Israel, a number of Israeli historians published books that questioned some of the established views. For example, these historians reassessed the reasons for the Israeli victory over the Arab states in 1948–49. They came to be called the 'Revisionist', or 'New', Israeli historians. They focused on issues such as the reasons for the mass departure of Palestinian refugees, and the relative strengths of the two sides in the war. Since then, other historians have re-examined events and issues in Israeli history, and Israel's relations with the Arab states. They have focused particularly on Israel's role in the ongoing hostilities. The primary sources that revisionist historians have used for their research are Israeli government papers that were declassified in 1988, 40 years after the founding of Israel. These historians acknowledge that it is to Israel's credit that it has allowed a free examination of these documents.

The views of the revisionists have been fiercely challenged in turn by pro-Zionist historians. As a result of the lively debate in Israeli historiography, many of the issues discussed in this book are the subject of ongoing re-examination – and sometimes controversial reinterpretation – by Israeli historians. You will read about these differing historical interpretations in the chapters that follow.

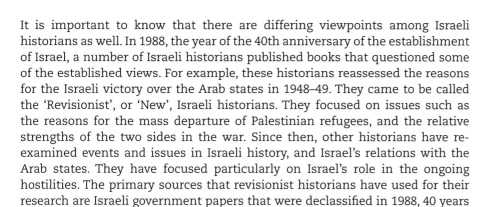

SOURCE C

One of the Israeli revisionist historians, Ilan Pappe, comments on the relationship between conflicting versions of history and 'historical truth'.

They represent historical narratives, powerful versions of history accepted as truth, whether told by child carers to kindergarten children or by university professors to students of history. The thickness of the narrative varies, but not its sequence or its heroes and villains. A concise history of Israel and Palestine must take into account these narratives, but cannot accept them as 'historical truth', if only because each is a mirror image of the other. If one version is historical truth then the other has to be a lie. If both are correct then there is no historical truth, only fictional versions of the past. Something else is needed: an alternative narrative that recognises similarities, criticises overt falsifications, and expands the history of the region to the areas not covered by the two historical narratives.

Pappe, I. 2006. A History of Modern Palestine (Second Edition). Cambridge, UK. Cambridge University Press. pp. 1–2.

 Theory of knowledge

'Historical truth'
As you use this book, you will find many opportunities to consider the questions that are at the core of history as a discipline. These include, what is 'historical truth'? Is there such a thing? What is the role of the historian? How can he or she avoid making subjective interpretations?

Terminology and definitions

You need to ensure that you understand certain words and concepts that are at the core of the Arab–Israeli conflict. These include the concept of nationalism itself, as well as the varieties of nationalism that developed in the Middle East and affected developments in the region. Key vocabulary for this topic will include terms relating to population movements, certain Hebrew and Arabic words, definitions related to international organisations, and some general political terminology.

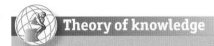

History as invention

Read Sources A (page 11) and C (page 15) again. In what ways can the 'historical narrative' that both sources refer to be considered an 'invented tradition'?

Nationalism

Nationalism means a sense of belonging to and identifying with a nation; that is, of being linked to other people you do not know, but who are all part of the same nation. It involves issues such as a common history and shared culture and values, as well as the belief that people of the same nation should have political self-determination. Some historians claim that a nation is an 'imagined community', in which people believe that they share values and traditions with others whom they do not know. Sometimes new nations have to develop a sense of national identity where none existed before, and they may use propaganda to do this by stressing heroic traditions, figures or events in the past. Historians refer to this as an 'invented tradition'.

Arab nationalism

Arab nationalism first emerged in the early 20th century as a response to Ottoman control and a desire to establish an independent and united Arab state. The term 'Arab nationalism' also refers to the heightened sense of political awareness, and the growth of popular nationalism, that emerged in Arab countries in the 1950s and 1960s. Some historians refer to it as 'Arabism', and focus on the emergence of a sense of common identity based on a shared language, culture and heritage. Others speak of 'pan-Arabism', and stress the attempts to forge links and political unity between Arab states.

Anti-Semitism

This term refers to prejudice, discrimination or acts of hostility towards Jews or Judaism.

Zionism

Zionism is a Jewish nationalist and political movement that started in Europe in the late 19th century, aimed at establishing a Jewish state in Palestine. It was formed as a response to the anti-Semitism that many Jewish communities encountered in Europe. Originally, some Zionists suggested Africa or the Americas as possible sites for a national home. It was only in the 1890s that Zionists formally adopted the idea of Palestine as the place for this homeland. The Zionists worked to get international support for this ideal from Western governments and the general public. They achieved their aim with the establishment of the state of Israel in 1948, but Zionism has remained a powerful political force since this time.

Palestinian nationalism

Palestinian nationalism arose out of the displacement of the Palestinian people that resulted from the establishment of Israel. By the late 1950s, many Palestinians began to believe that the restoration of their homeland would depend on their own efforts, instead of relying on Arab governments. This new national consciousness was especially evident among the younger generation in the Palestinian diaspora, who saw themselves as a nation and not simply a part of the wider Arab world.

Population movements

The establishment of the state of Israel, and the subsequent Arab–Israeli conflict, involved large-scale movements of people.

Demographics

This is the scientific study of a population, and the statistics that describe it. It includes aspects such as size, structure and distribution of the population. A demographic shift is a change in one or more of these features. Millions of Jews moved from Europe and the Arab states, as well as other parts of the world, to live in Israel. At the same time, large numbers of Palestinian Arabs moved to surrounding Arab countries. These demographic shifts altered the population structure of the Middle East.

Diaspora

This term literally means the scattering of people from their homeland or place of origin. When the term is spelt with a capital 'D', it usually refers to the Jewish population outside Palestine after their defeat by the Romans in the 2nd century CE. The Palestinian diaspora refers to those who were scattered as a result of the Arab–Israeli conflict. Currently, over 9 million Palestinians are estimated to be living in the diaspora.

Hebrew and Arabic terms

Some Hebrew and Arabic words occur frequently in this book.

Yishuv

Yishuv is the Hebrew word for the Jewish community in Palestine before the state of Israel was established. Large numbers of Jews immigrated to Palestine, especially during the 1930s after Hitler came to power in Germany, and became part of the *Yishuv*. The Jewish population rose from less than 60,000 at the end of the First World War to 600,000 in 1948.

Jewish settlers hand-plough fields on a kibbutz in Palestine, 1935

Eretz Israel (or *Yisrael*)

This is the Hebrew term used by Zionists for the Land of Israel, as it was in biblical times. This includes the parts of Palestine that are home to the Palestinian Arabs. Some Zionists were prepared to use extreme measures to achieve this. Political and religious support for the concept has led to the controversial expansion of Jewish settlements into the areas occupied by Israel in the 1967 War.

Al-Nakba

This is an Arabic word meaning 'the disaster' or 'the catastrophe'. It refers to the flight and expulsion of the Palestinian Arabs between 1947 and 1949, when the state of Israel was established and the Arab states were defeated.

Fedayeen

This is an Arabic word for those who sacrifice themselves for another person or for a cause. It refers to the Palestinian guerrilla fighters who launched raids across the border into Israel, especially after the formation of the Palestine Liberation Organisation in 1964.

Intifada

This is an Arabic word that means 'uprising'. In this book, it refers specifically to the two Palestinian uprisings in the West Bank and Gaza against continued Israeli occupation of these territories. The first *intifada* was between 1987 and 1993, and the second *intifada* was between 2000 and 2005.

International organisations

You need to understand the structure and functions of significant international organisations and their relationship to the conflict.

League of Nations

The League of Nations was established in 1920 with the main aim of maintaining world peace by settling disputes through negotiation. One of its functions was to supervise the administration of the 'mandates', the former colonies of Germany and Turkey that were taken away from them after the First World War. Palestine was a British mandate between 1920 and 1948. The League was weakened by the American decision not to become a member, and by having no means of enforcing its decisions. It was formally dissolved in 1946.

United Nations (UN)

The UN was formed in 1945 as the successor to the League of Nations. It assumed responsibility for Palestine, and proposed its partition into separate Jewish and Palestinian states in 1947. The UN was unable to prevent the four Arab–Israeli wars. It only succeeded in calling for and monitoring ceasefires, and in sending observers and peacekeeping forces to the region. Since 1948, the UN has maintained refugee camps for the displaced Palestinians. It has also passed numerous resolutions calling for the establishment of a Palestinian state.

General political terms

Finally, some general political terms you need to understand.

Lobby

To 'lobby' means to get support for a cause by trying to influence people in authority. A lobby acts as a pressure group. A powerful Jewish and pro-Israeli lobby in the USA had a significant effect on US foreign policy in the Middle East.

Secular

This term means 'not connected to any religion'. Secularism is the view that religion should be separate from government and from public education.

Fundamentalism

This describes a religious movement or point of view that supports returning to the fundamental principles of that religion, and observing them strictly. Fundamentalists are often intolerant of other views, and are opposed to secularism. Support for Jewish, Islamic and Christian fundamentalism has increased in recent decades, and has complicated the conflicts in the Middle East.

Summary

By the time you have worked through this book, you should be able to:

- understand and explain the development of the Arab–Israeli conflict between 1948 and 1979, and the causes and consequences of the military clashes that occurred
- understand and explain the role of outside powers and organisations in the conflict, either as agents of tension or as mediators of peace
- understand the political, economic and social issues behind the dispute, and the impact of social and economic developments on the populations living in Palestine/Israel
- compare and contrast, and evaluate, the various explanations and interpretations of these issues and developments that have been put forward by different historians
- use and assess – as historical evidence – a range of different types of sources relating to the conflict, by considering aspects such as comparison and contrast, and value and limitations
- combine evaluation of sources with relevant knowledge of your own to develop supported arguments, explanations and judgements about the nature of the conflict between Israel and the Arab states, and between Israel and the Palestinians.

19

Timeline

1915–16 letters between McMahon and Sharif Husayn

1916 May: Sykes–Picot Agreement

Jun: Arab Revolt

1917 Nov: Balfour Declaration

1919 Jun: Treaty of Versailles

1920 Apr: San Remo conference; Palestine becomes a British mandate

1921 Iraq and Transjordan become British mandates

1925 formation of Jewish Agency

1929 Aug: Arab riots in Palestine

1932 Oct: independence of Iraq

1933 Jan: Hitler becomes chancellor of Germany

1936 Apr–Oct: Arab general strike

1936–39 Arab Revolt

1937 Jul: Peel Commission recommends partition of Palestine

1939 White Paper limits Jewish immigration

1945 Mar: formation of the Arab League

Sep: end of Second World War

Introduction

The Arab–Israeli conflict has its roots in the rise of two forces of nationalism, one Arab and the other Jewish, in the late 19th and early 20th centuries. These two nationalist movements came into conflict because they had incompatible ambitions for the same area of land in the Middle East – that is, Palestine. The issue was further complicated by British ambitions and actions during and after the First World War. By 1945, tensions and the potential for conflict had increased substantially as a result of increasing Jewish immigration into Palestine, rising Arab opposition to it, and changing and contradictory British policies.

Key questions

- What was the situation in the Middle East at the beginning of the 20th century?
- How did the First World War affect Palestine?
- What happened in Palestine between 1919 and 1939?
- How did the Second World War affect Palestine?

Overview

- Before the First World War, Palestine was part of the Ottoman Empire. An awakening Arab nationalist movement saw an opportunity for independence when Turkey became involved in the war.
- In a reaction against persecution and anti-Semitism, Jews in Europe formed the Zionist Organisation. This group aimed to establish a Jewish state in Palestine.
- British interest in the Middle East principally focused on the Suez Canal, the supply of oil, and concerns about the expansion of Russian influence into the area. To a lesser extent, France shared similar concerns.
- During the First World War, the British government committed itself to three contradictory agreements concerning Palestine – with the Arabs, the French and the Zionists.
- After the war, Palestine became a British mandate. There were increasing tensions and clashes between Arabs and Jews in Palestine as more Jewish immigrants arrived.

- In 1936, an Arab general strike followed by a three-year uprising resulted in a state of civil war and harsh British reprisals.
- The 1937 Peel Report, recommending the partition of Palestine into two separate states, signalled a change in British policy. The proposal was totally rejected by the Arabs.
- With the approach of the Second World War, Britain tried to secure Arab support by issuing a White Paper that abandoned the idea of partition and placed limits on Jewish immigration.
- During the war, most Jews in Palestine co-operated with the Allied war effort to defeat Nazi Germany. However, a minority used extremist measures to force the British to leave Palestine.
- By the end of the war, international sympathy and support for the Zionist cause had increased. By contrast, the Palestinian Arabs found themselves in a weak position.

Developments before 1945 are not part of the IB curriculum. However, it is important for you to be aware of the origins of the conflict, in order to understand the issues involved and the events that unfolded after 1945.

British police clear streets in Jaffa during the Arab Revolt in 1936

What was the situation in the Middle East at the beginning of the 20th century?

In 1900, most of the Middle East was part of the **Ottoman Empire**. However, there were three forces at work that had a significant impact on later developments. These were: the rise of Arab nationalism in the areas under Ottoman control; the birth of the Zionist movement in Europe; and increasing European interest in the Middle East, for strategic and economic reasons.

The Ottoman Empire and Arab nationalism

From the 7th century CE, Palestine was part of a vast Arab empire that included much of the Middle East, North Africa and Spain. Although Palestine was ruled by the Ottoman Turks from the beginning of the 16th century, it remained a predominantly Arab country. The Arab population of Palestine in 1900 is estimated to have been 500,000.

From the 1880s onwards, various movements emerged among the Arabs, demanding greater independence from Turkish rule. One of these was the League of the Arab Fatherland. In 1905 one of its members, Najib Azouri, an Arab living in Paris, published a book called *The Awakening of the Arab Nation* that outlined the aim of the League to establish an independent Arab empire. In this book, Azouri made pertinent observations about the situation in Palestine at the time, as new groups of Jewish refugees from Russia moved there to settle.

SOURCE A

Two important phenomena, of identical character but nevertheless opposed, which till now have not attracted attention, are now making their appearance in Asian Turkey: these are the awakening of the Arab nation and the latent efforts of the Jews to re-establish, on an extremely large scale, the ancient Kingdom of Israel. These two movements are destined to struggle continuously with one another, until one prevails over the other. The fate of the entire world depends on the result of this struggle between the two peoples, which represent two contradictory principles.

Azouri, N. 1905. Le Réveil de la Nation Arabe dans l'Asie Turque. Paris, France. p. 5. Quoted in Rose, N. 2009. 'A Senseless, Squalid War': Voices from Palestine 1945–1948. London, UK. The Bodley Head.

In 1908, a reformist movement called the Young Turk Revolution brought some liberal reforms to parts of the Ottoman Empire. There was greater freedom of the press, and two Palestinian newspapers were established – *Filastin* and *al-Karmil*. The beginnings of a Palestinian nationalist movement were starting to emerge. Some Arabs in the Turkish Empire regarded **Sharif Husayn bin Ali** of Mecca, and his sons, Faisal and Abdullah, as leaders of the Arab cause. When the Ottoman Empire became involved in the First World War on the side of Germany, Arab nationalists saw this as an opportunity to achieve their independence and bring about the creation of an Arab state.

Ottoman Empire The Ottoman Empire, or Turkish Empire, ruled a vast area from its capital in Constantinople (Istanbul). It was the dominant Muslim power for nearly 500 years. At its height, it controlled south-eastern Europe, North Africa and much of the Middle East. The regime collapsed after Turkey's defeat in the First World War, and the loss of its empire. In 1922, Kemal Ataturk established a modern secular state in its place.

Sharif Husayn bin Ali (1854–1931) Sharif Husayn (also Sherif Hussein) was a member of the Hashemite dynasty. This dynasty traced its lineage to the Prophet Muhammed, and its members were the traditional 'Guardians' of Mecca and Medina, the two holy cities of Islam in the Hejaz. Husayn led the Arab Revolt against Ottoman rule in 1916, and proclaimed himself king of Hejaz. However, he was deposed in 1924 when Ibn Saud united Hejaz with the province of Nadj, to form the kingdom of Saudi Arabia. Husayn died in exile in Jordan.

The birth of Zionism

The Jews lived in Palestine in biblical times, until their conquest by the Romans in 130 CE. After this, Jewish communities were dispersed throughout the Middle East, Europe and North Africa, where they managed to maintain their religious traditions and cultural identity. Persecution towards Jewish communities in Europe ranged from discriminatory restrictions to expulsion and violent attacks on Jewish lives and property. The situation was especially bad in Tsarist Russia, where violent **pogroms** forced millions of Jews to flee. These pogroms became more frequent in the 1880s. A small number of these refugees went to Palestine, but the vast majority went to Western Europe or the USA. However, even in Western Europe they did not feel safe from the effects of anti-Semitism.

It was out of this situation that the Zionist movement (see page 16) developed. Many Jews began to question whether they would ever be secure as long as they were seen as an alien minority. Amongst them was an Austrian–Jewish journalist, **Theodor Herzl,** who organised the first Zionist Congress at Basel, Switzerland, in 1897. The Congress declared that the aim of the Zionist movement was to create a home for the Jewish people in Palestine.

SOURCE B

The Basel Declaration, a statement issued by the first Zionist Congress in 1897.

1 The aim of Zionism is to secure for the Jewish people a home in Palestine secured by public law. The Congress contemplates the following means to the attainment of this end:
2 The promotion, on suitable lines, of the colonisation of Palestine by Jewish agricultural and industrial workers.
3 The organisation and binding together of the whole of Jewry by means of appropriate institutions, local and international, in accordance with the laws of each country.
4 The strengthening and fostering of Jewish national sentiment and consciousness.
5 Preparatory steps towards obtaining government consent, where necessary, to the attainment of the aim of Zionism.

Quoted in Laqueur, W. and Rubin, B. (eds). 2001. The Israel–Arab Reader. New York, USA. Penguin. pp. 9–10.

A small but growing number of Jews had already settled in Palestine, mainly from Tsarist Russia. By 1900, there were an estimated 50,000 Jews in Palestine. They had begun to purchase land from local Arab landlords. The increase in Jewish immigration and land purchases was beginning to alarm the local Arab population, who attempted to persuade the Turkish administrators to limit Jewish immigration and land transfers. By 1914, there were over 40 Jewish farming settlements (*kibbutzim*) in Palestine, and communities in Jerusalem and Tel Aviv. Nevertheless, at the outbreak of the First World War, Zionism was a limited and struggling movement and the Jewish community in Palestine formed less than 10% of the population.

pogroms These were organised persecutions or massacres of religious or ethnic minorities, especially Jewish communities in the Russian Empire. Pogroms were often condoned or encouraged by the authorities as a means of deflecting attention from economic and social problems. Today the terms 'ethnic cleansing' or 'genocide' are more commonly used for similar attacks.

Theodor Herzl (1860–1904)
Herzl was an Austrian–Jewish writer. While working as a journalist in Paris in 1894, Herzl was deeply shocked by the Dreyfus Affair, an event that revealed the extent of anti-Semitism in supposedly enlightened France. Dreyfus, a Jewish officer in the French army, was falsely accused and convicted of treason in a case that caused an outburst of anti-Semitic sentiment and actions. When the case was reviewed in 1906, Dreyfus was found to be innocent. Herzl came to the conclusion that Jews would never be safe unless they had a state of their own.

23

Many Jews in other countries did not support Zionism, and there was considerable opposition among these Jews to the concept of migration to Palestine. They wanted instead to be assimilated into the populations of the countries in which they lived, and believed that the creation of a separate Jewish state would confirm the claims of anti-Semites that Jews and Christians could not live together as part of the same nation.

British and French interests in the Middle East

British interests in the Middle East were initially focused on the Suez Canal, which had been built in 1869. The Suez Canal provided quick and easy access to trade in the Indian Ocean, and to Britain's empire in India. The British government had bought a controlling interest in the Suez Canal Company, and in 1882 had extended a 'protectorate' over Egypt. The British were anxious to maintain stability and control in this key region.

This map shows the routes between Britain and India via the Suez Canal and via the Cape of Good Hope

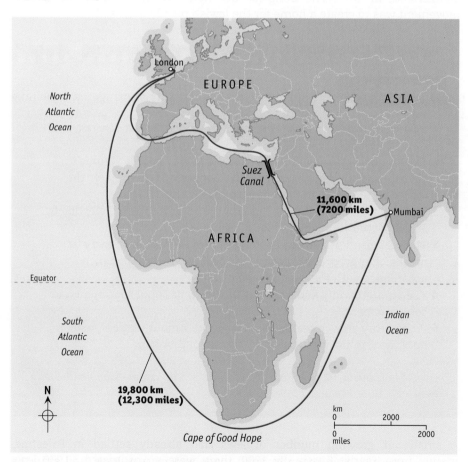

British interest in the Middle East was also based on oil. A British geologist discovered oil in Persia (now Iran) in 1908, and in 1911 the British–Persian Oil Company was set up to exploit the oilfields. This was the first of several substantial oil discoveries in the Middle East. The Royal Navy, as well as other European navies, was in the process of converting to the use of oil in its ships, and so Britain wanted to maintain its authority and presence in the area to ensure steady supplies of oil. By 1914, Britain had control of most of the areas around the Persian Gulf, including Kuwait, Bahrain, Qatar, the Trucial States (now the United Arab Emirates), Oman and Aden (now Yemen).

Britain was concerned about growing Russian influence in Persia, and was anxious to ensure that Russian expansion did not threaten trade in the eastern Mediterranean, the Suez Canal or the oilfields. For this reason, the British had provided diplomatic support to the Ottoman Empire as it gradually declined in the late 19th century, because they viewed it as a useful barrier to Russian ambitions and expansion. They feared that a collapse of the Ottoman Empire would be against British interests in the region. But when the Ottoman Empire allied itself with Germany in the First World War, this posed a new kind of threat.

France also had interests in the Middle East, although not to the same extent as Britain. A French engineer had designed and built the Suez Canal, and France had a proportion of the shares in the Suez Canal Company. France had colonial control over Algeria and Tunisia, Arab countries in North Africa. It also had commercial interests in Syria, where many French businesses operated. France similarly feared any extension of Russian or German influence into the Middle Eastern region.

Activities

1   Design a spider diagram to illustrate the reasons why each of the following had an interest in the Middle East before 1914: the Zionists, the Ottoman Empire, Britain and France.

2   Write brief notes to identify each of the following historical figures, explaining how each is linked (even indirectly) with the history of the Middle East:
   • Sharif Husayn
   • Kemal Ataturk
   • Theodor Herzl
   • Alfred Dreyfus
   • Najib Azouri.

3   'To what extent can the conviction of Dreyfus for treason be attributed to anti-Semitism in French society at the time?' Find out the details of the 'Dreyfus Affair' to write an answer to this question.

4   Write a paragraph to explain why, even before the First World War, there was potential for conflict over Palestine between the Arabs and the Jews.

How did the First World War affect Palestine?

When the First World War started in 1914, the Ottoman Empire joined on the side of Germany and Austria against Britain, France and Russia. Palestine suffered a brutal Ottoman occupation during the war, as military commanders took what they could to support the Turkish war effort. They forcibly conscripted young men into the army or into forced labour battalions.

These conscripts were made to build roads and railway lines, and strip the forests of timber to build an ambitious railway line to the south, from where the Turks planned to invade British-controlled Egypt. The occupying forces also executed anyone suspected of Arab nationalist sympathies. In response to the harsh conditions of the wartime occupation, many Arabs were prepared to support a movement to overthrow Ottoman control.

During the war, Britain made three separate agreements concerning Palestine, each expressing some kind of commitment to a particular viewpoint. The roots of later disputes over Palestine lay in these contradictory agreements.

T. E. Lawrence (1888–1935)

Lawrence was a British scholar, writer and soldier, who became disillusioned with Britain's treatment of the Arabs. He fought in the 1916 Arab Revolt, leading a small but highly effective guerrilla group that obstructed Turkish communications and supply routes, and attacked thousands of Turkish soldiers. He developed a deep sympathy for the Arab cause, and spent the post-war years trying to rally support for it. The 1963 film *Lawrence of Arabia* is the story of the Arab revolt and Lawrence's part in it.

Fact

When the Tsarist government was overthrown in 1917, the new Bolshevik government published the details of several secret agreements in which the Tsarist government had been involved. One of these was the Sykes–Picot agreement. The contradiction between the Husayn–McMahon letters and the Sykes–Picot Agreement became public knowledge, and the Arabs realised that they had been deceived by the British.

Pledges of support for Arab independence

Britain was afraid that the Ottoman Empire, with its German ally, might threaten British control of the Suez Canal and oil supplies from Persia. So the British decided to encourage the Arabs to rise against their Turkish rulers, and in this way weaken the Ottoman Empire through internal revolt. During 1915 and 1916, there was an exchange of letters (the McMahon letters) between the Arab leader in Mecca, Sharif Husayn, and the British high commissioner in Egypt, Henry McMahon. McMahon informed Husayn that Britain was 'prepared to recognise and support the independence' of the Arabs. Assured of British support, the Arabs began their revolt against Turkish rule in June 1916. They were led by Faisal, one of Husayn's sons, and aided by a British officer, Colonel **T. E. Lawrence** – the legendary Lawrence of Arabia. The Arabs attacked Turkish supply lines and troops. Together with a British force from Egypt, they succeeded in defeating the Turks by the end of the First World War. The Arabs now expected the British to honour the commitment they had made to support Arab independence. The correspondence was vague, however, about the precise geographic details of this future Arab state.

The Sykes–Picot Agreement

However, Britain had other plans for the region. Even before the Arab Revolt had started, Britain had made a conflicting deal with France. In a secret agreement reached in May 1916, the two countries agreed to divide up the Ottoman Empire between them. The arrangement was sanctioned by the Tsarist government. Under the Sykes–Picot agreement, which was named after the British and French politicians who made it, Britain and France would control the Middle East. Part of the Arab lands would come under direct British or French rule, while the rest would be made up of self-governing Arab states under indirect British or French control or 'influence'. By the terms of this agreement, Britain would control Palestine, an arrangement that obviously contradicted the undertakings made in the McMahon letters.

Pledges of support to the Zionists

From the beginning of the war, British Zionists – led by **Chaim Weizmann** (see page 27) – had been trying to secure the support of the British government for the concept of a Jewish homeland. This support finally came in November 1917, in a letter written by Arthur Balfour, the British foreign secretary, to Lord Rothschild, a prominent banker and leading member of the Jewish community in Britain. This letter became known as the Balfour Declaration, and it indicated the support of the British government for a 'national home' for the Jewish people in Palestine. The wording of the letter was carefully chosen: it spoke of a 'national home' rather than 'state', and it specified that nothing should be done to 'harm the civil and religious rights of existing non-Jewish communities in Palestine'. However, it conflicted in spirit, if not in detail, with the commitments already made in the McMahon letters. Various motives have been suggested for the publication of this controversial document, the most accepted being that Britain was trying to gain support from the influential Jewish community in the USA, both in the war against Germany and for Britain's post-war ambitions to be the controlling power in the Middle East.

The Zionists welcomed the Balfour Declaration as the first step towards the realisation of their ambitions. Avi Shlaim, a leading Israeli revisionist historian, explains its significance: '... the Balfour Declaration, despite its ambiguities and limitations, handed the Jews a golden key to unlock the doors of Palestine and to make themselves the masters of the country.'

SOURCE C

The letter written by the British foreign secretary, Lord Balfour, to Lord Rothschild, a leading British Zionist, on 2 November 1917. This letter became known as the Balfour Declaration.

Foreign Office
November 2nd, 1917

Dear Lord Rothschild,

I have much pleasure in conveying to you, on behalf of His Majesty's Government, the following declaration of sympathy with Jewish Zionist aspirations which has been submitted to, and approved by, the Cabinet.

His Majesty's Government view with favour the establishment in Palestine of a national home for the Jewish people, and will use their best endeavours to facilitate the achievement of this object, it being clearly understood that nothing shall be done which may prejudice the civil and religious rights of existing non-Jewish communities in Palestine or the rights and political status enjoyed by Jews in any other country.

I should be grateful if you would bring this declaration to the knowledge of the Zionist Federation.

Yours,
Arthur James Balfour

www.jewishvirtuallibrary.org/jsource/History/balfour.html

Britain's attempts to reconcile these three contradictory agreements influenced the situation in the Middle East after the First World War, and resulted in almost three decades of conflict-ridden British rule in Palestine.

Activities

1 Compare the three agreements reached by Britain regarding the Middle East. How did they contradict each other?

2 Design a spider diagram to summarise the reasons why the British government made such conflicting commitments.

3 The writer Gregory Harms has described the Balfour Declaration in these words:

   'The Balfour Declaration is without a doubt the most controversial document to come out of the entire history of the Palestine–Israel conflict. Interpretations of its meaning, and views of its legitimacy, vary widely and greatly.'

   Explain and comment on this view.

4 Write an argument to support or oppose this statement:
   'British policies and actions regarding Palestine during the First World War were motivated entirely by self-interest.'

Theory of knowledge

History, the 'truth', and ethics
When the Bolsheviks came to power in Russia, they were keen to expose the 'evils' of the former Tsarist regime, which is why they publicised the details of the Sykes–Picot Agreement and other secret dealings. A similar motivation may have been behind the decision by Wikileaks to publish secret American government correspondence on the internet in 2010. Supporters of Wikileaks claim that the public has the right to know this confidential information. Opponents claim that publishing secret documents may put lives in danger and jeopardise delicate diplomatic negotiations. Should historians seek to get hold of the 'truth' by whatever means? Or are there ethical issues that should be taken into consideration?

Chaim Weizmann (1874–1952) Weizmann was born in Russia, studied chemistry in Germany and Switzerland, and moved to Britain to lecture in science at Manchester University. Weizmann played a leading role in the negotiations between the British Zionists and the British government that led to the Balfour Declaration. He was later criticised for his moderate approach by more extreme Zionists, who accused him of pro-British sympathies. In 1948, he became the first president of Israel.

> **mandates** These were the former colonies of Germany and Turkey that were taken away from these countries after the First World War. Under the supervision of the League of Nations, they became 'mandates' of the Allied powers, with a view to eventual self-determination. Most of the former German or Turkish colonies in the Middle East and Africa became mandates of Britain and France. Critics of this system saw it as a disguised form of colonialism. 'Protectorates' were weaker states under the protection and control of a stronger nation. Imperial powers sometimes established a protectorate before colonising certain regions.

What happened in Palestine between 1919 and 1939?

After the First World War, the Allies dictated the terms of the peace settlements, and the essence of the Sykes–Picot Agreement was implemented in the Middle East. The Ottoman Empire was broken up, and the Arab lands divided between Britain and France as **mandates**, under the authority of the League of Nations. Syria and Lebanon were given to France, and Britain took Iraq, Transjordan (later called Jordan) and Palestine. These details were confirmed at the San Remo conference in 1920. French and British troops moved into the areas that were now mandates. Arab hopes of independence and unity were ignored. It seemed to many Arabs in the Middle East that they were simply exchanging one set of rulers for another, European instead of Ottoman. Only the kingdom of Hejaz and the province of Najd were recognised as independent Arab states. Ibn Saud, the ruler of Najd, united the two states into the Kingdom of Saudi Arabia. In doing this, he drove out Sharif Husayn of Mecca – the leader of the Arab Revolt – who went into exile. Husayn's sons fared better: Faisal became king of Iraq, and Abdullah king of Transjordan.

A map of the Middle East after the First World War showing the British and French mandates and protectorates

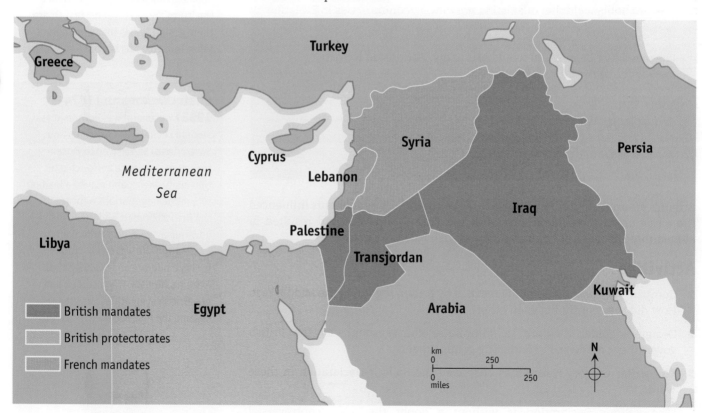

The British mandate

The League of Nations specified that Britain must govern its mandate in Palestine in the spirit of the Balfour Declaration. The British therefore had to fulfil the contradictory promises of creating a 'national home' for the Jews in Palestine, and ensuring for the Arabs that nothing was done to 'harm the civil and religious rights of existing non-Jewish communities in Palestine'. Britain soon found that it was impossible to honour both of these conditions.

The population of Palestine in 1920 was about 700,000. Less than 10% of this number were Jewish. Of the 60,000 Jews who were in Palestine, most had migrated there since the 1880s to escape persecution in Russia. These Jews had bought up land, often from absentee Arab landlords, and established farming settlements. In the terms of the mandate, a **Jewish Agency** was set up to advise the British administration on the establishment of the 'national home'.

Jewish immigration

The aim of the Zionists was to create a Jewish majority in Palestine. The Jewish Agency, under the leadership of **David Ben Gurion**, set out to boost immigration. Initially, the number of immigrants was small, but after Adolf Hitler came to power in Germany in 1933 the numbers increased substantially. Neither the USA nor Western European countries welcomed Jewish refugees, so to many of those trying to escape from the Nazis, Palestine seemed the only option. From just 4000 Jewish immigrants in 1930, the numbers rose to 30,000 in 1933, and 61,000 in 1935. By 1936, Jews formed over 25% of the population of Palestine.

Large numbers of these Jewish immigrants went to work on the land, but many also went to the cities, especially Tel Aviv and Jerusalem. In the cities, they established factories and businesses, employing Jewish workers and providing goods and services for the Jewish community in Palestine. They also set up their own schools and hospitals for the growing Jewish population of the *Yishuv* (see page 17). To many Palestinian Arabs it seemed that the capital and skills brought by the new immigrants benefited only the Jews. Many Arabs saw the Jews as an alien community growing in their midst like a colonial élite.

The Jews also set up their own defence organisation, called the Haganah (meaning 'defence') to defend Jewish settlements, and this provided useful military experience for a future army. By the time the Second World War broke out in 1939, there were 430,000 Jews in Palestine, forming nearly one-third of the population.

SOURCE D

Under the British mandate, the *Yishuv* swelled with refugees from European anti-Semitism – first Polish, then German – and established social, economic, educational institutions that in a short time surpassed those furnished by Britain. By the 1940s, the *Yishuv* was a powerhouse in the making: dynamic, inventive, ideologically and politically pluralistic. Drawing on Western and Eastern European models, the Jews of Palestine created new vehicles for agrarian settlement (the communal *kibbutz* and cooperative *moshav*), a viable socialist economy with systems for national health, reforestation, and infrastructure development, a respectable university, and a symphony orchestra – and to defend them all, an underground citizens' army, the *Haganah*. Though the British had steadily abandoned their support for a Jewish national home, that home was already a fact: an inchoate, burgeoning state.

Oren, M. 2002. Six Days of War: June 1967 and the Making of the Modern Middle East. New York, USA. Ballantyne Books. p. 3.

Jewish Agency The Jewish Agency was the governing body of the Zionist movement in Palestine during the British mandate, linked to the World Zionist Organisation.

David Ben Gurion (1886–1973) Ben Gurion was born in Poland, but emigrated to Palestine in 1906. He was the leader of the Jewish Agency and helped to organise the Haganah, the Jewish defence organisation. Ben Gurion was prime minister of Israel from 1948 to 1953, and from 1955 to 1963. He is regarded as the architect of modern Israel.

Historical interpretation

In his book, *Israel: A Colonial-Settler State?*, the radical French scholar Maxime Rodinson describes the establishment of a Jewish state in Palestine as 'the culmination of a process that fits perfectly into the great European–American movement of expansion in the nineteenth and twentieth centuries whose aim was to settle new inhabitants among other peoples or to dominate them economically and politically'.

Question

How does Oren's description of the Jewish settlement in Palestine differ from Rodinson's perception of it?

29

Hadj Amin al-Husayni (1897–1974) Husayni was a spiritual authority and a leading Palestinian Arab. He was appointed as the Mufti of Jerusalem by the British in 1921. A mufti is a Muslim scholar who interprets Islamic law. Husayni was an outspoken critic of Jewish immigration. When the Arab Revolt broke out in 1936, the British removed him from his position and he went into exile. During the Second World War, Husayni travelled to Nazi Germany, where he tried unsuccessfully to persuade Hitler to support the Arabs against the British in the Middle East.

Arab Higher Committee This committee was formed by Hadj Amin al-Husayni in 1936, after the start of the general strike by the Palestinian Arabs. It consisted of the leaders of the main Palestinian clans, and was the most important political body representing the Arab community in Palestine.

Arab protests

To the Palestinian Arabs, Jewish immigration represented a threat. At the basis of their fears was the issue of land, as farms were increasingly bought up by Jewish settlers. In many cases, the land was sold by wealthy Arab landlords who lived in the cities and were not directly affected by Jewish immigration. It was the small landowners and tenant farmers who were. The new Jewish farms employed Jewish workers, so the landless Arabs were poverty-stricken and bitter. These Palestinian Arabs increasingly associated Zionism with European imperialism. They accused the British of being pro-Zionist in their administration of the mandate.

Another factor that fuelled discontent among Arabs in Palestine was frustrated nationalism. Many of them had taken part in the Arab Revolt of 1916–18 against Turkish rule in order to gain their independence (see page 122 for information on the two Arab Revolts). Now they found themselves under direct British rule, while around them other Arab states had achieved, or were moving towards, independence. In 1922, Egypt had become independent and in 1932 Britain gave up its mandate over Iraq, which became a fully independent state. Although Transjordan remained a British mandate, it had some degree of self-government.

In 1921, there were violent clashes in Jaffa, the main port for Jewish immigration into Palestine. In two days of rioting, 200 Jews and 120 Arabs were killed or wounded. The British government immediately suspended further immigration, but soon allowed it to resume. Although the rate of immigration was slow during the 1920s, by the end of the decade the Jewish population had grown from 60,000 in 1919 to 160,000 in 1929. As the number of immigrants rose, the problems increased. An area of acute tension was Jerusalem, a city holy to both Arabs and Jews (see page 9), and in 1929 serious clashes between the two groups broke out there. There were also Arab attacks on Jewish settlements in other parts of Palestine.

In 1936, **Hadj Amin al-Husayni**, the Mufti of Jerusalem, called for a general strike. During the strike, the Arab community stopped co-operating with the British authorities or the Zionists (for example, by refusing to pay taxes). It demanded an immediate end to Jewish immigration and land sales. Although the Arab economy was crippled by the strike, the Jewish Agency took advantage of the situation to develop a Jewish economy by establishing more settlements and building new roads and ports. A port was built at Tel Aviv as an alternative to the Arab-controlled port of Jaffa, and was opened in 1938.

The strike ended after six months, but it was followed by an uprising that lasted for three years. Arab bands engaged in guerrilla warfare against the British and attacked Jewish settlements, and widespread fighting broke out. In an effort to maintain control, the British used harsh tactics to crush Arab unrest. They banned the **Arab Higher Committee**, imposed collective fines on villages, destroyed houses suspected of giving shelter to Arabs involved in the revolt, imprisoned and tortured people, and executed several Arab leaders. At the same time, the British army used Jewish settlers in police units to help crush the uprising. Over the next three years, many on both sides were killed in what was effectively a civil war. By 1939, the British forces had managed to restore order by sending more troops and better weapons to Palestine. By then, over 500 Jews and 3000 Arabs had been killed in the uprising and its suppression. The British authorities' harsh response, and their co-operation with the Jews, alienated the Arabs even further.

Changing British policies

From 1923 to 1929, Britain supported Jewish immigration. However, as violence increased in the 1930s the British found the policy difficult to uphold. Unrestricted immigration would mean further violent reactions from the Arabs. After the clashes in 1929, a British commission of enquiry suggested limiting immigration. This was never implemented, because of pressure from influential Jewish groups in Britain and the USA.

The Arab Revolt in 1936 forced Britain to rethink its policies in Palestine. In 1937, a British government commission, the Peel Commission, recommended the partition of Palestine into two separate states – one Arab and one Jewish. It also suggested an international zone, which included Jerusalem and Haifa, to be placed under the authority of the League of Nations. The Jewish Agency officially accepted the plan, although some Zionist leaders hoped to create a Jewish state in the whole of Palestine. The plan was totally rejected by the Arabs, who insisted that Palestine should remain an Arab country. They wanted the same right to self-determination and independence that Britain had recognised in Egypt and Iraq, and would soon grant in Transjordan. The Arabs argued that Palestine should not be used as a solution to the problems faced by the Jews in Europe.

SOURCE E

To both Arabs and Jews Partition offers a prospect – and there is none in any other policy – of obtaining the inestimable boon of peace. It is surely worth some sacrifice on both sides if the quarrel which the Mandate started could be ended with its termination. It is not a natural or old-standing feud. The Arabs throughout their history have not only been free from anti-Jewish sentiment but have also shown that the spirit of compromise is deeply rooted in their life. Considering what the possibility of finding a refuge in Palestine means to many thousands of suffering Jews, is the loss occasioned by Partition, great as it would be, more than Arab generosity can bear? In this, as in so much else connected with Palestine, it is not only the peoples of that country who have to be considered. The Jewish Problem is not the least of the many problems which are disturbing international relations at this critical time and obstructing the path to peace and prosperity. If the Arabs at some sacrifice could help to solve that problem, they would earn the gratitude not of the Jews alone but of all the Western World.

From Chapter X of the Report of the Palestine Royal Commission *(Peel Commission Report). From the United Nations Information System on the Question of Palestine (UNISPAL) website. http://domino.un.org/unispal.nsf/0/0 8e38a718201458b052565700072b358?OpenDocument*

Question

What techniques are used in this extract from the Peel Report in an attempt to get Arab support for its proposal of partition?

Questions

What options did Britain have in trying to solve the ongoing crisis in Palestine? Would any solution have satisfied both sides?

Britain found itself in an increasingly difficult situation. It was unable to satisfy either Arab or Zionist demands, and was forced to station a large military force to maintain order in Palestine at a time when the situation in Europe was deteriorating.

In the months before the Second World War, Britain was concerned about any alliance between Germany and Arab leaders. They did not want the Suez Canal or the Persian and Iraqi oilfields, on which the British and other European economies had become increasingly dependent, to fall into hostile hands. Britain therefore considered it essential to win the support of the Arabs.

The result of this was the 1939 **White Paper**, which showed a distinct change in British policy. It abandoned the idea of partition, and proposed an independent Palestine within ten years. In this state, Jews and Arabs would share responsibility for government. The White Paper also placed restrictions on Jewish immigration, limiting immigrant numbers to 75,000 in total over the next five years. After this, immigration would stop altogether unless the Arabs agreed to its continuation.

White Paper This is an official government report, originally bound in white paper, which sets out government policy on a matter before parliament.

SOURCE F

This extract from Section 11 of the 1939 White Paper explains the British government's decision to limit further Jewish immigration.

It has been the hope of British Governments ever since the Balfour Declaration was issued that in time the Arab population, recognizing the advantages to be derived from Jewish settlement and development in Palestine, would become reconciled to the further growth of the Jewish National Home. This hope has not been fulfilled. The alternatives before His Majesty's Government are either (i) to seek to expand the Jewish National Home indefinitely by immigration, against the strongly expressed will of the Arab people of the country; or (ii) to permit further expansion of the Jewish National Home by immigration only if the Arabs are prepared to acquiesce in it. The former policy means rule by force … Moreover, the relations between the Arabs and the Jews in Palestine must be based sooner or later on mutual tolerance and goodwill; the peace, security and progress of the Jewish National Home itself requires this. Therefore His Majesty's Government, after earnest consideration, and taking into account the extent to which the growth of the Jewish National Home has been facilitated over the last twenty years, have decided that the time has come to adopt in principle the second of the alternatives referred to above.

www.jewishvirtuallibrary.org/jsource/History/paper39.html

Activity

Analyse the British government's decision to impose limits on further Jewish immigration. How does Source F show that there was an official change in its attitude towards the Arabs between 1936 and 1939?

The Zionists were furious at this change in British policy. To many of them, it marked the end of the alliance between the British government and the Zionists. This had a significant effect on the Zionists' tactics: they began to focus on the USA, rather than on Britain, to gain support for their cause.

Some Zionists thought that the best option now would be to work actively to force Britain to withdraw and end the mandate, and then to seize power and establish a Jewish state. However, the outbreak of war in 1939 postponed any large-scale organised resistance to British rule in Palestine.

SOURCE G

A table showing the relative size of the Jewish population in Palestine during the period of the British mandate.

Date	Total Population	Jewish population	% of Jews
1918	700,000	60,000	9%
1931	1,036,000	175,000	18%
1939	1,500,000	429,605	28%

Statistics taken from Schools Council History 13–16 Project. 1977. Arab–Israeli Conflict. Edinburgh, UK. Holmes McDougall. p. 30.

Theory of knowledge

History and statistics
How do statistics such as those in Source G help historians to understand the tensions building up in Palestine, and the dilemma facing the British? What are the dangers of using statistics as historical evidence?

Activities

1 Find out what you can about the causes, events and results of the Arab Revolt (1936–39). Design a spider diagram to summarise this information.

2 Divide into two groups. One group represents the Jewish Agency and the other the Arab Higher Committee. Each group should prepare a presentation of its case to make to the 1937 Peel Commission, which has been sent by the British government to investigate the unrest in Palestine.

3 Write a speech to support or oppose this statement: 'By 1939, the British government had good reason to be critical of the policies and actions of its predecessors concerning Palestine.'

How did the Second World War affect Palestine?

Most Jews in Palestine were prepared to co-operate with Britain to defeat Germany, and thus put an end to the persecution of the Jews in Nazi-occupied Europe. Thousands volunteered for active service in a Jewish Brigade to support the Allies.

Soldiers in the Jewish Brigade of the British Army, November 1944

33

Irgun The full name of this group was Irgun Zvai Leumi – the National Military Organisation. Irgun was a Jewish underground group that used terrorist tactics against the British and the Arabs. It was involved in the Deir Yassin Massacre in 1948 (see page 53).

Lehi Also known as the Stern Gang, Lehi was the smallest and most extreme Jewish underground organisation. It was founded by Avraham Stern, and was an offshoot of Irgun. It was responsible for the assassinations of Lord Moyne (the British representative in the Middle East) in Cairo in 1944, and of UN mediator Count Bernadotte in Jerusalem in 1948. A former member of Lehi, Yitzhak Shamir, became prime minister of Israel in 1983.

Menachem Begin (1913–92)

Begin was born in Poland and moved to Palestine in 1942, where he became leader of Irgun. After 1948, he founded the right-wing Herat Party and was elected to the Knesset. As leader of Likud, Begin served as prime minister of Israel from 1977 to 1983. Despite his uncompromising views on negotiating with the Arab states, he signed the Camp David Accords (1978) and the Peace Treaty with Egypt (1979).

The war provided valuable training opportunities for future Jewish military commanders. Arms and ammunition found their way into the secret stores of the Haganah, the Jewish defence organisation that was later transformed into a national army.

A small minority of Jews in Palestine decided to use the opportunity provided by the distraction of the Second World War to drive the British out of the country immediately. Two extremist groups, **Irgun** and the more radical **Lehi** (or Stern Gang), committed acts of sabotage and assassination. The leader of Irgun, **Menachem Begin**, openly declared the start of a Jewish revolt in 1944. He said that the Jewish people were prepared to fight to force the British to transfer power immediately to a provisional Jewish government.

During 1944 and 1945, Irgun and Lehi increased their efforts to force the British out. They blew up roads and bridges, raided banks and post offices to get funds, and attacked British soldiers and the local police force. Lehi made several unsuccessful attempts to assassinate the British high commissioner in Palestine. In Cairo in 1944 they killed Lord Moyne, the British government minister representing British policy in the Middle East. Lord Moyne was the first high-ranking British official to be assassinated in the Palestine conflict. This action hardened British government attitudes towards the Zionists, and relations between the Jews in Palestine and the British deteriorated.

As news got out about the massacre of Jews in Nazi-occupied Europe, it strengthened the determination of the Zionists to create a Jewish state in Palestine. The news also increased support in the USA for the Zionists' aims. A strong Jewish lobby existed in the USA: there were more than 5 million Jewish voters in the north-eastern states, and 2 million in New York alone. Support for the Zionists also came from other sources, such as the American Palestine Committee and the Christian Council on Palestine. In May 1942, American Zionists held a conference at the Biltmore Hotel in New York, hoping to unite the various pro-Zionist groups and strengthen their voice and influence. The decisions reached at the conference were known collectively as The Biltmore Program, and they called for an immediate end to restrictions on immigration.

The Biltmore Program helped to unite American Jews behind the Zionist movement, and their influence began to have an impact on American politics. In the 1944 presidential election, both the Republicans and the Democrats made references to their support for the establishment of a Jewish state. By contrast, the Palestinian Arabs were in a weak position by the end of the war. Some Arab leaders, such as Amin al-Husayni, were discredited in Allied eyes by their willingness to support Nazi Germany as a way of gaining independence. Ilan Pappe, an Israeli revisionist historian, observes that al-Husayni's connections with the Nazis 'did a great service to Zionist propaganda after the war'.

Some members of the Arab Higher Committee, who were imprisoned by the British during the Arab Revolt of 1936–39, also went into exile. Other leaders who remained in Palestine were disunited. Independent Arab governments tried to create some form of Arab unity, and met in Alexandria, Egypt in 1944. They adopted the Alexandria Protocol, declaring their support for the Palestinian Arabs (see page 40), but their attempts to form a united front were not successful until shortly before the end of the war. In March 1945, Egypt, Iraq, Syria, Lebanon, Transjordan and Saudi Arabia formed the Arab League in Cairo.

By this stage, France had virtually given up its mandate over Syria and Lebanon, and Britain was preparing to do the same in Transjordan. Of the former Ottoman Empire in the Middle East, only the future status of Palestine remained uncertain.

SOURCE H

An extract from the Declaration adopted by the Extraordinary Zionist Conference at the Biltmore Hotel in New York City, 11 May 1942.

In our generation, and in particular in the course of the past twenty years, the Jewish people have awakened and transformed their ancient homeland; from 50,000 at the end of the last war their numbers have increased to more than 500,000. They have made the waste places to bear fruit and the desert to blossom. Their pioneering achievements in agriculture and in industry, embodying new patterns of cooperative endeavour, have written a notable page in the history of colonization …

The Conference calls for the fulfillment of the original purpose of the Balfour Declaration and the Mandate which recognizing the historical connection of the Jewish people with Palestine was to afford them the opportunity, as stated by President Wilson, to found there a Jewish Commonwealth. The Conference affirms its unalterable rejection of the White Paper of May 1939 and denies its moral or legal validity … The policy of the White Paper is cruel and indefensible in its denial of sanctuary to Jews fleeing from Nazi persecution.

www.jewishvirtuallibrary.org/jsource/Zionism/BiltProg.html

Activities

1 Draw up a table to summarise the relationship each of the following people had to the history of Palestine before 1945:
- Arthur Balfour
- Chaim Weizmann
- Amin al-Husayni
- David Ben Gurion.

2 Find out about the policies, tactics and actions of the extremist underground organisations that operated in Palestine during the Second World War.

3 Explain the significance of each of the following:
- the assassination of Lord Moyne
- the relations of Amin al-Husayni with the Nazi regime
- the Biltmore Program
- the formation of the Arab League.

4 Design a spider diagram to illustrate the origins of the Arab–Israeli conflict before 1945.

End of chapter activities

Summary

You need to ensure that you have a good understanding of the origins of the Arab–Israeli conflict. Firstly, this involves knowing how British policies during the First World War influenced subsequent developments in Palestine. You also need to consider how the policies and actions of governments and politicians can affect the lives of ordinary people. For example, what were the desires and problems of the Jewish and Arab communities in Palestine? Were they mutually exclusive? Above all, you must be able to explain clearly what the situation was in Palestine in 1945. This is the date at which the IB History course begins its study of the Arab–Israeli conflict. You will be examined on the events that took place after 1945, which are covered in the following chapters.

Summary activity

Copy the spider diagram below. Using the information in this chapter and from other sources, make brief notes under each heading.

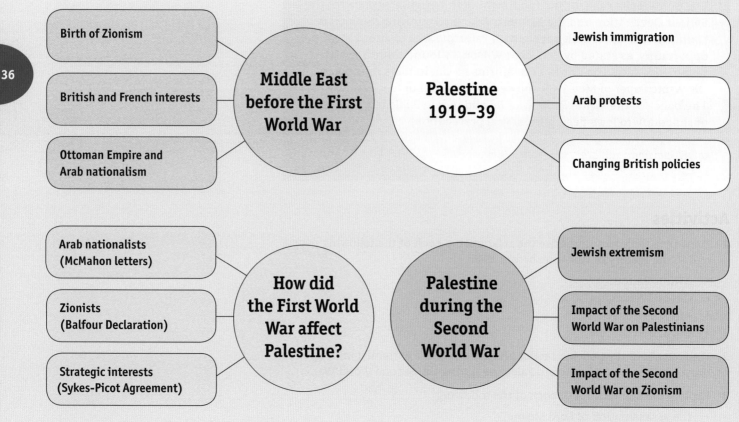

Paper 1 exam practice

Question

What does Source A below suggest about the situation in the British mandate of Palestine?
[2 marks]

Skill

Comprehension of a source

Before you start

Comprehension questions are the most straightforward questions that you will face in Paper 1. They simply require you to understand a source *and* extract two or three relevant points that relate to the particular question. Before you attempt this question, refer to pages 217–18 for advice on how to tackle these questions, and a simplified markscheme.

SOURCE A

Try as Britain did to strike a balance, the incompatible interests of the Arabs (independence), the Zionists (a Jewish state), and Great Britain (colonial control) created an untenable situation that eventually – and unsurprisingly – turned violent.

Harms, G. 2005. *The Palestine–Israel Conflict: A Basic Introduction.* London, UK. Pluto Press. p. 76.

Student answer

Source A suggests that the Arabs, the Zionists and the British government wanted completely different things in Palestine, and that these were incompatible because they conflicted with each other.

Examiner comments

The candidate has explained one of the key issues mentioned in the source – that the aims of the Arabs, the Zionists and the British government in Palestine were incompatible – and this is certainly enough to gain 1 mark. However, the answer does not refer to the untenable (or unworkable) nature of the situation, which resulted in violence.

Activity

Look again at Source A and at the student answer above. Now, using information from the source, explain how the situation was 'untenable', and so obtain the other mark available for this question.

Paper 2 practice questions

1   Assess the roles of Arab nationalism and Zionism as causes of conflict in the Middle East.

2   Examine British policy towards Palestine between 1914 and 1939.

3   Account for the growing tensions in the British mandate of Palestine by 1939.

4   Analyse the impact of the Second World War on the situation in Palestine.

3 The last years of the British mandate and the war of 1948–49

Timeline

1945 Mar: formation of Arab League in Cairo

May: end of Second World War in Europe

Jul: Labour government comes to power in Britain

Aug: Zionist conference supports active opposition to British rule

Nov: establishment of Anglo–American Committee of Inquiry

1946 May: report of Anglo–American Committee of Inquiry

Jul: Irgun attack on King David Hotel

1947 Feb: Britain refers Palestine issue to UN

Jul: *Exodus* turned back; two British soldiers hanged by Irgun

Aug: UNSCOP recommends partition

Nov: UN General Assembly supports partition; outbreak of civil war

1948 Apr: Haganah launches Plan Dalet; massacre at Deir Yassin

May: British withdrawal completed

14 May: declaration of state of Israel

15 May: start of first Arab–Israeli war

Sep: assassination of Bernadotte (UN mediator)

1949 Jan–Jul: separate armistice agreements between Israel and Egypt, Lebanon, Transjordan and Syria

Introduction

The years 1945 to 1949 were a critical time in Palestine, during which the status and population structure of the country fundamentally changed. In 1945, Palestine was a British mandate in which Jews formed less than half of the population. By 1949, 78% of Palestine had become the Jewish state of Israel, and more than half of the Palestinian Arab population had fled. The years 1945 to 1949 were a time of tension, violence, civil war, and war between Israel and the Arab states. The origins of future conflict and crises in the Middle East, which remain unresolved nearly 70 years later, is in this period.

Key questions

- What was the situation in Palestine after the Second World War?
- How did UNSCOP and the United Nations Partition Plan affect the situation?
- What happened during the civil war between 1947 and 1948?
- How did the British withdrawal and the establishment of Israel lead to war in Palestine in 1948–49?

Overview

- After the Second World War, Britain maintained limits on immigration into Palestine, despite the large number of Jewish refugees in Europe wanting to move there.
- The Zionists stepped up their efforts to establish a Jewish state by smuggling immigrants into Palestine, launching a propaganda campaign to gain support in the USA, and using terror tactics to force the British to give up the mandate.
- In February 1947, as a result of the mounting violence in Palestine, post-war economic problems at home, and changes in global priorities, the British government referred the issue of Palestine to the United Nations.
- The UN special committee, UNSCOP, recommended the partition of Palestine into two separate states – one Arab and one Jewish. Although the Arabs rejected the plan outright, it was accepted by the United Nations.
- There was increasing violence in Palestine as the Jews sought to strengthen their position before the mandate ended. This escalated into full-scale civil war in April 1948, when the Haganah launched Plan Dalet to secure the area designated as the future Jewish state.

- Jewish forces occupied more than 200 Arab villages, especially in the area between Jerusalem and Tel Aviv. They also took over the coastal towns of Jaffa and Haifa, and the Arab areas of West Jerusalem.
- In the most controversial incident of the civil war, over 250 civilians in the Arab village of Deir Yassin were killed by Irgun commandos – an event that became significant in the subsequent flight of Arab refugees.
- On 14 May 1948, the final British forces withdrew from Palestine and the Jewish Agency declared the establishment of the state of Israel. On the following day, the armies of five Arab countries invaded, and the first Arab–Israeli war began.
- By the end of the war, Israel occupied 78% of Palestine rather than the 56% allocated to the Jewish state in the UN Partition Plan. The areas that had been designated as the Palestinian state were under Israeli, Jordanian or Egyptian control.
- The Israeli military victory was due to Israel's larger force of experienced soldiers, rivalry and distrust between Arab leaders, Arab disunity, and ineffective organising structures among the Palestinians themselves.

The immigrant ship President Warfield, *or* Exodus, *seized by the British Royal Navy on 20 July 1947; crammed on board were 4500 Jewish immigrants who were trying to enter Palestine illegally*

What was the situation in Palestine after the Second World War?

The situation in Palestine in 1945

In 1945, Palestine was still a mandate under British administration, and its Jewish population remained less than a third of its total population. During the Second World War there had been limited Jewish immigration into Palestine, in spite of the desperate situation of the Jews in Nazi-occupied Europe. At the end of the war, however, this changed. There were hundreds of thousands of Jewish survivors of the Nazi death camps in Europe, as well as large numbers of displaced Jews whose communities had been destroyed. Sympathy for these people's plight increased international support for the Zionist demand to allow more Jewish immigrants into Palestine immediately. The urgency of the situation of the Jews in Europe therefore had direct implications for Palestine.

At the same time, the Arab League – which was formed in 1945 – warned against any relaxation of the limits on Jewish immigration set out in the 1939 White Paper (see page 32). In the Alexandria Protocol in 1944, the Arab states had declared their support for the Palestinian Arabs' cause, arguing that Palestine should not be used as a solution to a problem that originated in Europe.

Fact

According to a 1990 study by Justin McCarthy on Palestinian population statistics, in 1946 there were 1.3 million Arabs, 600,000 Jews and 30,000 people classified as 'other' living in Palestine.

Question

What are the different forms of 'injustice' referred to in Source A?

Question

How do you think the Zionist Organisation would have responded to the statement in Source A by the governments of the Arab states?

SOURCE A

An extract from the Alexandria Protocol, signed by the governments of Egypt, Syria, Transjordan, Iraq and Lebanon on 7 October 1944.

The Committee also declares that it is second to none in regretting the woes which have been inflicted upon the Jews of Europe by European dictatorial states. But the question of these Jews should not be confused with Zionism, for there can be no greater injustice and aggression than solving the problem of the Jews of Europe by another injustice, i.e., by inflicting injustice on the Arabs of Palestine of various religions and denominations.

www.jewishvirtuallibrary.org/jsource/Peace/alexpro.html

There was little change in British policy in Palestine after the Second World War, despite the fact that the Labour Party – which came to power in Britain in July 1945 – had previously declared its support for the Zionist cause. The new British government, under Clement Attlee, was acutely aware that any increase in Jewish immigration would provoke a reaction from the Palestinian Arabs. This would in turn require a greater British military presence in Palestine, in order to keep the peace between the two communities. The British government therefore announced that it would not change its policy towards Jewish immigration into Palestine. The British foreign secretary, Ernest Bevin, also believed that an Arab-controlled Palestine under British supervision would better serve British interests in the Middle East. In November 1945, he proposed the establishment of an Anglo–American Committee of Inquiry to investigate the situation in Palestine. In this way, Bevin hoped to force the American government to become involved in solving the Palestine issue.

Zionist policies and actions after the Second World War

The Zionists set up highly efficient networks in Europe to organise the movement of Jewish refugees to Mediterranean ports, and from there to Palestine. Apart from humanitarian motives, the Zionists also had a political aim. They wanted to increase the size of the Jewish population in Palestine, in order to strengthen the Zionist demand for a Jewish state. The Zionists actively discouraged schemes to settle Jewish refugees in any other countries. In an effort to prevent the outbreak of civil war between Jews and Arabs, the British stopped immigrants from landing in Palestine. When boatloads of refugees tried to evade the British naval blockade, they were intercepted and sent to refugee camps in Cyprus. In the aftermath of the Nazi death camps and the Holocaust, the issue of the Jewish refugees was an emotive one. British actions were regarded by many in the international community as heartless and inappropriate. They provided powerful ammunition for Zionist propaganda.

At the same time, the Zionists focused on a propaganda offensive in the USA, where there was a strong Jewish lobby in the US Congress. Zionists hoped that the USA would exert enough pressure on the British government to force the latter to change its policies in Palestine. American Zionists held rallies, and Jewish leaders from Palestine addressed meetings to raise public support and funding for their cause. These efforts paid off when US President **Harry S. Truman** announced his support for the Zionist demand that Britain immediately admit 100,000 Jewish immigrants into Palestine. When the British government rejected Truman's demand, there were further violent reactions from the Zionists in Palestine.

To put pressure on Britain, in August 1945 the Zionist conference adopted a policy of more active opposition to British rule. It urged the Haganah, the defence force organised by the Jewish Agency, to work together with the extremist underground groups Irgun and Lehi to end British rule as soon as possible. They launched terror attacks on British military bases, police stations, refineries, railway lines and bridges. In 1946, attacks and acts of sabotage targeting the British administration increased. The British responded with tighter security. During Black Saturday on 29 June 1946, the British authorities in Palestine used 100,000 soldiers and 10,000 police to occupy the Jewish Agency's headquarters in Jerusalem, make raids on 25 Jewish settlements, and detain 2700 individuals. This resulted in even more violence, including the Irgun bombing of the King David Hotel, which housed the British military headquarters in Jerusalem. These attacks provoked a stern reaction from Britain, but also weakened British morale.

SOURCE B

A much tougher kind of Zionism was forged during World War II, and the commitment to Jewish statehood became deeper and more desperate in the shadow of the Holocaust. On the one hand, the Holocaust confirmed the conviction of the Zionists that they had justice on their side in the struggle for Palestine; on the other, it converted international public opinion to the idea of an independent Jewish state.

Shlaim, A. 2000. The Iron Wall: Israel and the Arab World. London, UK. Penguin. p. 24.

Harry S. Truman (1884–1972)

Truman was president of the USA from 1945 to 1953. The Zionist lobby in the USA put a great deal of pressure on him while he was in power. Truman later noted in his memoirs that the White House had never been subjected to as much pressure and propaganda as it was in this instance. His verbal support for the Zionist cause is seen as a key factor in the movement's success.

41

Question

According to Source B, what impact did the Holocaust have on the Zionist cause?

British policy towards Palestine

As violence escalated in Palestine, the British government found its position increasingly difficult. Britain was economically weak after six years of war. There were urgent problems to be addressed at home: wartime bombing had destroyed thousands of houses and factories, which needed to be rebuilt. Food shortages and the continuation of wartime rationing added to the problems facing the government. Britain could no longer afford to keep a large military presence in Palestine at a time of severe post-war economic problems. The Labour government was also anxious to focus on domestic reforms to create a welfare state. Many people in Britain began to feel that the situation in Palestine was taking up too much money and attention.

This 1948 photograph shows armed British soldiers on lookout duty in the Jewish quarter of Jerusalem; by this time, many in Britain disapproved of the army's continued presence in Palestine

The changing British attitude towards Palestine was influenced by other factors besides the difficulties and costs of coping with the mounting violence. The late 1940s were the beginning of an era of decolonisation. Britain had already committed itself to withdrawal from India, and during 1947 and 1948 the British colonies in India, Pakistan, Ceylon and Burma became independent. The Second World War also stimulated the rise of nationalism in other colonies, and there were demands from the Egyptians for the removal of British troops from Egypt. With Britain's global empire coming to an end, domination of the Middle East was no longer a major consideration in British foreign policy.

The start of the Cold War (see page 13) also influenced British policy, and forced the government to reassess its priorities. The USA and the USSR were the new superpowers in the post-war world, and the development of a Western alliance to contain the USSR was crucial. Britain's good relationship with the USA was threatened by the unresolved situation in Palestine.

The Anglo–American Committee of Inquiry

The Anglo–American Committee of Inquiry was appointed in November 1945 to investigate the issue of Jewish migration to Palestine. It heard presentations from a number of different viewpoints. The Palestinian Arabs repeated their opposition to unrestricted immigration and to the establishment of a Jewish state in Palestine.

SOURCE C

The whole Arab people is unalterably opposed to the attempt to impose Jewish immigration and settlement upon it, and ultimately to establish a Jewish state in Palestine. Its opposition is based primarily upon right. The Arabs of Palestine are descendants of the indigenous inhabitants of the country, who have been in occupation of it from the beginning of history; they cannot agree that it is right to subject an indigenous population against its will to alien immigrants, whose claim is based upon a historical connection which ceased effectively many centuries ago. Moreover, they form the majority of the population; as such they cannot submit to a policy of immigration which if pursued for long will turn them from a majority into a minority in an alien state; and they claim the democratic right of a majority to make its own decisions in matters of urgent national concern …

It cannot be too often repeated that Zionism is a political movement aiming at the domination of at least the whole of Palestine; to give it a foothold in part of Palestine would be to encourage it to press for more and to provide it with a base for its activities. Because of this, because of the pressure of population and in order to escape from its isolation, it would inevitably be thrown into enmity with the surrounding Arab states and this enmity would disturb the stability of the whole Middle East.

Extract from the evidence submitted by the Arab Office, Jerusalem, to the Anglo–American Committee of Inquiry, March 1946. Quoted in Laqueur, W and Rubin, B. 1969. The Israel–Arab Reader. London, UK. Weidenfeld and Nicolson. pp. 94 and 104.

Activity

How would the Jewish Agency have challenged the issues raised by the Arab Office in Source C? Make a list of the points that you think they would include in a presentation to the Anglo–American Committee to support the Zionist claim for the establishment of a Jewish state.

Question

What are the values and limitations of Source C for understanding the situation facing the Anglo–American Committee of Inquiry?

There was a small group of Zionists who supported the establishment of a national state of both Arabs and Jews that would be based on equality and co-operation in social, economic, political and cultural relations. The most prominent supporter of this view was the philosopher Martin Buber. Together with other Zionist intellectuals, he formed the League for Arab–Jewish Rapprochement and Cooperation in 1939, which aimed to build bridges between the two communities. Buber was also a member of Ihud, a political movement that tried to rally support for this bi-national solution, with equal rights for Arabs and Jews, and a federal union of Palestine and the neighbouring Arab countries. These views had little support from either the Jewish or Arab communities.

SOURCE D

The whole history of Palestine shows that it just has not been made for uni-lateral sovereign independence. This is an inescapable fact which no one can disregard … we contend that the sovereign independence of tiny Palestine, whether it be Jewish sovereignty or Arab sovereignty, is a questionable good in this post-war period, when even great States must relinquish something of their sovereignty and seek union, if the world is not to perish. We contend that for this Holy Land the idea of a bi-national Palestine is at least as inspiring as that of an Arab sovereign Palestine or a Jewish sovereign Palestine … the hard facts of the situation are that this is not a Jewish land and it is not an Arab land – it is the Holy land, a bi-national country – and it is in the light of such hard facts that the problem must be appreciated.

Extract from a presentation to the Anglo–American Committee made by Martin Buber and Dr Judah L. Magnes, leading members of the Ihud movement. Quoted in Laqueur, W. and Rubin, B. 1969. The Israel–Arab Reader. London, UK. Weidenfeld and Nicolson. p. 105.

SOURCE E

In the light of its long history, and particularly the history of the last thirty years, Palestine cannot be regarded as either a purely Arab or a purely Jewish land.

The Jews have a historic connection with the country. The Jewish National Home, though embodying a minority of the population, is today a reality established under international guarantee. It has a right to continued existence, protection and development.

Yet Palestine is not, and never can be, a purely Jewish land. It lies at the crossroads of the Arab world. Its Arab population, descended from long-time inhabitants of the area, rightly look upon Palestine as their homeland.

It is, therefore, neither just nor practicable that Palestine should become either an Arab state, in which an Arab majority would control the destiny of a Jewish minority, or a Jewish state, in which a Jewish majority would control that of an Arab minority. In neither case would minority guarantees afford adequate protection for the subordinated group.

Extract from the Report of the Anglo–American Committee, 1946. Quoted in Laqueur, W. and Rubin, B. 1969. The Israel–Arab Reader. London, UK. Weidenfeld and Nicolson. p. 89.

Question

Why would the views expressed in Source D not have much support in post-war Palestine?

United Nations (UN) The UN was formed as a peacekeeping organisation in 1945, as the successor to the League of Nations. The League of Nations had ceased to function effectively during the 1930s, and was formally dissolved in 1946. One of the groups within the UN was the Trusteeship Council, which was established to supervise the former mandates of the League and to prepare them for independence.

After interviewing displaced persons in Europe and hearing presentations from a range of groups with conflicting interests in Palestine, the Anglo–American Committee of Inquiry finally published its report in May 1946. It recommended that 100,000 Jewish refugees in Europe be allowed into Palestine immediately, and that the British mandate should continue until a system of trusteeship under the supervision of the **United Nations (UN)** could be set in place. However, apart from rejecting partition as unworkable, the report was vague about the future of Palestine.

The committee's findings were rejected by the Arabs as well as the Jewish Agency, and received little support from either the British or American governments. Bevin was annoyed that his attempts to force the USA to share responsibility for Palestine had failed.

Britain decides to end the mandate

As the situation in Palestine deteriorated, the British government decided to refer the issue to the United Nations.

SOURCE F

There are in Palestine about 1,200,000 Arabs and 600,000 Jews. For the Jews the essential point of principle is the creation of a sovereign Jewish State. For the Arabs, the essential point of principle is to resist to the last the establishment of Jewish sovereignty in any part of Palestine. The discussions of the last month have quite clearly shown that there is no prospect of resolving this conflict by any settlement negotiated between the parties …

His Majesty's Government have of themselves no power, under the terms of the Mandate, to award the country either to the Arabs or to the Jews, or even to partition it between them. It is in these circumstances that we have decided that we are unable to accept the scheme put forward either by the Arabs or by the Jews, or to impose ourselves a solution of our own. We have, therefore, reached the conclusion that the only course now open to us is to submit the problem to the judgment of the United Nations. We intend to place before them an historical account of the way in which His Majesty's Government have discharged their trust in Palestine over the last 25 years. We shall explain that the Mandate has proved to be unworkable in practice, and that the obligations undertaken to the two communities in Palestine have been shown to be irreconcilable … We shall then ask the United Nations to consider our report, and to recommend a settlement of the problem. We do not intend ourselves to recommend any particular solution.

Announcement made by the British foreign secretary, Ernest Bevin, in the House of Commons, 18 February 1947. http://hansard.millbanksystems. com/commons/1947/feb/18/palestine-conference-government-policy#S5CV0433P0_19470218_HOC_314

Questions

Why had the mandate proved to be 'unworkable in practice', as it is described in Source F? What is ironic about Bevin's statement that the 'obligations undertaken to the two communities in Palestine have been shown to be irreconcilable'?

At this stage, the British government had not yet decided to withdraw from Palestine altogether. It was still trying to force other countries, especially the USA, to play a more constructive – rather than a critical – role in resolving the situation. However, as the violence in Palestine continued, the British public increasingly supported the idea of withdrawal.

Activities

1 Draw up a table to summarise the differences between the various Jewish military organisations operating in Palestine. Use the information in this unit as a start, but use other sources to find out more details. Copy the table below, and add any other categories that you think are important.

	Haganah	Irgun	Lehi
Background/origins			
Leadership			
Numbers			
Tactics/strategies			
Political outlook/ ideology			

2 Find out what you can about the bombing of the King David Hotel in Jerusalem in July 1946, and write a brief essay on the incident. Include information on the circumstances of the attack itself, the reactions to it, and its consequences. Why do certain aspects of the incident remain controversial?

3 Write an argument to support or oppose the following statement:

'The issue of Jewish survivors of the Nazi death camps could not be solved on humanitarian grounds alone; there were other considerations that had to be taken into account as well.'

4 Design a spider diagram to show which factors led the British government to hand the Palestine issue over to the United Nations.

How did UNSCOP and the United Nations Partition Plan affect the situation?

The formation of UNSCOP

Palestine was the first serious regional conflict that the newly formed United Nations had to face. In response to the British request, the General Assembly of the UN appointed a special committee to investigate the Palestine issue. This was the United Nations Special Committee on Palestine, or UNSCOP. The committee travelled to Palestine to collect evidence, and also visited Holocaust survivors in camps around Europe. The Zionists in Palestine welcomed the opportunity to promote their case for partition to the committee members, but the Palestinian Arabs refused to meet them. Historian Ilan Pappe believes that this imbalance contributed to UNSCOP's decision to support the Zionist demand for partition as the most logical solution to the problem.

While the UNSCOP fact-finding mission was in progress, the violence continued, with radical Zionist groups carrying out bombing attacks on both the Arabs and the British. In July 1947, Irgun kidnapped and hanged two British soldiers, and booby-trapped their bodies. This was an act of retaliation for the execution of three Irgun commandos, and was condemned by the Jewish Agency and the Haganah. The incident had a powerful impact on British public opinion. It caused widespread outrage and set off anti-Jewish rioting in several British cities, which included attacks on 300 Jewish properties in Liverpool. Many people saw the incident as a sign that British control in Palestine had virtually collapsed, and there was growing public support for the mandate to end.

British soldiers dig their way through the debris in search of survivors after the bomb attack by Irgun at the King David Hotel in Jerusalem in July 1946

At the same time, more moderate Zionists continued their attempts to land illegal immigrants in Palestine, despite the British blockade. In the most famous incident, the British authorities refused entry to a refugee ship, the *Exodus*, carrying 4500 refugees. Many of the people on board were survivors of the Nazi death camps, and the British decision to send them back to their port of departure – Hamburg in Germany – provoked international condemnation. This event further strengthened the Zionist position.

The UNSCOP Partition Plan

UNSCOP presented its report in August 1947. The UNSCOP plan, which was supported by the majority of its members, recommended that the British mandate should be terminated and that Palestine should be partitioned into separate Jewish and Arab states, with Jerusalem under international control. Although the Jews numbered under one-third of the population, they were to receive 56% of the land, in anticipation of further Jewish immigration. Much of the fertile coastal land, including the ports of Tel Aviv and Haifa, would be part of the Jewish state. The Arab state would be divided into three sections and would have no major outlet to the sea. Jaffa – the main Arab port – would be cut off from the rest of the Arab territory, and surrounded by the Jewish state.

Questions

What were the options facing Britain with regard to immigration into Palestine at this time? What were the implications of each option?

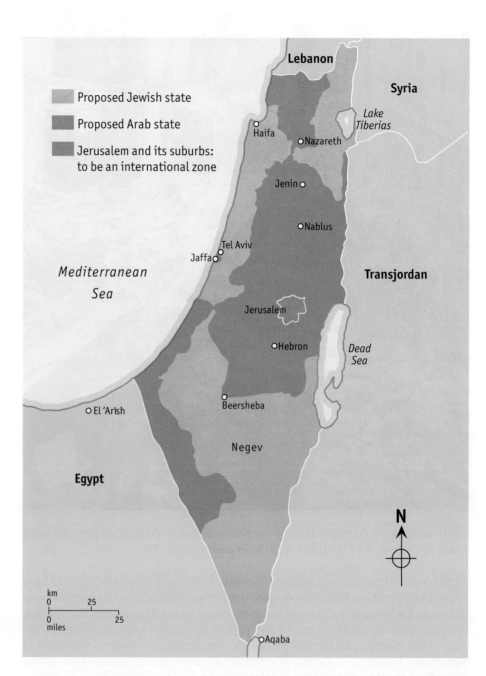

A map showing the areas set aside for the Arab and Jewish states in Palestine in the UN Partition Plan of 1947

UNSCOP produced two plans. The partition plan was supported by the majority of the committee's members (and later adopted by the United Nations). Another plan, supported by India, Iran and Yugoslavia, recommended the establishment of a federation of Arab and Jewish states, with a central authority in control of matters such as foreign policy and defence.

Reactions to the UNSCOP Partition Plan

The partition plan was totally rejected by the Arabs. In a statement, the Arab Higher Committee accused the UN of violating its own Charter by suggesting a partition that was 'absurd, impracticable, and unjust' in the same way that the Balfour Declaration contradicted the Covenant of the League of Nations by being 'immoral, unjust and illegal'.

Fact

The UN Charter is an agreement that was adopted by the 51 founder members of the United Nations at a conference in San Francisco in 1945. It outlines the aims and principles of the UN: to maintain international peace and security, to promote economic and social development, and to uphold and promote fundamental human rights.

SOURCE G

UNSCOP explains its reasons for supporting the idea of partition as the only viable solution for Palestine.

The basic premise underlying the partition proposal is that the claims to Palestine of the Arabs and Jews, both possessing validity, are irreconcilable, and that among all of the solutions advanced, partition will provide the most realistic and practicable settlement, and is the most likely to afford a workable basis for meeting in part the claims and national aspirations of both parties.

It is a fact that both of these peoples have their historic roots in Palestine, and that both make vital contributions to the economic and cultural life of the country. The partition solution takes these considerations fully into account.

The basic conflict in Palestine is a clash of two intense nationalisms … Only by means of partition can these conflicting national aspirations find substantial expression and qualify both peoples to take their places as independent nations in the international community and in the United Nations.

Jewish immigration is the central issue in Palestine today and is the one factor, above all others, that rules out the necessary co-operation between the Arab and Jewish communities in a single State. The creation of a Jewish State under a partition scheme is the only hope of removing this issue from the arena of conflict.

It is recognized that partition has been strongly opposed by Arabs, but it is felt that that opposition would be lessened by a solution which definitively fixes the extent of territory to be allotted to the Jews with its implicit limitation on immigration. The fact that the solution carries the sanction of the United Nations involves a finality which should allay Arab fears of further expansion of the Jewish State.

Extract from the official records of the UN General Assembly. UNSCOP Report to the General Assembly. Volume 1 Chapter V1. New York, USA. 1947. http://unispal.un.org/ unispal.nsf/181c4bf00c44e5fd85256c ef0073c426/07175de9fa2de56385256 8d3006e10f3?OpenDocument

Questions

Compare the UNSCOP report with the submissions made to the Anglo–American Committee of Inquiry by the Arab Office (Source C on page 43) and the Ihud movement (Source D on page 44). How would these two groups have reacted to the UNSCOP plan? What would the reactions of the Jewish Agency, and the British and American governments have been?

49

SOURCE H

Historian Mark Tessler explains the Arab response to the UNSCOP Partition Plan.

They adhered to their long-held position that Palestine was an integral part of the Arab world and that from the beginning its indigenous inhabitants had opposed the creation in their country of a Jewish national home. They also insisted that the United Nations, a body created and controlled by the USA and Europe, had no right to grant the Zionists any portion of their territory. In what was to become a familiar Arab charge, they insisted that the Western world was seeking to salve its conscience for the atrocities of the war and was paying its own debt to the Jewish people with someone else's land.

Tessler, M. 1994. A History of the Israeli–Palestinian Conflict. Bloomington, USA. Indiana University Press. p. 259.

Fact

In 1947, the UN had only 56 member states. The organisation's membership increased substantially in the 1950s and 1960s, after former European colonies in Asia, Africa and the Caribbean became independent and joined the UN as separate members. In 2012, it had 193 members.

The Jewish Agency officially accepted the plan, although there were aspects of it that the organisation did not like. The proposed boundaries put Jerusalem at the heart of the Arab zone: although the city itself would be administered by the UN, the Arabs would control access to and from the city. The proposed Jewish state would also contain a large number of Arabs: there would be roughly 500,000 Jews and 400,000 Arabs. Hardliners such as Menachem Begin, the leader of Irgun, were determined that the whole of ***Eretz Israel*** should become part of the Jewish state, with Jerusalem as its capital.

The Zionists mounted a major diplomatic campaign to convince member countries of the UN to support the partition plan. President Truman came under intense pressure from American Zionists. The US government in turn put pressure on other UN members. Fearing a boycott by Jewish customers, some American corporations also used what influence they had to gather support for the plan.

The partition plan needed a two-thirds majority in the UN General Assembly in order to be adopted. Many initially assumed that the plan would be rejected, as it was not clear whether the USSR and its allies would support it. However, when the vote was taken on 29 November 1947, there were 33 votes in favour and 13 against, with 10 abstentions. Both the USA and the USSR supported the partition plan, while Britain abstained from voting. Six of the seven member states of the Arab League voted against the plan, but Transjordan abstained.

The plan was adopted by the United Nations as UN Resolution 181. The news of the UN vote was welcomed by overjoyed Jewish communities in Tel Aviv and other parts of the world. In contrast, the Arab League threatened to resist the implementation of the partition plan by force, and the Arab Higher Committee declared a three-day general strike that was accompanied by attacks on Jewish civilians. As tensions and violence mounted, the British government announced the date for its withdrawal from Palestine: 15 May 1948.

SOURCE 1

Historian Norman Rose explains his view of the failure of the British mandate.

Britain had undertaken responsibility for the Palestine mandate when its empire, territorially at least, was at its apogee [highest point] – though cracks were already appearing, particularly in India. It had done so believing firmly that the mandate was workable, despite warning signs to the contrary. All that was needed [it believed] was a spirit of compromise, a measure of goodwill and cooperation between the interested parties, behaviour in accordance with the presumed British tradition of resolving thorny political problems. Unfortunately, the belligerent, extra-European nationalisms, gaining in militancy in the aftermath of the Second World War, were in no mood to adhere to this practice. So Britain stumbled along, at odds with its closest allies, subject to withering criticism at home and abroad, persisting in a policy it scarcely believed in. By 1948, it had neither the will nor resources to continue the mandate: it was a classic case of imperial overreach: psychologically, emotionally and materially.

Rose, N. 2009. 'A Senseless, Squalid War': Voices from Palestine 1945–1948. London, UK. The Bodley Head. pp. 215–16.

Activity

What are the main reasons suggested in Source 1 for the failure of the British mandate in Palestine? Draw a simple spider diagram to summarise these reasons.

SOURCE J

A cartoon from the British magazine Punch, *published on 31 March 1948; the G.B. on the nurse's case stands for Great Britain, and the doctors represent the most powerful member states of the United Nations*

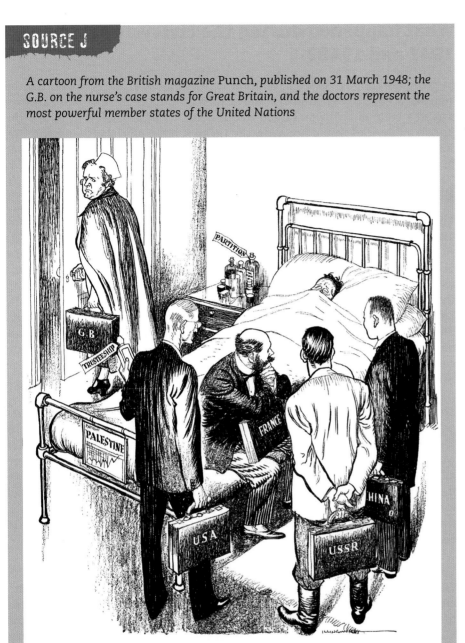

NURSE GIVES NOTICE.

"And now, gentlemen, we shall have to get something done ourselves, instead of telling *her* what to do."

Activities

1   Work in groups to prepare a presentation that UNSCOP could have made to defend its proposal to partition Palestine. Use the map on page 48 as part of the presentation. The rest of the class should ask critical questions to determine how the partition will work in practice.

2   Examine Source H on page 49. Explain what is meant by the charge that the Western world wanted to 'salve its conscience' and pay 'its debt'. Assess the validity of this source.

3   Study the cartoon in Source J and answer these questions:

   a   Why do the doctors look so serious? Do they have authority over the nurse?

   b   What message is the cartoonist trying to convey?

King Abdullah (1882–1951)

King Abdullah of Jordan was a son of Sharif Husayn, the Arab leader who negotiated with the British during the First World War. He was the leader of Transjordan (and later Jordan) from 1921 until he was assassinated in 1951 while attending Friday prayers at the Dome of the Rock in Jerusalem. His assassin was a Palestinian who feared that Abdullah was about to sign a separate peace treaty with Israel.

Abd al-Qadir al-Husayni (1907–48)

Husayni was a Palestinian nationalist leader. After his leading role in the Arab Revolt against the British (1936–39), he went into exile in Iraq and Egypt. He returned to Palestine in secret, early in 1948, to lead irregular Palestinian troops. For a while, Abd al-Qadir al-Husayni succeeded in cutting the road between Tel Aviv and Jerusalem, but he was killed by Haganah forces fighting for control of the villages along this route.

What happened during the civil war between 1947 and 1948?

Between the adoption of UN Resolution 181 and the departure of the British, the violence in Palestine escalated. In the last few months of the mandate, Palestine was in a state of civil war. British troops could do little to prevent it, and the British authorities would not allow the UN to send in officials to supervise the transition. This meant that there was no effective peacekeeping force in place in the last, violent days of the mandate.

Background to civil war

The Jewish forces were determined to strengthen their position while the mandate was still in place. They conscripted young men and women into the Haganah, and made arrangements to buy large quantities of arms from the Škoda armaments works in Czechoslovakia – including rifles, machine guns and 25 fighter aircraft. There were still differences between the approaches of the Haganah and Irgun. Many members of Irgun had a fanatical belief in the Zionist cause, and were prepared to use violence against Arab communities. They saw the Arabs as an obstacle to the creation of a Jewish state. Acts of terror multiplied, involving more and more civilians. Previously, the war that Irgun conducted against the British was an undercover affair, based on secret attacks. Now, the Irgun war against the Arabs was carried out far more openly.

The Palestinian Arabs outnumbered the Jews in the mandate, but they did not prevent Jewish forces from establishing control over large areas of Palestine by the time the mandate expired. It was more difficult for the Arabs to prepare for war due to their losses in the Arab Revolt of 1936–39, when more than 3000 were killed – including many leaders. The Arab League tried to help the Palestinians: it declared the UN Partition Plan illegal, gave the Palestinians 10,000 rifles, and formed an Arab Liberation Army of 3000 volunteers to support them. However, there were divisions among members of the Arab League, and there was no central Arab command.

The best Arab military force in the region was the Arab Legion, the army of Transjordan, but many Palestinians were suspicious of **King Abdullah**'s ambitions to dominate the Palestinian cause. Some suspected that he wanted to unite Palestine under his own rule. He was opposed in this ambition by the Mufti of Jerusalem, the spiritual leader of the Palestinians (see page 30), who was supported by irregular troops under the command of his cousin **Abd al-Qadir al-Husayni**. However, the Arab position was further weakened when Abd al-Qadir was killed by a Jewish patrol. According to historian Rashid Khalidi, Abd al-Qadir's death 'deprived the Palestinians of their most gifted military leader and an important unifying figure'. Members of the Palestinian élite had already started to leave for safer places, such as Beirut or Damascus, and more Palestinians left the mandate as the situation became increasingly dangerous for them.

The Haganah and Plan Dalet

In April 1948, the fighting became a full-scale civil war when the Haganah launched Plan Dalet (often shortened to Plan D). The overall aim of Plan D was to secure the area that was designated as a Jewish state, before the British withdrew. In the process, Haganah members expelled as many Palestinians as possible from the proposed Jewish state. An immediate goal was to ensure access to Jerusalem, where a Jewish community of 100,000 was surrounded by Arab areas, and could only receive supplies by means of a single road from Tel Aviv.

At first, the Haganah had limited success in getting convoys of provisions through to the city. They decided to go on the offensive by attacking and capturing Arab villages along the road linking Jerusalem and Tel Aviv. This would split the Arab state even further, and would give the Jews access to Jerusalem before it came under UN control.

Between the beginning of April and 15 May 1948, Jewish forces attacked and occupied nearly 200 Arab villages in Palestine. Many villagers were killed in these attacks, and others were forcibly moved to Transjordan. Hundreds of thousands more people fled. The Haganah took over several coastal towns with large Arab populations – Haifa, Acre and Jaffa – and occupied most of the Arab areas of West Jerusalem.

The massacre at Deir Yassin

The most notorious event during this period occurred on 9 April 1948, in the Arab village of Deir Yassin. This village lay 8 km (5 miles) west of Jerusalem, and was inside what was designated to be the Arab state in the UN Partition Plan. A combined force of Irgun and Lehi fighters attacked the village and killed 254 civilians – men, women and children. People were robbed, houses were looted, and some dead bodies were thrown down wells. Afterwards, a number of survivors were packed on trucks and paraded through the streets of other villages as a warning.

Deir Yassin was certainly not the only massacre that occurred in this civil war, and the Arabs also carried out atrocities. For example, a week later Arab forces attacked a Jewish medical convoy, killing 77 nurses and doctors. However, the Deir Yassin massacre had significant repercussions.

Child survivors of the Deir Yassin massacre, recovering in the government hospital in Jerusalem

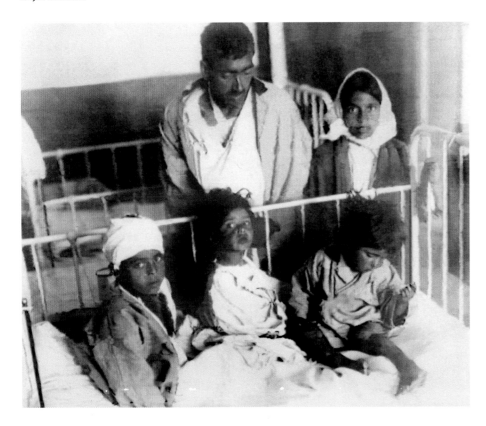

There are different views on the significance of what happened at Deir Yassin, as Sources K and L show.

SOURCE K

The point in examining one Zionist attack is not for the sake of emphasizing Zionist terrorism; Arab fighters, too, carried out appalling attacks on defenceless civilians during this period. But, aside from being an instance of savage atrocity, both the severity of Deir Yassin and its promulgation and propaganda by Arabs and Zionists alike created vast Arab panic. This terror and flight affected the demographics of the UN-designated territories along with the outcome of the war. As Arab radio stations broadcast news of Deir Yassin, Zionist forces in trucks with loudspeakers further terrorized Arab peasants and villagers with threats of similar violence. By the end of the civil phase of the war in 1948, 300,000 Arabs had fled their homes for other areas in Palestine, or entered surrounding Arab states. This was the start of a Palestinian refugee problem that changed the course of Palestinian-Israeli history and has yet to be resolved.

Harms, G. 2005. The Palestine–Israel Conflict: A Basic Introduction. London, UK. Pluto Press. p. 94.

SOURCE L

This extract is from the memoirs of Menachem Begin, the former commander of Irgun. Originally published in 1952, a revised edition of the book was published in 1979, when Begin was prime minister of Israel.

Apart from the military aspect, there is a moral aspect to the story of Dir Yassin. At that village, whose name was publicised throughout the world, both sides suffered heavy casualties. ... The fighting was thus very severe. Yet the hostile propaganda, disseminated throughout the world, deliberately ignored the fact that the civilian population of Dir Yassin was actually given a warning by us before the battle began ... Throughout the Arab world and the world at large a wave of lying propaganda was let loose about 'Jewish atrocities'. To counteract the loss of Dir Yassin, a village of strategic importance, Arab headquarters at Ramallah broadcast a crude atrocity story, alleging a massacre by Irgun troops of women and children in the village ... Out of evil, however, good came. This Arab propaganda spread a legend of terror amongst Arabs and Arab troops, who were seized with panic at the mention of Irgun soldiers. The legend was worth half a dozen battalions to the forces of Israel. The 'Dir Yassin Massacre' lie is still propagated by Jew-haters all over the world.

Begin, M. 1979. The Revolt. London, UK. W. H. Allen. pp. 163–64.

Activities

1 Draw up a table to compare the advantages and disadvantages facing the Jewish and Arab sides in the civil war of 1947–48. Use the categories below as a guide, but add any other factors that you think are relevant.

	Jewish forces	Arab forces
Numbers		
Arms		
Outside support		
Organisation		

2 Explain clearly the differences between the Arab League, the Arab Legion and the Arab Higher Committee.

3 Read Sources K and L on page 54, and compare and contrast them:
- On which points of factual information do the two sources agree?
- Both writers say that the events at Deir Yassin were significant, but for different reasons. Contrast their views of the significance of the event.
- Explain why Source L is not an objective account. Refer to its origin and purpose, and also quote phrases from the source to support your answer.

4 Divide the class into two groups. One group should prepare an argument to support the view that the Haganah's Plan D was necessary and acceptable. The other group should build a case for the idea that it was immoral and ruthless.

How did the British withdrawal and the establishment of Israel lead to war in Palestine in 1948–49?

The British withdrawal from Palestine

During 1948, the British gradually withdrew their troops towards the port of Haifa, and the withdrawal was completed on 14 May 1948. The British departure was widely welcomed by Jews in Palestine, who could not forgive the limitations that the British authorities placed on immigration. Many Jews also regarded Britain with suspicion, believing that it intended to maintain its influence in the Middle East by supporting King Abdullah of Transjordan and his British-led army, the Arab Legion. Some Zionist leaders were outspoken in their criticism of British actions in Palestine, and accused Britain of favouring the Arabs.

The attitudes of British officials towards the Zionists varied. Some regarded them as terrorists who had committed unforgivable atrocities against British troops; others were genuinely sympathetic to Zionist aims. Colin Shindler is one of several historians who believe that there was a general feeling that supporting the Arabs suited British interests better (see Source M).

Questions

What 'economic interests' did Britain have in the Middle East? In what ways could the Balfour Declaration be considered a 'mistake of monumental proportions' from this perspective, as Shindler suggests in Source M?

SOURCE M

Regardless of personal feelings, successive British administrations in Palestine had demonstrated their belief that economic interests pushed them inexorably [inevitably] towards the Arab world. Many believed that the window of opportunity for the Zionists, briefly opened by Lloyd George [British prime minister during the First World War] and Balfour, was a mistake of monumental proportions and muddied the waters between Britain and the Arab world.

Shindler, C. 2008. *A History of Modern Israel. Cambridge, UK. Cambridge University Press. p. 41.*

55

In the last months of the British mandate, there were secret talks between the Jewish Agency and King Abdullah of Transjordan. According to the Israeli revisionist historian Avi Shlaim, who has made a detailed study of these talks, they shared a common interest in repressing Palestinian nationalism. King Abdullah and Golda Meir (a future prime minister of Israel) of the Jewish Agency met secretly on at least two occasions. The first of these was before the UN vote for partition, and the second was a few days before the declaration of the state of Israel. In the second of these meetings, it became clear that Transjordan was under pressure from other Arab states to act with them. However, Shlaim suggests that by then King Abdullah and Golda Meir had reached an understanding that they would partition Palestine between Transjordan and Israel.

The establishment of Israel

The US government put some last-minute pressure on the Jewish Agency to postpone Israel's declaration of independence, in an attempt to prevent an all-out war in the Middle East. However, although there was some support for this, the majority of Jewish leaders – including the influential David Ben Gurion – pushed strongly for proceeding as planned. On 14 May 1948, the same day that the last British forces withdrew, Ben Gurion proclaimed the state of Israel. He became the prime minister of a provisional government, with the veteran Zionist Chaim Weizmann as the first president. Within hours the new state was formally recognised by the USA, and the USSR followed two days later. It was eight months before Britain formally recognised the state of Israel.

SOURCE N

Historian Ritchie Ovendale analyses the international political and strategic context to the establishment of Israel.

The state of Israel came into being because, in the end, two of the Great Powers, Russia and the USA, for conflicting reasons, strategic and domestic, thought it would be in their interests. Britain, concerned to maintain its paramountcy in the Middle East, opposed the move. British morale was eroded by a combination of Zionist terrorism, and a feeling that an American President dictated a policy in the interests of Zionism and his re-election, that led to the deaths of British troops. In any case this was the period of the twilight of the British Empire and the replacement of the *pax Britannica* by the *pax Americana*. After 15 May 1948 the situation in the Middle East was not determined just by Great Power politics, but by a local fight for possession of land. Britain's imperial position there, established between 1917 and 1923, was eroded.

Ovendale, R. 1984. The Origins of the Arab–Israeli Wars. London, UK. Longman. p. 125.

pax Britannica This is a Latin term, meaning literally 'the British peace'. It refers to the period during much of the 19th century and early 20th century when British power was dominant and unchallenged. The term comes from *pax Romana*, a long period of peace and stability under the Roman Empire.

On 15 May 1948, the armies of Egypt, Transjordan, Syria, Iraq and Lebanon, supported by Saudi Arabia, invaded the new state of Israel. This turned what had until then been a civil war into an international war – the first in a series of Arab–Israeli wars.

The 1948–49 War

The first Arab–Israeli war was called the War of Independence by the Israelis, and *Al-Nakba* by the Arabs. Neither side had enough forces to maintain a long offensive, so the war was a series of clashes between small units, usually lasting a few days each. The main fighting happened in three phases, with UN-sponsored ceasefires in between.

To meet the Arab invasion, the Haganah was transformed into the Israeli Defence Force (IDF). In the first phase of the war, the main fighting was the battle for Jerusalem between the IDF and the Arab Legion, the army of Transjordan. Although the Israeli army captured West Jerusalem, it was unable to defeat the Arab Legion in the eastern part, the Old City, which remained under Arab control. In June, the UN managed to arrange a ceasefire, which lasted for only a month. During this time, the Israelis trained more troops, and obtained more arms from Czechoslovakia – despite a UN arms embargo, which was ignored by the countries of Eastern Europe under Soviet influence. However, the UN arms embargo prevented the Arab armies from replenishing their arms supplies.

When fighting broke out again in July, the Israeli army captured large areas of the proposed Arab state. This included parts of Galilee in the north, the Negev in the south, and a large area of land near Jerusalem. Once again, however, the Israelis were unable to capture the Old City of Jerusalem from the Arab Legion. By the time the UN arranged a second ceasefire, the Israelis were in a strong position.

The UN sent a special mediator, Count Bernadotte of Sweden, to negotiate a compromise solution. Bernadotte's proposed plan meant that Israel would lose the Negev, that Jerusalem would remain an international city under UN control, and that 300,000 Palestinian refugees who had been displaced by the fighting would be able to return to their homes. The Israelis were totally opposed to the plan, and the day after its announcement, members of Lehi assassinated Bernadotte. This action provoked outrage from the UN and the rest of the world. There were also many Israelis who felt that the extremists had gone too far, and had discredited the Zionist cause. In an effort to maintain international support, the Israeli government officially dissolved Irgun and Lehi. Many of their members joined the IDF. However, the Israeli government still rejected the idea of giving up any of the gains it had made, or allowing the refugees to return.

When the third round of fighting broke out again in October, the Israelis captured the rest of Galilee. They pushed the Egyptian forces back into the Sinai desert, which left the Arabs with a small area near Gaza. Under American pressure, the Israelis withdrew from Egyptian territory before the final ceasefire was arranged in January 1949.

The results of the war

The Israelis succeeded in defeating the Arab armies and extending their frontiers considerably beyond those outlined in the UN Partition Plan. By the end of the war, the state of Israel had acquired 78% of Palestine, instead of the 56% allocated to it by UNSCOP. The borders of Israel in January 1949 included many areas intended for the Palestinian Arabs. Israel also controlled half of the city of Jerusalem, which had been designated in the partition plan as international territory. About 6000 Jews had been killed in the war, which was about 1% of the Jewish population of Israel at the time. Arab losses were higher: 8000 Palestinian Arab deaths, and another 4000 killed in the Arab states' armies.

> *Al-Nakba* In Arabic, this term means 'the disaster' or 'the catastrophe'. It refers to the events of 1947–49, and especially to the dispossession and flight of the Palestinian Arabs. Each year, Palestinians commemorate these events on 15 May – Nakba Day. On Nakba Day in 2011, demonstrators moved into Israel across the border from Syria, to protest against the continued occupation of Palestinian land. Sixteen protestors were killed by Israeli troops, and hundreds more were wounded.

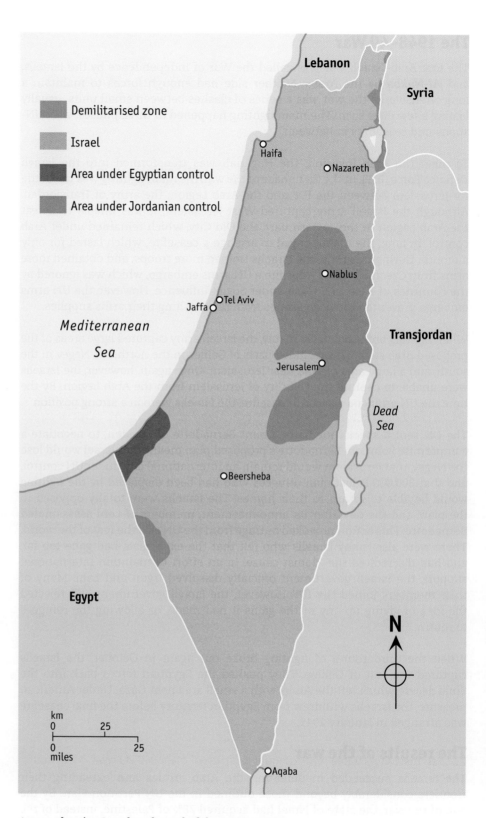

A map showing Israel at the end of the 1948–49 War

Between January and July 1949, Israel signed separate armistice agreements with Egypt, Lebanon, Transjordan and Syria (but not Iraq). However, no formal peace treaties were signed because the Arab governments refused to recognise Israel.

SOURCE O

To the Arabs, Israel is a temporary phenomenon, the invasion of lands, traditionally Arab, by an alien culture, supported by outsiders. There is no Israel, only Palestine … Like other crusader states, Israel, seen through Arab eyes, is not a natural growth; she represents the outcomes of policies of those Western powers who first created her and then protected her. To the Arab, the much vaunted western concept, the right of self-determination, has in Palestine been brutally cast aside, for Arabs were clearly the majority. The Arabs brush aside as irrelevant the Jewish claim that historically this was their land, that their civilisation was nurtured here … To the Arab, 'Europeans' have once again colonised a 'non-European' area; 'Europeans' have been forced out of Kenya, out of Algeria: they will also be expelled from Palestine.

Browne, H. 1971. *Flashpoints: Suez and Sinai. London, UK. Longman. pp. 8–9.*

Questions

What do the terms 'crusader state' and 'self-determination' mean? What is the link suggested by Source O between the establishment of Israel and colonialism?

In the armistice agreements, it was accepted that the Gaza area of Palestine would come under Egyptian control, but that the Negev would be part of Israel. The Old City of Jerusalem and the large area west of the Jordan River, which had been designated as part of the Palestinian state in the UN Partition Plan, went to Transjordan – which was renamed Jordan. This area became known as the West Bank, confirming its status as an extension of Jordan. The city of Jerusalem was divided between Israel and Jordan. Israel rejected a later UN resolution, in December 1949, that declared the permanent international status of Jerusalem.

The UNSCOP Partition Plan was abandoned as a result of these UN-sponsored armistice agreements, and there were no attempts to create a Palestinian state. The areas originally set aside for Palestine in the partition plan had been swallowed up by Israel, Jordan and Egypt. The Palestinian Arabs, who fled or were forced from their homes, were scattered and homeless. By the end of the war, 760,000 Arabs had left Palestine for neighbouring countries as refugees, where they were placed in camps run by the United Nations. Most of these Palestinians ended up in Gaza and the West Bank, under Egyptian or Jordanian control respectively. The reasons for the mass departure of the Palestinian refugees remain a subject of controversy – you will learn more about this in Chapter 4.

The reasons for the Israeli victory

Zionist historians have traditionally portrayed the 1948–49 War as a heroic Israeli victory over insurmountable odds by a small and dedicated force: a re-enactment of the victory of David over Goliath in the biblical story, with Israel as the victim of Arab aggression. In this view, Israel succeeded in defeating the Arab armies because of better training, leadership and morale, and greater determination. The historian Avi Shlaim sees this interpretation as a 'prime example of the use of a nationalistic version of history in the process of nation-building. In a very real sense history is the propaganda of the victors, and the history of the 1948 war is no exception.'

 Theory of knowledge

History and truth

Is it accurate to say that 'history is the propaganda of the victors'? Is it acceptable for a country to use history for the purpose of nation-building? How does this link to the search for historical 'truth'?

Other historians challenge the traditional Zionist view of the reasons for the Israeli victory, as they believe that it overlooks other factors. Firstly, they point out that although the population of surrounding Arab countries did indeed vastly outnumber the population of Israel, the Israeli Defence Force actually had more soldiers involved in the fighting than the Arabs did. Many of these IDF soldiers had gained useful experience fighting with the Allies during the Second World War. The Israeli forces were better prepared than the Arab armies. They had a centralised and well-organised system of command, and were fighting over a relatively smaller area, which enabled them to operate quickly and efficiently.

In contrast to this, there was a lack of military experience among the Arab soldiers. The Arabs were also affected by a lack of unity in command, and there was no central authority to focus on exploiting the weak points of the Israelis. Some Arab armies, such as the Egyptians and the Iraqis, were operating at a distance from their home bases, unlike the Israelis. The Arabs also lacked a common purpose. There was rivalry and distrust between different leaders. Some historians suggest that the intervention by Arab armies was motivated largely by their own self-interest, rather than by support for the Palestinian cause. Transjordan wanted the West Bank as part of Jordan, Egypt wanted Gaza, and Syria and Lebanon wanted Galilee. These internal conflicts and separate agendas considerably weakened the Arab cause.

In particular, historians have critically examined the role of King Abdullah of Transjordan. Transjordan had the best-equipped and best-trained army in the Arab world, and Abdullah was made commander-in-chief of the Arab armies. However, his forces did little more than occupy the area of the designated Palestinian state west of the Jordan River, and defend the Old City of East Jerusalem. They never crossed into the Jewish state to fight the Israeli army there. As has since been revealed, Abdullah met secretly with representatives of the Jewish Agency and discussed a future partition of Palestine between Israel and Transjordan. The prime minister of Transjordan also travelled to London in January 1948, and reached an agreement with the British government that Transjordan would take over the area of Palestine that UNSCOP designated as the Arab state.

The Palestinians themselves were divided. They had not set in place structures that might have united them politically, and helped them to organise resistance to defend their position. They had no real national body to represent their interests, and so they were effectively sidelined by the Arab League.

SOURCE P

Even if the Palestinians were occasionally nominally represented in the post-World War II deliberations that sealed their fate as a people, in practice they were effectively ignored. Most frequently, if spoken for at all, they were spoken for by the Arab states, each of which had its own considerations and calculations, all of which were weak, and some of which, like Lebanon, Syria and Transjordan, had only just won a precarious independence. Even such limited Palestinian efforts to speak for themselves internationally as took place were entirely dependent on the support of Arab states. These efforts ultimately foundered because of these states' inconsistency and because of divisions among them (as well as among the Palestinians themselves). It is clear that for most of the actors dealing with Palestine at this stage, the Palestinians were considered a negligible factor if they were considered at all.

Khalidi, R. 2006. The Iron Cage: The Story of the Palestinian Struggle for Statehood. Oxford, UK. Oneworld. pp. 125–26

Question

According to Source P, what disadvantages did the Palestinians face in their efforts?

Historical interpretations of the 1948–49 War

For 40 years, the standard Zionist interpretation of the Israeli victory in the 1948–49 War went largely unchallenged by Israeli historians. However, in 1988 – the year of the 40th anniversary of the establishment of Israel – a number of Israeli historians published books that questioned some of the assumptions behind this view, and analysed the myths and realities of the Israeli victory. They came to be called the 'Revisionist', or 'New', Israeli historians. Initially, the chief names among them were Benny Morris, Ilan Pappe and Avi Shlaim.

These revisionist historians focused in particular on issues such as the reasons for the flight of Palestinian refugees, the relative strengths of the two sides, and the role of King Abdullah of Transjordan in the war. Since then, other Israeli historians have similarly reassessed other events and issues in their country's history. They have considered Israel's relations with the Arab states, in particular its role in the ongoing hostility between them.

The re-examination of these events was made possible by Israel's policy of making official documents available to the public after 30 years, and allowing researchers access to its archives. The new historians have acknowledged that it is to Israel's credit that it allows access to its records, making such critical studies possible. The writer Jonathan Mahler also believes that the rise of revisionism was partly due to the younger age of Israel's new historians. Unlike the majority of the traditional historians who 'were firsthand participants in the country's nation-building effort', most of the revisionist historians were born after the 1948–49 War, and grew up in an 'increasingly self-critical society'.

Pro-Zionist historians, such as Efraim Karsh – the director of the Mediterranean Studies programme at King's College at the University of London – have fiercely challenged the views of the revisionists. Karsh is highly critical of the methods and conclusions of these 'new historians'.

SOURCE Q

For quite some time, Israeli historiography has been subjected to a sustained assault by a cohort of self-styled 'new historians' vying to debunk what they claim to be the distorted 'Zionist narrative' of Israeli history in general, and of the Arab–Israeli conflict in particular. Deriding alternative interpretations as 'old' or 'mobilized', they have portrayed Zionism as the 'original sin' underlying the region's violent history. To some, Zionism is an archaic remnant of Western colonialism destined to wither away sooner or later as Israel will enter its 'post-Zionist' phase. To others it is 'merely' an exploitative and aggressive movement which brought about the Palestinian tragedy and bears responsibility for perpetuating the conflict with its Arab neighbours, failing time and again to seize the extended hand for peace.

Karsh, E. 2000. Fabricating Israeli History: The 'New Historians' (Second Revised Edition). London, UK. Frank Cass. p. 1.

As a result of the lively debate in Israeli historiography, many of the issues discussed in this book are the subject of ongoing re-examination, and sometimes controversial reinterpretation, by Israeli historians.

Activities

1   Compare the map of Palestine after the 1948–49 war (on page 58) with the map showing the UN Partition Plan (on page 48). Apart from gaining more territory, what other advantages does the map show that the new state of Israel gained as a result of its victory in the war?

2   Select one of the revisionist historians and prepare an oral presentation to explain how his or her views challenged the traditional historiography of Israeli history. Some suggestions are: Avi Shlaim, Benny Morris, Ilan Pappe, Tom Segev and Simha Flapan. However, you may want to find out about one of the less well-known historians.

3   Design a spider diagram to illustrate the reasons for the Israeli victory in the 1948–49 War.

4   At the website link below, read the relevant parts of this account of the assassination of the UN mediator Count Bernadotte in Jerusalem in 1948.

http://www.independent.co.uk/news/world/middle-east/israels-forgotten-hero-the-assassination-of-count-bernadotte--and-the-death-of-peace-934094.html.

According to the writer of this article, what was the motivation for Bernadotte's assassination? In what ways was the Israeli investigation into the murder flawed?

End of chapter activities

Summary

You have seen that there were fundamental changes in Palestine between 1945 and 1949. You should understand how and why these changes happened. You should be able to explain why there was escalating violence in the last years of the mandate. In particular, you should be able to show how the UN Partition Plan resulted in civil war, and how the declaration of the state of Israel led to the first war between Israel and the Arab states. You should understand that there are different interpretations of why Israel won the 1948–49 War. You should also recognise the significance of the Israeli victory in this war.

Summary activity

Copy the diagram below and, using the information in this chapter and from other sources, make brief notes under each heading.

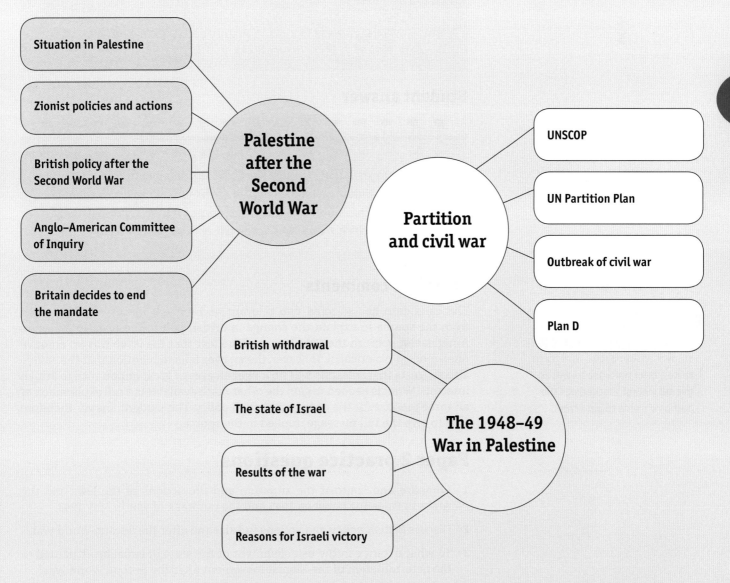

- Situation in Palestine
- Zionist policies and actions
- British policy after the Second World War
- Anglo–American Committee of Inquiry
- Britain decides to end the mandate

Palestine after the Second World War

Partition and civil war
- UNSCOP
- UN Partition Plan
- Outbreak of civil war
- Plan D

- British withdrawal
- The state of Israel
- Results of the war
- Reasons for Israeli victory

The 1948–49 War in Palestine

63

Paper 1 exam practice

Question

What reasons does Source A below imply were responsible for the change in British policy towards Palestine?
[3 marks]

Skill

Comprehension of the message of a source

SOURCE A

Most historians agree that given the Cold War context, in which the need for Anglo-American amity was seen as paramount, Whitehall [the British government] could ill afford to alienate Washington [the US government] over a highly emotional issue that, when all was said and done, was not a vital British interest.

Morris, B. 2001. *Righteous Victims: A History of the Zionist–Arab Conflict, 1881–2001. New York, USA. Vintage Books. p. 181.*

Student answer

Source A suggests that because the Cold War had begun, Britain needed to make sure that it remained on good terms with America. It could not risk annoying the Americans (over the issue of Jewish refugees), which was an issue which many Americans felt very strongly about.

Examiner comments

The candidate has selected **two** relevant and explicit pieces of information from the source to explain the change in British policy (the need to maintain American support in the Cold War, and the fact that the issue was an emotive one amongst Americans). However, the answer fails to mention that the source also suggests that Palestine was no longer an area of great importance to British interests. What is needed to gain the other mark available is a full explanation of all three reasons for the change in British policy. The student answer therefore fails to give the full message implied in the source.

Paper 2 practice questions

1   Compare and contrast the situation and the actions of the Jews and the Arabs in Palestine between 1945 and the outbreak of war in May 1948.

2   Discuss British policy and actions in Palestine after the Second World War.

3   To what extent can the establishment of the state of Israel be attributed to the determination of the Zionist movement after the Second World War?

The Palestinian diaspora and the state of Israel 1948–56

Introduction

During and after the 1948–49 War, there was a substantial demographic shift in the Middle East. Vast numbers of Palestinian Arabs left their homes in Palestine and fled to surrounding Arab countries, where most of them lived in refugee camps run by the United Nations. The new Israeli government promoted the immigration of even larger numbers of Jewish immigrants from other parts of the world, many of them from Arab countries. In this way, the demographic make-up of the region changed significantly within a few years.

Key questions

- What happened to the Palestinians?
- How did Israel encourage immigration and promote economic development?

Overview

- The establishment of Israel had significant effects on the demography of the region: nearly a million Arabs left Palestine for surrounding Arab states, and Jewish immigrants from many countries moved to Israel.
- The mass departure of Palestinians started in 1947, and continued during and after the 1948–49 War. Recent research has caused a fierce debate among historians about the degree of Israel's responsibility for this flight.
- Palestinian refugees ended up in camps run by the UN Relief and Works Agency in surrounding Arab countries, and their presence was subject to tight controls and restrictions. There are conflicting views about why these Palestinians were not assimilated by the Arab countries.
- Israel refused to allow the Palestinian refugees to return, believing that they would threaten the security and stability of the state. New Jewish settlements were built on the sites of deserted Palestinian villages and farms.
- Younger Arabs were dissatisfied with their governments after the Arab defeat. They joined nationalist movements, demanding economic and social reform, and an end to foreign interference. This resulted in political instability and changes of government in several Arab countries.

Timeline

1947 Nov: Palestinian Arabs begin leaving Palestine

1948 14 May: declaration of state of Israel

15 May: start of first Arab–Israeli war; flight, expulsion and exile of Palestinians accelerates

Jun: Irgun transformed into political party, Herut

1949 Jan: first Israeli elections; Ben Gurion becomes prime minister

Jan–Jul: armistice agreements between Israel and Arab states

Dec: establishment of UNRWA to assist refugees

1950 Apr: West Bank officially annexed to Jordan

Jul: Law of Return in Israel

1951 Jul: assassination of King Abdullah of Jordan

1952 Apr: Citizenship Law in Israel

Jul: coup in Egypt; King Farouk overthrown

Sep: Reparations Treaty between West Germany and Israel

1953 Aug: Hussein becomes king of Jordan

- The Mapai party won the elections in Israel for the first parliament. The party's leader, David Ben Gurion, became Israel's first prime minister.
- Huge numbers of Jewish immigrants, mainly from Eastern Europe and Arab countries, doubled the population of Israel within three years. They were encouraged by laws that granted them immediate citizenship.
- Israeli government measures tried to assimilate all these new Jewish immigrants from widely different cultural backgrounds. Despite this, Jews from Arab countries remained in inferior political, social and economic positions.
- Economic growth in Israel was boosted by defence spending and the large workforce resulting from immigration. However, the state's economic survival was dependent on foreign aid, mainly from America and West Germany.
- The Palestinians who remained in Israel were placed under military rule until 1966. They were subjected to discriminatory laws and practices, and struggled to survive economically.

Women and children carry their possessions in sacks as they flee their homes in Palestine

What happened to the Palestinians?

The establishment of Israel had far-reaching consequences for the Palestinians. Before 1948, the Arabs made up well over half of the total population of Palestine; after the 1948–49 War, only 160,000 Arabs remained, compared to a Jewish population of 650,000. During the course of the war, more than 75% of the Palestinian population fled, or were forced from their homes, into surrounding Arab countries. No Palestinian state was created, and these refugees became the Palestinian diaspora (see page 17).

The flight of Palestinian refugees

In the early stages of the civil war in 1947, upper- and middle-class Palestinian Arabs – those who had the financial resources to enable them to do so – started to leave Palestine, intending to return once the violence had ended. Many of them went to cities such as Beirut in Lebanon or Damascus in Syria. According to the historian Gregory Harms, this 'set a precedent for the peasant classes to emulate'. The pace of the mass flight picked up in the last two months of the mandate, and continued during the war between Israel and the Arab armies. By the end of the war, about 760,000 Palestinians had fled into surrounding Arab countries, abandoning their property and possessions in the areas that were incorporated into the state of Israel. The remainder of the Palestinian population was distributed between Israel (160,000), the West Bank (400,000) and Gaza (20,000). More than 500 Arab villages were abandoned, and many of them were destroyed. Arab urban neighbourhoods in cities such as Haifa, Acre and Jaffa were virtually deserted.

This map shows the flight of Palestinian refugees, 1947–49

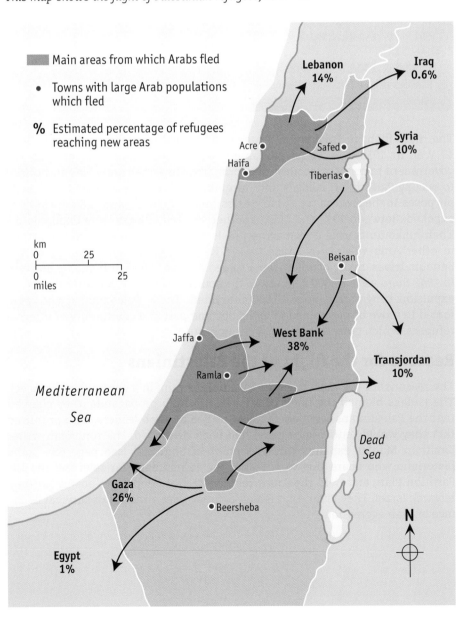

SOURCE A

Historian Rashid Khalidi analyses the impact of the mass dispersal on the national identity of the Palestinian people.

These results marked the end for many decades of Palestine as a predominantly Arab country, as well as of the ability of the Palestinians to operate as independent actors. They marked as well the beginning of decades in the wilderness for the Palestinians. Far from being able to dream of a state of their own, they were now faced with an existential test of whether they would be able to remain together as a people. Paradoxically, later events showed that the traumatic impact of the shared experience of 1948 on the entirety of Palestinian society helped to weld it together even more strongly, obliterating much that had transpired before 1948, rendering many earlier divisions irrelevant, and creating a sort of tabula rasa [clean slate] on which Palestinian identity could be re-established.

Khalidi, R. 2006. The Iron Cage: The Story of the Palestinian Struggle for Statehood. Oxford, UK. Oneworld. p. 135.

The mass flight of Palestinian refugees continued after the end of the 1948–49 War. In 1950, the Israeli parliament passed legislation that allowed the government to confiscate Palestinian property. The Israeli army was authorised to occupy Palestinian villages and farmland, and use these areas for security purposes. In the process, many more Palestinians lost their land and were forcibly expelled. Between 1949 and 1952, another 40 Arab villages were depopulated. Their inhabitants were driven across the Israeli border, or dispersed and settled in other Arab villages in Israel. In the Negev, a similar situation faced the Bedouin tribes, many of whom were forced to abandon their nomadic lifestyle. In 1947 there were 80,000 Bedouin in the south of Palestine, but after the Israeli expulsion programme only 13,000 remained. Those Palestinians who were forced to move but remained in Israel became part of a community of internal refugees, which grew in number over the years.

Reasons for the flight of the Palestinians

The reasons for the mass flight of Palestinians remain a controversial subject. The Israelis blamed the flight of refugees on Arab propaganda: they claimed that the Palestinians were encouraged to flee by Arab leaders, who promised that they would return once Israel had been destroyed. The American writer Jonathan Mahler explains this viewpoint in Source B (see page 69). Some historians who share this view blame the Palestinians for rejecting the UN Partition Plan, and hold the Arabs responsible for adopting a hostile attitude towards Israel. They claim that Israeli actions were a matter of survival in the face of Arab aggression.

SOURCE B

To the first generation of Israeli scholars, Palestine's early Jewish settlers were idealistic pioneers who arrived in pre-state Israel with every intention of living in peace alongside their Arab neighbors and upgrading the quality of life for all of the land's inhabitants. Years later, Zionist leaders worked furiously to help their Jewish brethren escape Nazi-occupied Europe. And when the War of Independence erupted in 1948, the narrative continues, local Palestinian Arabs left their villages not under threats from invading Israeli troops but at the behest of the Arab rulers of surrounding states who assured them they would be able to return to their homes once the Arab armies emerged victorious. As for the war itself, early histories of Zionism characterized the outcome as a major upset: Jewish David defeats Arab Goliath … Over the years, such collective memories have played an important role in shaping Israeli policy toward the Palestinians. If, for example, the Palestinians fled voluntarily after the Arab states declared war on Israel, why should Israel feel guilty about its reluctance to repatriate them?

Mahler, J. 1997. 'Uprooting the past: Israel's new historians take a hard look at their nation's past'. Lingua Franca. New York, USA. http://linguafranca.mirror.theinfo.org/9708/mahler.9708

SOURCE C

There is no convincing evidence of a Zionist plot to ethnically cleanse, or transfer, the Palestinians from their homeland, as has been argued by some. The by now notorious 'Plan Dalet', the supposed blueprint of this plot, reveals, after careful and responsible scrutiny, nothing of the kind. 'The objective of this plan', it read, 'is to gain control of the areas of the Hebrew state (according to the partition frontiers) and defend its borders' – against an impending all-Arab attack. From June 1946, the Haganah had been preparing in earnest for such an eventuality. That month an Arab conference, held in Bluden, Syria, called for the mobilisation of all Arab resources, money, arms and volunteers, the use of force – an army of 100 000 was mentioned – even anti-Western sanctions, all to thwart a Zionist occupation of Palestine. The Jewish Agency, and Ben Gurion in particular, took these threats extremely seriously. 'Plan Dalet' was the latest manifestation of the measures intended to counter an inevitable Arab assault on the Jewish state.

Rose, N. 2009. 'A Senseless Squalid War'; Voices from Palestine 1945–1948. London, UK. The Bodley Head. pp. 212–13.

69

The Arabs claimed that the success of Zionism depended on the expulsion of the Palestinians. In this view, acts of terrorism – such as the massacre at Deir Yassin (see page 53) – were deliberately staged to encourage the flight of Palestinian refugees, who feared for their safety in a Jewish-dominated state.

Historians who support this view suggest that the expulsion of the Palestinians was long part of Zionist thinking, and they accuse the Zionists of a deliberate policy of **ethnic cleansing**.

ethnic cleansing This term refers to the forced displacement of an ethnic or religious minority, involving the expulsion of a population from a certain area. The term was first widely used to refer to events in the civil wars in Yugoslavia in the 1990s.

The reasons for the flight of the Palestinian refugees was one of the issues that the Israeli revisionist historians re-examined in their new histories, published from 1988 onwards. These studies challenged the accepted Zionist interpretation of events by showing that Israeli actions before and during the 1948–49 War were indeed a factor that caused the Palestinians to flee. Since then, there has been a lively debate among historians about the degree of Israel's responsibility for this flight. Benny Morris concluded that there were several causes for the mass departure, including deliberate pressure from the Zionists, and that Israel was therefore partly – but not fully – responsible. However, Ilan Pappe maintains that the Zionists had a master plan for the expulsion of the local Arabs, and that the dispossession of the Palestinians was therefore part of a deliberate and calculated policy.

SOURCE D

The Palestinian refugee problem was born of war, not by design, Jewish or Arab. It was largely a by-product of Arab and Jewish fears and of the protracted, bitter fighting that characterised the first Arab–Israeli war; in smaller part, it was the deliberate creation of Jewish and Arab military commanders and politicians ... What happened in Palestine/ Israel over 1947–49 was so complex and varied, the situation radically changing from date to date and place to place, that a single-cause explanation of the exodus from most sites is untenable.

Morris, B. 1988. The Birth of the Palestinian Refugee Problem, 1947–1949. Cambridge, UK. Cambridge University Press. pp. 286 and 294.

SOURCE E

[On] 10 March 1948, a group of eleven men, veteran Zionist leaders as well as young military Jewish officers, put the final touches to a plan for the ethnic cleansing of Palestine. That same evening, military orders were dispatched to the units on the ground to prepare for the systematic expulsion of the Palestinians from vast areas of the country. ... Once the decision was taken, it took six months to complete the mission. When it was over, more than half of Palestine's native population, close to 800 000 people, had been uprooted, 531 villages had been destroyed, and eleven urban neighbourhoods emptied of their inhabitants. The plan decided upon on 10 March 1948, and above all its systematic implementation in the following months, was a clear-cut case of an ethnic-cleansing operation, regarded under international law today as a crime against humanity.

Pappe, I. 2006. The Ethnic Cleansing of Palestine. Oxford, UK. Oneworld. pp. xii–xiii.

Activity

Compare and contrast the views in Sources B–E (pages 69–70) of the reasons for the flight of the Palestinian refugees. In what respects do they differ? Are there any issues on which they agree?

Historical interpretation

Benny Morris was the first of the revisionist historians to examine the issue of the Palestinian mass flight, in *The Birth of the Palestinian Refugee Problem, 1947–1949*. Other historians, such as Norman Finkelstein, are critical of the conclusions that Morris drew from his research. They believe that there is evidence of greater Zionist responsibility than Morris suggests. Ilan Pappe maintains that Israel is fully responsible for a pre-planned policy of Palestinian expulsion and dispossession: the title of his 2006 book, *The Ethnic Cleansing of Palestine*, reflects this conviction.

After the start of the second *intifada* (Palestinian uprising) in 2000, and renewed suicide-bombing attacks on Israeli civilians, Morris changed his views. He came to the conclusion that Israel made a mistake in allowing even a small number of Palestinians to remain in Israel. This new viewpoint is seen in his revised work, *The Birth of the Palestinian Refugee Problem Revisited*. According to another revisionist historian, Avi Shlaim, the significance of this change of views was that Morris was 'effectively terminating his membership of the club' of New Historians.

Life for Palestinians in the diaspora

Palestinian refugee camps

Most of the Palestinian refugees went to the West Bank and Gaza; many others went to Transjordan, Lebanon and Syria. Wherever they went, they ended up living in refugee camps that were initially funded by donations from American welfare agencies and international aid organisations. In December 1949, when this aid ran out, the United Nations set up a single body to deal with the Palestinian refugee problem – the United Nations Relief and Works Agency, known as **UNRWA**. The UN defined a Palestinian refugee as a 'needy person and his direct descendants, who as a result of the war in Palestine has lost his home and his means of livelihood'. In terms of this definition, 750,000 Palestinians qualified as refugees.

> **UNRWA** This organisation was originally set up as a temporary means of dealing with the refugee crisis following the 1948–49 War. However, its responsibilities have been repeatedly renewed by the UN General Assembly. UNRWA now provides education, health services, social services and other forms of assistance to Palestinian refugees. In 2009, these refugees numbered 4.8 million. UNRWA administers more than 50 camps in Jordan, Lebanon, Syria, the West Bank and Gaza.

> **repatriation** This term describes the act of return or restoration to one's country of birth or origin.

The focus in these camps was on providing emergency aid and welfare for the refugees, and the most permanent structures built to house them were simple huts, built of materials such as mud. This seemed to symbolise their temporary refugee status in the eyes of the UN. The camp inhabitants generally shared this view, as they had hopes of being repatriated. Although the United Nations undertook to protect the Palestinian refugees and their rights, it never succeeded in making **repatriation** a reality.

In this 1949 photo, a woman teaches Arabic to young Palestinian refugees in a makeshift tent classroom inside a refugee camp in Transjordan

The Palestinian refugees came from all sections of society, but most of them were farmers. Now they found themselves in the refugee camps, without land to farm and lacking skills or experience to do other work. They were dependent on the UN for everything, as they had abandoned their property and possessions in Palestine. A notable feature of the camps was the UNRWA flag that flew on every public building, including schools, clinics, administration offices and food shops. The UNRWA became the main employer in the camps, paying the wages of teachers, doctors and social workers. The camps were small and overcrowded, and became more so as the population grew. They lacked basic infrastructure such as roads, water, electricity, sewerage and proper housing. According to Ilan Pappe, the camps were the poorest dwellings in the Arab world, where 'violence and despair were channelled into guerrilla activity' by the late 1950s.

The reception of Palestinian refugees in the Arab states

The refugees were not welcome in most of the countries to which they fled, because of the strain that they put on resources. They were treated with suspicion, and their movements were strictly monitored. However, their situation varied from country to country. When the Transjordan government annexed the West Bank and created the Kingdom of Jordan in 1950 (see page 75), Jordan had more than half the total number of Palestinian refugees. These refugees were allowed to leave the camps as long as they showed loyalty to the Jordanian regime. In this way they could obtain Jordanian citizenship, which entitled them to passports enabling some of them to travel and seek education and employment abroad. The majority, however, remained in refugee camps. Only Jordan allowed the refugees to become citizens; in other countries, they remained stateless refugees.

The Palestinian refugees were generally better educated than the Jordanian population, and filled posts in education and in the civil service. Many of the refugee farmers were better adapted to modern methods of agriculture than the Jordanians, a lot of whom were nomadic desert Bedouin. The underlying social differences meant that the Jordanians never fully trusted the Palestinians, and denied them access to top positions in government. The Jordanian authorities feared a future Palestinian breakaway, and so political activity of any kind was ruthlessly crushed. This created an uneasy relationship between the refugees and the Jordanian authorities, both under King Abdullah and later under his grandson, **King Hussein bin Talal**, who came to power in 1953.

About a quarter of the total number of Palestinian refugees were under Egyptian military control in the Gaza Strip. Egypt maintained tight controls on their movement, and prevented the refugees from entering Egypt itself. The Egyptian military authorities did not want to risk damaging Egypt's armistice agreement with Israel, so they allowed only limited political activity among the Palestinians.

More than 100,000 Palestinian refugees fled to Lebanon. Most of these refugees were self-sufficient peasant farmers from Galilee, or people who were expelled from urban centres such as Haifa and Acre. The government of Lebanon was afraid that their arrival would upset the delicate ethnic and religious balance of the Lebanese population (see page 127). Lebanon therefore adopted a policy of oppression and exclusion: the refugees were confined to their camps, and banned from more than 40 types of occupation. Only the most menial forms of unskilled labour were open to them. Palestinian children were denied access to Lebanese schools, and the camps were regularly entered and patrolled by Lebanese troops. As a result of these measures, life in Lebanon was extremely hard for the refugees.

King Hussein bin Talal (1935–99) King Abdullah's grandson, Hussein, became king of Jordan in 1953, at the age of 18. He was with his grandfather when the latter was assassinated in 1951. His appointment as king followed the short reign of his father, who abdicated due to mental health problems. King Hussein was perceived by the West as an ally and a moderate Arab leader, and for most of his long reign he followed a policy of peaceful co-existence with Israel.

Conditions were better in Syria, where the relatively smaller number of Palestinian refugees was given access to schools and skilled occupations. They were also allowed to set up small businesses. However, they were denied access to any form of unskilled work, as there were too many poor and unemployed Syrians. A small number of the refugees went to the Persian Gulf states, but had to have employment to be allowed to remain there. Some also went abroad to study or work, to countries such as the USA, but their numbers made up a very small minority of the total number of refugees.

SOURCE F

Rashid Khalidi analyses the impact of the mass Palestinian dispersal on the unity and political consciousness of the Palestinians.

From this point onwards and for many decades, most Palestinian political activity would take place outside Palestine rather than inside it. The reasons for this had to do with the policies of the three states that controlled the territory of the former Mandate for Palestine. The state of Israel kept a tight rein on the 150 000 Palestinians in the 78% of Palestine that had been brought under its control by the time of the 1949 armistice, maintaining a military government and oppressive movement and political restrictions on them until 1966. The Jordanian authorities saw virtually any independent Palestinian organisation as subversive and as a threat to the unity of the kingdom, and ruthlessly combated political activity of most kinds, making the West and East banks of the Jordan highly inhospitable for independent Palestinian political action. The Egyptian military authorities, in control of the Gaza Strip at the end of the war, allowed only limited Palestinian activity, and none that could jeopardise Egypt's armistice agreement with Israel. Among the now dispersed Palestinians, scattered in tents in refugee camps or in rented accommodations, living among relatives or precariously scratching out a living in their new places of exile, a new generation of political activists took the stage, and soon found themselves forced to operate further afield because of controls on their activities by these three states.

Khalidi, R. 2006. *The Iron Cage: The Story of the Palestinian Struggle for Statehood. Oxford, UK. Oneworld. p. 136.*

Questions

What were the attitudes of the Israeli, Jordanian and Egyptian authorities towards political activity among the Palestinian refugees? How did these attitudes differ between the three countries?

The problem of assimilation

There are conflicting views on why the vast majority of Palestinian refugees were not assimilated by their host countries. One view, from an Israeli perspective, is that **assimilation** should have been relatively easy. The refugees spoke the same language and followed the same religion as their host nations. This view maintains that it should have been an easier process than Israel's assimilation of Jewish immigrants, who spoke different languages and came from widely different social and economic backgrounds. Writers who support this view claim that the refugees were deliberately kept as an embittered minority, to be used as political pawns by the Arab governments in their conflict with Israel.

assimilation This term means becoming part of the mainstream community; being absorbed or integrated into society; adopting the customs and culture (and in some cases the religion) of the dominant population group.

Question

What options did the Palestinian refugees in the camps have?

fifth column This term describes a subversive element, an organised body working for the enemy within a country at war. The term was first used during the Spanish Civil War, which was fought between nationalists and republicans from 1936 to 1939. The nationalist general who was besieging Madrid with four columns of troops boasted that Madrid would fall because he had a 'fifth column' of supporters inside the city, who were intent on undermining republican control.

The other view is that the Arab countries themselves had economic problems, and simply could not cope with hundreds of thousands of refugees. Their economies were underdeveloped and could not provide enough jobs for their own people, so they found it difficult to absorb the refugees or to assimilate them into the local populations. Writers who support this view also point out that the Palestinians themselves did not wish to be assimilated. They saw themselves as victims of injustice, and they wanted to return to their own villages and farms in Palestine.

The issue of return

After the 1948–49 War, the Israeli government introduced a policy to prevent the repatriation of Palestinians who fled or were expelled. Palestinian Arab villages were destroyed, and became sites for new settlements or were turned into fields for cultivation. The empty Palestinian neighbourhoods in the cities were either destroyed or left vacant for the expected arrival of Jewish immigrants.

The Israeli government believed that if the Palestinian refugees were allowed to return, they would act as a **fifth column** and threaten the security and stability of Israel. The right of the Palestinian refugees to return to their homes was one of the three issues that formed the basis of United Nations peace proposals. The other two issues were the international status of Jerusalem, and the partitioning of the land according to the distribution of the population. Jewish extremists rejected all three of these issues. This had resulted in the assassination of Bernadotte, the UN representative behind the peace proposals (see page 57).

In December 1948, the UN adopted Resolution 194 (see Source G). These proposals were rejected by Israel, and the UN had no means of enforcing them. After the 1948–49 War was over, Israeli leaders believed that it would be dangerous for Israel to allow the refugees to return at all, given the hostility towards Israel from the Arab world. This remains Israeli policy to this day.

SOURCE G

The General Assembly,
Having considered further the situation in Palestine,

Resolves that the refugees wishing to return to their homes and live at peace with their neighbours should be permitted to do so at the earliest practicable date, and that compensation should be paid for the property of those choosing not to return and for loss of or damage to property which, under principles of international law or in equity, should be made good by the Governments or authorities responsible;

Instructs the Conciliation Commission to facilitate the repatriation, resettlement and economic and social rehabilitation of the refugees and the payment of compensation, and to maintain close relations with the Director of the United Nations Relief for Palestine Refugees and, through him, with the appropriate organs and agencies of the United Nations.

Extract from UN General Assembly Resolution 194, 11 December 1948.
http://unispal.un.org/unispal.nsf/a06f2943c226015c85256c40005d359c/c7585 72b78d1cd0085256bcf0077e51a?OpenDocument

Question

Read the extract from UN Resolution 194 in Source G. What exactly was the General Assembly asking the Israeli government to do?

SOURCE H

Historian Colin Shindler sums up the situation of the Palestinian refugees at the end of the 1948–49 War.

The failure to achieve peace with the Arab world in 1949 left the refugees in a limbo between an Israel which did not want to readmit them and Arab states which did not wish to absorb them ... The stalemate left the refugees in an unenviable, parlous [dangerous] situation. Neither Israel nor the Arab states recognised the Palestinians as a national entity ... The refugees were marooned in a political no-man's land defined by the seemingly insurmountable hostility between Israel and the Arab states ... In this political stand-off where neither return nor integration was offered, the Palestinians began to define themselves as a nation and not merely as part of a wider Arab world.

Shindler, C. 2008. A History of Modern Israel. Cambridge, UK. Cambridge University Press. pp. 51–53.

> **Question**
>
> According to Source H, how did the status of the refugees lead to the development of a Palestinian national identity?

Almost 20 years after the flight of refugees first began, the number of people living in the Palestinian diaspora increased substantially. As a result of the 1967 War between Israel and the Arab states, over a million more Palestinians came under Israeli control in the West Bank, the Gaza Strip and the Golan Heights area of Syria. More than 200,000 Palestinians from areas of the West Bank and the Old City of Jerusalem became refugees, some of them for the second time. You will learn more about this in Chapter 7.

Developments in the Arab states after 1948

By 1948, the Arabs had not realised the dream of independence and unity that inspired the Arab Revolt against Ottoman rule in 1916. Of the vast area of the Middle East granted to Britain and France as mandates at the end of the First World War, only Iraq was granted full independence (in 1932). The other states remained linked to the colonial powers. In the Anglo–Egyptian Treaty of 1936, Britain recognised the independence of Egypt but retained the right to station troops there in times of war. During the Second World War, there were 250,000 British and Allied troops in Egypt, and Britain dictated policy to the government of the Egyptian king, Farouk. This caused great resentment among Egyptian nationalists.

The independence of Lebanon and Syria was recognised in 1943 and 1946 respectively, after lengthy resistance to French rule. Lebanon was unique among the Arab countries in that it had a Christian population almost equal in number to Muslims. It was hoped that stability and unity would be maintained by granting the presidency to the Christian community, and the premiership to the Muslims.

The British mandate of Transjordan was in a difficult position economically, and relied heavily on subsidies from Britain. Its army was trained and led by British officers. During the 1948–49 War, the Arab Legion held on to the Old City of Jerusalem and much of the West Bank. After the war, this area was incorporated into Transjordan, which became the independent Hashemite Kingdom of Jordan in 1950. Approximately half of the Palestinian refugees were living in villages and camps in Jordan.

Muslim Brotherhood The Muslim Brotherhood was formed in Egypt in 1928, as a religious organisation that opposed Western influences in Egyptian society and supported a return to traditional Islamic values and practices. Although it initially concentrated on social projects, teaching literacy and setting up hospitals, it became involved in politics by opposing British control in Egypt. By the 1930s, the Muslim Brotherhood had a membership of about 1 million. The movement spread to other Arab countries, but was banned in some of them because of its perceived support for violence. In 1987 a Palestinian political party, Hamas, was formed as a branch of the Muslim Brotherhood. The stated aim of Hamas was to liberate Palestine from Israeli occupation.

Ba'athist movement This movement was established in Damascus, Syria in 1943. Its programme was a mixture of socialism and Arab nationalism, and it was strongly opposed to Western interference. Ba'athist parties have ruled Syria since 1963. They were also in power in Iraq from 1968 until 2003, when the Ba'athist government of Saddam Hussein was toppled in a US-led invasion. There are Ba'athist parties in several other Arab countries.

Activity

What were the reasons for the political instability in many Arab states, and for the lack of unity between them? Compare and contrast the views expressed on these issues in Sources I and J.

Although the Arab states formed the Arab League in 1945, there was little unity between them. A deep divide existed between the Kingdoms of Iraq and Jordan and the rest of the Arab states, which regarded the two countries' pro-British policies with suspicion. In the post-war period, a new generation of educated Arabs saw the ruling governments as ineffective and outdated. They joined nationalist movements that aimed to put an end to economic backwardness, social inequalities, and foreign control and influence. The **Muslim Brotherhood** and the **Ba'athist movement** were two of the most prominent movements. *Ba'ath* means 'renaissance' in Arabic, and the Ba'athists believed in achieving Arab unity through a form of Arab socialism.

After the defeat of the Arab armies by Israel in 1948–49, some of the younger generation of Arabs believed that their leaders had let them down. This led to political instability and revolution. In December 1948, the Egyptian prime minister was assassinated. During 1949, there was a series of military coups in Syria. In 1950, the Lebanese prime minister was assassinated, as was King Abdullah of Jordan in 1951. In 1952, King Farouk of Egypt was overthrown in a bloodless military coup, which would have significant repercussions throughout the Middle East. You will learn more about this in Chapters 5 and 6.

SOURCE I

The First Arab–Israeli War, however, did not unify the Arab world. Rather it led to upheavals in individual Arab countries, often fomented by a new, young and disillusioned generation which had been nurtured on what was considered the injustice of Zionist dispossession of Arab land with the assistance of the Western powers. This emerging Arab nationalism found a common focal point in the hatred of Israel. But it also disliked what it saw as the reactionary influence of the old dynasties.

Ovendale, R. 1984. The Origins of the Arab–Israeli Wars. London, UK. Longman. p. 130.

SOURCE J

The Arab nations were not domestically stable before the war, and defeat by Israel didn't help matters. For the younger generation this humiliation clearly indicated a lack of leadership. The attendant dismay at both the élite and popular levels resulted in severe instability, and finally revolution ... Postwar Arab attention was focused primarily on domestic concerns, and secondarily on competition with one another – Israel and Palestine were, at this point, something of an afterthought, though for saving face before the Arab populations a posture of anti-Israeli belligerency was generally struck.

Harms, G. 2005. The Palestine–Israel Conflict: A Basic Introduction. London, UK. Pluto Press. p. 103.

This photo from 1952 shows welders helping to construct an oil pipeline that will stretch for 900 km (560 miles), from Kirkuk in northern Iraq to Banjas on the Syrian coast

Oil would play a vital role in changing the economic structure and social attitudes in many Arab countries. Before the First World War, relatively small oil deposits were found in Iran. After the war, and especially during the 1930s, large oil deposits were discovered in Iraq, Saudi Arabia and the Persian Gulf states. In all of these places, exploration and drilling operations were owned and controlled by international oil companies – British, French, American and Dutch. They formed subsidiary companies that paid fees to local rulers for the rights to develop the oilfields and export the oil. Developments were delayed by the Second World War, but after 1945 vast oil discoveries made the Middle East the greatest oil-producing area in the world. During the 1950s, as production increased and the extent of the oil deposits was realised, local leaders demanded greater control and a larger share of the profits. They bought major shareholdings in the subsidiary companies, most of which later became fully state-owned. Before the 1960s, however, revenue from oil did not have any marked effects on government policies or social conditions in the Arab states.

The development of the Cold War after 1945 also influenced attitudes towards the Middle East. Both the USA and the USSR saw the possibility of more conflict between Israel and the Arab states as an opportunity to advance their own interests by supporting opposing sides. At the same time, each superpower feared that its Cold War rival would gain more power and influence by intervening in Middle Eastern affairs.

neo-colonialism This term refers to the economic control that Western powers and industrialised countries continue to exercise over their former colonies.

Question

How did the start of the Cold War affect the Middle East?

SOURCE K

After 1945, the Middle East became of vital concern to the super-powers because of its strategic position, its oil resources and the threat of the Arab–Israeli conflict to peace. Russia, with common frontiers with Turkey and Iran, renewed her traditional pressure on them and the USA replied with the Truman Doctrine, offering aid against the threat of Communist aggression. So the region became a theatre in the Cold War, yet without the clear-cut East-West division of the European scene; for the Arab states saw Israel as the greatest threat to their security and found little to choose between the USA and the USSR, both of whom had given immediate recognition to the new Jewish state. Moreover, recent experience of British and French imperialism, which Britain vainly tried to continue through the Arab League, hardly encouraged newly independent Arab states to commit themselves to the **neo-colonialism** of the West. On the other hand, the atheistic Communism of the East did not attract Muslims.

Kohler, J. and Taylor, J. 1985. Africa and the Middle East. London, UK. Edward Arnold. p. 127.

Activities

1 Draw up a table to summarise the information about developments in the Arab states after 1948, and the situation of Palestinian refugees within each state. Use the sections of the text on the Palestinians in the diaspora, and on political developments in each state, as your basic information. However, you should also look for information in other sources.

	Political developments	Situation of the Palestinian refugees
Jordan		
Egypt		
Lebanon		
Syria		
Other		

2 Design a spider diagram to summarise the views of different historians about the causes of the flight of the Palestinian refugees.

3 Find out about the current social and economic situation of the Palestinian diaspora. Find out the answers to questions such as:

- How many Palestinians are there?
- In which countries or areas do they live?
- Are they still living in refugee camps?
- Does the UNRWA still play a role in their lives?
- What is their standard of living? (Look for information about literacy rates, life expectancy, infant mortality rates, unemployment figures, average income per household and so on to determine this.)

How did Israel encourage immigration and promote economic development?

The form of government and the first elections

After the state of Israel was established, it was ruled by a provisional government until January 1949, when the first elections for the Knesset (parliament) of 120 members were held. A system of **proportional representation** made it possible for small minority parties to be represented in parliament, and even government. As a result, most governments ended up as coalitions, as it was difficult for a single party to attract enough support to govern alone. In this way, some of the small religious parties were able to gain an influence out of proportion to their actual support base, by being included in coalition governments.

Elections for the Knesset were to be held every four years. The Knesset would elect a president as head of state, but real power would be in the hands of the prime minister. Israel did not draw up a written constitution. This was partly because some Orthodox Jews believed that it would be in conflict with religious tradition, and partly because it would mean defining the borders of the new state, which Ben Gurion and other leaders preferred to leave unspecified at this stage.

The party that won the most number of seats in the Knesset was Mapai, with 36% of the vote. Mapai is the Hebrew acronym for the Workers Party of the Land of Israel. The party was led by David Ben Gurion, who became Israel's first prime minister. Many of the early Zionist leaders, including Ben Gurion, wanted Israel to be a secular state. However, the newly elected government realised that it would have to compromise with religious groups in order to create a stable coalition government. Mapai formed a coalition with the third largest party, the United Religious Front, and a few other small parties.

In return for the religious parties' support, the government introduced religious laws that applied to every Jew in Israel, whether they were religious or secular. However, religious views did not dictate all policy: in 1951, the Knesset passed the Women's Equal Rights Law recognising gender equality, despite objections from some of the religious parties and ultra-Orthodox Jews.

The largest opposition party was Mapam, the Hebrew acronym for the United Workers Party, which won 15% of the vote. Mapam was more left-wing in its policies than Mapai, and strongly pro-Soviet in its views. This was a key reason why Ben Gurion did not include Mapam in the coalition: he did not want to alienate America, Israel's main source of funding. The only other party to win more than 10% of the votes was the right-wing Herut, formed by Menachem Begin in 1948 as the successor to Irgun, the extremist paramilitary group.

The government declared Jerusalem as the capital of Israel, even though only the western half of the city was under Israeli control. This was in conflict with the UN resolution passed in December 1949 (see page 59), which confirmed the UN view that Jerusalem should be placed under international control. As a result, many countries did not recognise it as the capital, and maintained their embassies in Tel Aviv.

proportional representation
This is a system of voting in which each party gains representation in parliament according to the proportion of total votes that it receives in an election. In this system, people vote for the party whose policies they support, rather than for individual candidates.

Fact
In the first election in 1949, 87% of the electorate cast their votes. Only 10% of those who voted were born in Palestine, and 86 of the 120 members of parliament elected were born in Eastern Europe or the USSR. These figures highlight the significance of immigration in the composition of the Israeli population, and the dominant political role that immigrants from Europe played.

Fact
Many decades later, with growing support for ultra-Orthodox Judaism in Israel, discriminatory measures to separate women and men were introduced in certain areas, especially Jerusalem, where the size and influence of the Orthodox population had grown significantly. Among these were attempts to force women to sit at the back of buses, and the building of barriers to prevent men and women from walking on the same pavement. In 2011, both of these measures were successfully challenged in the Israeli Supreme Court.

79

The issue of immigration

Around 47,000 Jewish refugees left Yemen after anti-Jewish riots that followed the establishment of Israel in 1948; the Yemeni Jews in this photograph are lining up for their meal at a new immigrants' camp in Israel

Fact

By 2009, Israel had overtaken the USA in terms of the size of its Jewish population: 42.5% of the world's Jews lived in Israel, compared to 39% in the US. The other 18% live in many countries around the world, with the larger numbers in France, Canada and the United Kingdom.

In 1948, only 6% of the Jews in the world lived in Israel. The Israeli government wanted to change this by encouraging Jewish immigration in the hope of consolidating Israel's possession of the land. By the Law of Return (1950), the government recognised the right of any Jew to settle in Israel. The Citizenship Law (1952) granted immediate citizenship to Jewish immigrants. There was a huge influx of immigrants and within three years the Jewish population had more than doubled. According to historian Martin Gilbert, this was the largest single migration of people during the 20th century, in relation to the size of the population of the state to which they moved. The steady flow of immigrants continued for some years.

The first to come were survivors of the Holocaust, followed by immigrants from Eastern European countries. The USSR had a Jewish population of 2 million, but Stalin's government refused to allow them to emigrate. Between 1948 and 1952 about 300,000 Jews from Eastern Europe, especially from Poland and Romania, entered Palestine. Many of them wanted to take the opportunity to do so before their countries' borders were closed by the new communist governments that had come to power in Eastern Europe. Only 2% of the Jews from other parts of the world – the USA, Western Europe, Latin America, Australia and South Africa – migrated to Israel.

SOURCE L

Historian Martin Gilbert describes the desperate state of many of the first immigrants.

The pre-war Zionist hope of bringing trained agriculturalists and pioneers zealous to establish new settlements and to till the soil and raise cattle and cultivate their fields and orchards had to be set aside in the realization that most of the survivors of the Holocaust were people who had no such ideals, had never intended to go to Palestine, and would require a world of their own in which to recover as best they could from the physical and mental devastation of their wartime torment. Many of the tens of thousands of survivors who had wanted to get to Palestine were quite untrained, or broken by their terrible experiences in the war. The teenagers among them had lost up to six years' schooling and education in the ghettos and concentration camps. But they could not be excluded, and the Jewish Agency had to adjust its expectations and prepare for the arrival of those who would need considerable support.

Gilbert, M. 1998. Israel: A History. London, UK. Black Swan. p. 258.

SOURCE M

Historian Colin Shindler analyses the reasons for the relatively small numbers of Jewish immigrants from countries beyond Eastern Europe and the Arab states, and the implications this had for Zionism.

While half a million Jews left Eastern Europe and the Islamic countries for Israel, only 1682 left North America whose Jewish population was 5 201 000. Clearly, Jews in the more affluent countries did not wish to leave their place of residence for the uncertainty of the Middle East. However, they were willing instead to identify through paying for the enormous costs of the absorption and rehabilitation of those who had suffered persecution and discrimination. After 1945 the great centres of Zionist endeavour in Eastern Europe no longer existed and the victory of Stalinism left those Jews in a state of penury. In addition, the reaction of Arab nationalism to the establishment of Israel disenfranchised and impoverished Jews in the Arab world. The centres of immigration in the Diaspora now no longer coincided with the centre of capital. Many appeals to the Jewish community in the USA were answered extremely generously, but this was not exactly the fulfilment of Zionist ideology.

Shindler, C. 2008. A History of Modern Israel. Cambridge, UK. Cambridge University Press. p. 64.

Fact
Stalin supported the UN Partition Plan and was quick to recognise the establishment of Israel. However, he also banned emigration to Israel from the USSR, mainly for economic reasons, and made any Zionist activity punishable by imprisonment in labour camps. After Stalin's death, the Soviet government continued to restrict emigration to Israel. However, after the collapse of the USSR and the lifting of these restrictions, a million Jews from Russia moved to Israel in the 1990s.

Many Jewish communities had lived in Arab countries and other parts of the Middle East since Roman times, usually without fear of persecution. However, their position changed dramatically after the events of 1948. There were attacks and anti-Jewish riots in some cities, and many Jews became victims of discrimination and expulsion.

As a result, there was a wave of Jewish refugees from the Arab countries to Israel. More than half of the number of immigrants who reached Israel between 1948 and 1952 came from the Arab countries and other Muslim states, such as Iran and Afghanistan.

Many of the Jewish immigrants from Arab countries were settled in the border areas of Israel, in villages that had belonged to the Palestinians. By 1956 there were over 1,650,000 Jews in Israel, compared to an Arab population of 200,000.

SOURCE N

Martin Gilbert explains why as more immigrants arrived, it became less and less likely that the Israeli government would ever allow the Palestinians to return.

Simultaneously with UNWRA setting up facilities – at first minimal – to take over the refugee camps beyond Israel's borders, Israeli legislation made any realistic prospect of the return of more than half a million people increasingly unlikely ... As the number of refugees grew, through the natural increase of births over deaths, so the legislation designed to make the return of refugees more difficult, if not impossible, also increased ...

Among those who protested was the German-born Jewish philosopher, Martin Buber, who, in answer to the Israeli government's correct insistence that the Custodian of Absentee Property was granting leases rather than titles to land and houses, wrote to the Speaker of the Knesset [parliament] (on 7 March 1953), 'We know well, however, that in numerous cases land is expropriated not on grounds of security, but for other reasons, such as expansion of existing settlements etc. These grounds do not justify a Jewish legislative body in placing the seizure of land under the protection of the law. In some densely populated villages, two thirds and even more of the land have been seized.'

Within three years of independence, and two years before Buber wrote his letter of protest, 1,400,000 people, a quarter of the Jews of Israel, were housed on 'absentee' Arab property.

Gilbert, M. 1998. Israel: A History. London, UK. Black Swan. p. 258.

Discussion point

What is the role of philosophers in society? Is it their duty to provoke discussion about government policies? Should they raise ethical issues to ask critical questions about practical policies or political expediency? Why would Buber's comments have been unpopular with many Israelis at the time?

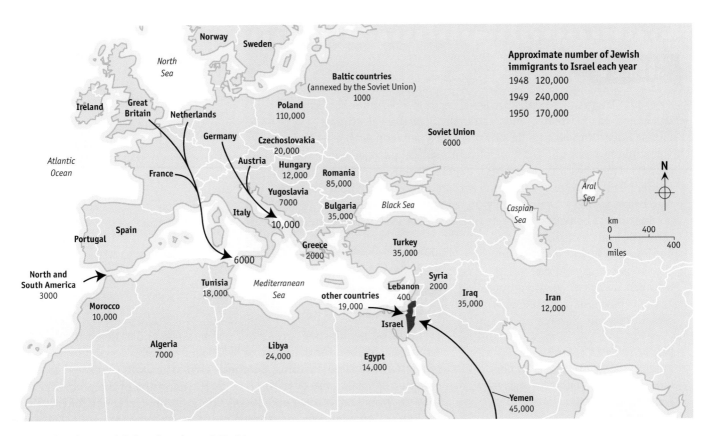

A map showing Jewish immigration, 1948–50

Ashkenazi, Sephardic and Mizrachi Jews

Jewish immigrants into Israel shared a common religion, but they came from different economic and cultural backgrounds and distinct religious traditions. There were three different groups: the Ashkenazi Jews, the Sephardic Jews and the Mizrachi (or Oriental) Jews. The Ashkenazi Jews were those whose ancestors came from central and eastern Europe, and Russia. The Sephardic Jews were those whose ancestors were expelled from Spain and Portugal by the Inquisition in the 1490s, and then settled mainly in North Africa and other Mediterranean countries. The Mizrachi Jews were the descendants of communities in North Africa and Middle Eastern countries. There are many similarities between the traditions and culture of the Mizrachi and Sephardic Jews, which is why the term Sephardim (or Sephardic) is often used to include both groups.

By 1956, the composition of the Jewish population had changed dramatically. European Jews, who had dominated the Zionist movement for decades, formed only one-third of the population. There were economic and cultural differences between the Ashkenazi and the Mizrachi Jews: the latter were referred to as 'Arab Jews' because they spoke Arabic and because other Israelis believed they were more Arab than Jewish. Many of the Mizrachi Jews were unskilled, and suffered far higher levels of unemployment. Positions of power and influence – political, economic and social – remained firmly in the hands of those with a European background, a fact that contrasted with the socialist ideals of the earlier settler communities. Many of the Mizrachi lived in poor-quality public housing, and did not receive the same benefits or pay as other Israelis.

Fact

So many Mizrachi Jews immigrated to Israel that by 1990 they made up 70% of the country's population. However, with the mass immigration of 1 million Ashkenazi Jews from Russia in the 1990s, the composition of the population changed. The Mizrachi Jews now make up about 50% of the Jewish population of Israel.

SOURCE O

They [the Mizrachi or Sephardic Jews] became a permanent cheap workforce, easily isolated and used to displace the Palestinian labour force. Competition for unskilled jobs between Arab Jews and Palestinians was exploited cynically for political purposes on Israel's borders. The Palestinians had been expelled from their villages near the borders, and Arab Jews were being settled on their land; now the latter also began taking jobs previously done by those Palestinians.

To this should be added the cycle of Palestinian infiltration and Israeli retaliation, all occurring on the borders and further heightening the tension and animosity between these two victim groups of the veteran Ashkenazi Jewish community and Zionism.

Pappe, I. 2006. A History of Modern Palestine (Second Edition). Cambridge, UK. Cambridge University Press. pp. 170–71.

Activities

Use Sources O and P to answer these questions:

1 Explain why the immigrants from Arab countries had not found 'the Zion of their dreams' (Source P).

2 On what issues do the sources agree with each other about the problems facing these immigrants?

3 Explain how the situation of the Mizrachi Jews contributed to tensions between this group and the Palestinians.

4 Why does Pappe say that Mizrachi Jews and Palestinians were both victims of Zionism?

SOURCE P

From the outset, the Sephardim felt undervalued and suffered from Ashkenazi disdain for their way of life. There was little respect for their religion and ancient customs. European civilisation was perceived as superior. Officials were overwhelmed by the enormity of the problems they were obliged to solve and life became a bureaucratic hell for the Sephardim – pawns moved into new positions by invisible hands. The difficulties of acculturation and the meeting with modernity had not produced the Zion of their dreams. Despite all the good intentions to integrate the Sephardim, the worsening economic situation was increasingly producing a generation of the disaffected. Most Sephardim fell to the bottom of the productive ladder ... If they were not unemployed, they became the human material for unskilled jobs and menial labour and often drifted into petty crime.

Shindler, C. 2008. A History of Modern Israel. Cambridge, UK. Cambridge University Press. p. 97.

The problem of assimilating immigrants from such widely different backgrounds was partly overcome by a common religion, and the adoption of Hebrew as the main official language. Although Arabic also had the status of an official language, the Jews from Arab countries were actively discouraged from speaking it. The Israeli Defence Force, in which women as well as men had to serve as conscripts, was another attempt to create national unity.

Economic development

In terms of economic policy, the new state was capitalist. However, the government owned a large sector of the economy and, to a certain extent, regulated economic affairs. The economy expanded rapidly, with the establishment of new industries producing chemical products, electronic equipment and processed foods. In time, most of Israel's export earnings came from citrus fruits and processed diamonds, although export markets were limited because of boycotts by Arab states and some communist countries. Economic growth was boosted by defence spending, and by the large workforce produced by immigration.

To promote development in agriculture, hundreds of new agricultural settlements were established – some in areas previously unsuited to agriculture, such as the Negev desert. There were two main types of settlement – the kibbutz (collective farm) and the moshav (co-operative village). The kibbutzim were communal enterprises that were jointly owned and controlled; they provided clothing, food, housing, health services and education for the people living and working there. In the moshavim, the land was also communally worked, but houses and land were individually owned. Many of the new settlements were placed in sensitive border areas, where they replaced villages abandoned by the Palestinians. As the population of Israel increased, and the amount of land under cultivation expanded, there was a further source of friction between Israel and its Arab neighbours: water. The governments of Syria and Jordan strongly protested when Israel implemented a scheme to divert the waters of the River Jordan towards dry agricultural land in Israel. In a region where water was scarce, this issue had the potential to cause further tension and conflict. In response to international pressure from the United Nations, the USSR and even the USA, Israel backed down.

Although Israel defeated the Arab armies in the 1948–49 War, there was an awareness that Israel's position was not secure. Some historians have described it as a country with a siege mentality. The government aimed to have an army in a constant state of readiness, equipped with the most up-to-date technology and weapons. Accordingly, Israel maintained one of the largest armies in the world in proportion to its population, conscripting men and women into the armed forces and as reservists. Defence spending was estimated to be as high as 44% of the budget in 1950, which put a considerable strain on the economy and curtailed spending on other developments. But the continuing state of tension in the region made it unthinkable for any Israeli government to cut military expenditure.

SOURCE Q

Gregory Harms describes the general feeling within Israel in the years following the 1948–49 War.

Israel, on the other hand, was aglow with confidence and defiance. But despite its recent military success, there still lingered the doubt over Arab desire to destroy Israel, and a general sense of vulnerability and isolation, creating a hyper-defensive mindset among the populace, and an assumed stance of aggressive defence or 'activism', at the top levels of government.

Harms, G. 2005. The Palestine–Israel Conflict: A Basic Introduction. London, UK. Pluto Press. p. 103.

Historical interpretation

Revisionist historians have paid a great deal of attention to the underlying causes of the ongoing tensions between Israel and the Arab states. The traditional Israeli view blamed the Arab states for their stubborn refusal to negotiate. However, revisionist historians say that Israel was not willing to negotiate a lasting peace because of the price it would have to pay – namely, giving up some of the land it had conquered and allowing the Palestinian refugees to return.

Theory of knowledge

History and education

In 2008, Avi Shlaim claimed that the 'new history' had an impact on the way history was taught in Israeli schools, and that textbooks had been re-written to incorporate some of the views of the revisionists. Why is it essential for students of history to be exposed to different and conflicting views of issues and events?

Question

How was Israel able to achieve significant economic growth?

Activity

The terms 'Israeli Arab' and 'Arab Jew' are used to refer to two different groups of people in Israel. Distinguish between the two.

SOURCE R

Avi Shlaim explains the two opposing views among Israeli historians as to why there was no proper peace settlement after the 1948–49 War.

The traditional Zionist answer to this question can be summed up in two words: Arab intransigence [stubbornness or inflexibility]. According to this version, Israel's leaders strove indefatigably [tirelessly] for a peaceful settlement of the conflict after the terrible ordeal of 1948, but all their efforts foundered on the rock of Arab intransigence. Israel's leaders were desperate to achieve peace, but there was no one to talk to on the other side …

Revisionist Israeli historians, on the other hand, believe that post-war Israel was more intransigent than the Arab states and that it therefore bears a larger share of the responsibility for the political deadlock that followed the formal end of hostilities … The real question facing Israel at that critical point in its history was not whether peace with its Arab neighbours was possible but at what price.

Shlaim, A. 2000. The Iron Wall: Israel and the Arab World. London, UK. Penguin. pp. 47–49.

Israel was heavily dependent on foreign aid for economic development and the accommodation of immigrants. Absorbing immigrants into the country was a costly process: in addition to houses and settlements, they needed schools, hospitals, jobs, factories, roads and other infrastructure. Ever since the Balfour Declaration in 1917 (see page 26), there had been regular contributions from Jewish communities in the Diaspora; the USA in particular had been a major source of support for Jewish settlements in Palestine. A $50 million donation made in response to an appeal by Golda Meir in the USA helped to fund the Israeli military preparations in the 1948–49 War. Soon after the establishment of Israel, the USA provided $65 million worth of aid to help Israel provide for its immigrants.

Israel had another source of income that was highly controversial: from 1952, Israel accepted reparations payments from the West German government. This was despite strong – and at times violent – opposition from Holocaust survivors, who were outraged that the suffering of the Jewish people under the Nazis should be considered atoned for in this way. But the Israeli government was acutely aware that without outside aid Israel could not survive.

The position of the Palestinians in Israel

The 160,000 Palestinians who remained in Israel after the 1948–49 War became known officially as 'Israeli Arabs'. Many of them lived in villages close to the borders. The Israeli authorities were concerned about possible alliances they might form with fellow Palestinians in neighbouring states. As a result, Israel imposed harsh military rule in these areas in October 1948, and maintained this for 18 years. Any person suspected of identifying with Palestinian nationalism was imprisoned or expelled.

Israeli Arabs voting in Israel's first election in 1949

The Kfar Qassem massacre on 29 October 1956 demonstrated the harshness of Israeli military rule. The Israeli authorities, without warning, imposed a curfew on all Palestinian villages in Israel. When villagers at Kfar Qassem, unaware of the order, returned to their homes after the curfew time of sunset, Israeli border guards shot and killed 48 men, women and children. Some influential Israelis, including the head of the Israeli secret service and the director-general of the Defence Ministry, argued against the continuation of military rule, believing that it was doing more harm than good. However, nothing was done to lift it in the years following the massacre. Some liberal Israeli politicians supported full citizenship for the Palestinians, but Ben Gurion and his advisors on 'Arab affairs' were firmly opposed to this. It was only after Ben Gurion was no longer in power, and his influence had diminished, that military rule was lifted in 1966.

The Israeli government tried to encourage Palestinian village and tribal leaders to co-operate with the authorities, in return for wealth and privileges. However, the policy was not effective because those leaders who agreed to become agents of government policy were shunned by their own communities. The government also attempted, without success, to create divisions among the Palestinians by treating Christians and Muslims differently, regarding Christian Palestinians as more loyal to Israel. However, religious identity did not play an important role in determining attitudes towards the government among the Israeli Arabs. Many Christians later played leading roles in the development of a Palestinian nationalist movement.

Certain basic laws passed by the Knesset in the early 1950s discriminated against Palestinians. The citizenship laws gave preference to Jewish citizens, even foreign-born ones, over indigenous Palestinians. The property laws declared most of the land for sale in Israel to be the property of the Jewish people. As a result of this, almost all Palestinian-owned land was taken over by the state to be sold or leased to Jewish people. In this way, Israeli Jews came to own 92% of the land. By 2000, the amount of land available to the Palestinians in Israel remained the same as it had been decades earlier. This was despite the fact that the Palestinian population had substantially increased.

Fact
According to population statistics, in 2010 there were 1,573,000 Israeli Arabs in Israel, forming just over 20% of the country's population. These people identified themselves as Israeli by citizenship, but Palestinian by nationality. The vast majority (82%) were Muslim, 9% were Christian and the other 9% were Druze (see page 88). This figure does not include Palestinians in the occupied territories (such as the West Bank and Gaza), who were regarded as permanent residents – but not citizens of Israel.

Druze The Druze are a religious sect with about 1 million followers in the world, most of them in Syria and Lebanon. Their religion is a branch of Shi'ite Islam, and the Druze consider their faith to be a new interpretation of Islam, Christianity and Judaism, in which a private relationship with God replaces religious ritual and ceremonies. The 104,000 Druze living in Israel are recognised as a distinct community. Their language is Arabic and their culture Arab, but many Druze fought on the Israeli side in the 1948–49 War.

Fact
Historian Ilan Pappe notes that among the Palestinians living in Israel, poetry became an outlet for the expression of their identity. Poets could write about issues that political activists could not express openly. They included issues such as dispossession and state oppression into their poetry and aired them in public at poetry festivals. The Israeli secret service was unsure whether these were simply cultural events or to view them as subversive. Pappe suggests that 'poetry was the one area in which national identity survived the Nakbah unscathed'.

Histradut This was the Israeli labour organisation. It was established by the Jewish Agency in 1920 as a trade union for Jewish workers.

Military service was another issue that put Palestinians at a disadvantage in Israel. The only members of the Palestinian population who were conscripted for national service were the **Druze**. This was the result of an agreement reached between Druze religious leaders and the Israeli government in 1956. The rest of the Palestinians did not do national service, and this had serious implications: only people who had served in the army qualified for state benefits such as loans, mortgages and reduced university fees. There was also discrimination in employment against those who had not served in the army. As a result, more than 50% of jobs in industry were closed to Palestinians.

Economic and social conditions for the Palestinians in Israel were difficult. Surveys indicated significant differences in education levels and health care between Arabs and Jews. The Palestinians had the highest levels of unemployment: this was partly because many had been peasant farmers who now had no land, and were forced to do unskilled and poorly paid work. An added difficulty was that the Palestinians had to return home to their own communities every day, as they were not allowed to stay overnight in a Jewish area. The Palestinian communities were struggling to survive, so more women had to find jobs outside the home. This brought about a relative improvement in some women's lives, as it gave them greater freedom and access to education.

One basic right that the Palestinians in Israel had was the right to vote and to be elected. This was something that was not available to many Palestinians in the diaspora. In the first Israeli elections held in 1949, three Arabs were elected to the Knesset. Mapai and other political parties were in favour of the Palestinian right to vote because they believed it would broaden their base of support in elections. Since 1966, Palestinians in Israel also have the same legal rights as other Israelis. Historians J.A. Kohler and J.K.G. Taylor suggest that there were some positive features of Israeli rule for the Palestinians living in Israel (see Source S below).

SOURCE S

The Arabs who remained in Israel were promised in the Declaration of Independence, 'full and equal citizenship and due representation in all its institutions'. Thus they could vote, and Arab parties put forward their lists of candidates, some of whom were elected and joined coalitions in government or opposition. Arab citizens, Christian or Muslim, had religious freedom and control over their churches and townships, and could have separate schools. In the 1960s, they were allowed full membership of the *Histradut*. At the same time the military administration of the border was removed, and this ended restrictions on daily life which Arabs had found most irksome. Israeli law forbade polygamy and marriage for girls under 16, and the Arabs reluctantly accepted this. For obvious reasons, Arabs were excused military service.

Kohler, J. and Taylor, J. 1985. Africa and the Middle East. London, UK. Edward Arnold. p. 94.

88

Activities

1 Design a spider diagram to illustrate the political, social and economic challenges facing the state of Israel in the first few years of its existence.

2 Research the role played by David Ben Gurion, and evaluate his influence on shaping the type of state that emerged in Israel.

3 Explain each of these terms in the context of the history of modern Israel:
   • immigration
   • assimilation
   • discrimination
   • repatriation
   • reparation.

4 Find information about Israel today, and determine how successfully it has overcome the challenges of promoting national unity in a country where the population has come from such vastly different backgrounds.

5 Use the information in this chapter, or do further research, to carry out the following activities based on the table in Source T below:

   a The table does not show the population figures for 1948. Use the information in this chapter to estimate what the figures would have been. Explain the trends shown by the figures for 1949.

   b Explain the substantial increase in the Jewish population between 1949 and 1967, and between 1990 and 2000.

   c Despite the steady Jewish immigration to Israel reflected in this table, the percentage of Jews in the total population has been declining. Find out the possible reasons for this.

   d How would the Israeli government use the figures in this table to justify its policy regarding the return of Palestinian refugees?

SOURCE T

Israel: Arab/Jewish population, 1949–2006

Year	Jews	Arabs	Total	% of Jews to total
1949	1,013,900	159,100	1,173,000	86.436%
1967	2,383,600	392,700	2,776,300	85.855%
1973	2,845,000	493,200	3,338,200	85.225%
1983	3,412,500	706,100	4,118,600	82.855%
1990	3,946,700	875,000	4,821,700	81.853%
2000	4,955,400	1,188,700	6,144,100	80.652%
2006	5,393,400	1,413,300	6,806,700	79.237%

Israeli Central Bureau of Statistics. 'Statistical Abstract of Israel, No. 55' (2004) and 'Statistical Abstract of Israel 2007: Population by district, sub-district and religion'. ICBS website accessed on 20 September 2007. http://israelipalestinian.procon.org/view.resource.php?resourceID=000636#graph4

End of chapter activities

Summary

You have learnt about the demographic shifts that resulted from the 1948–49 War. You should understand why the Palestinian Arabs fled, what conditions were like for them in the diaspora, and why they did not return to Israel after the war. You should be able to discuss different views about the causes of their flight. You have also read about the political, economic and social developments in Israel in the early 1950s. You should understand the problems as well as the advantages associated with large-scale immigration to Israel. Above all, you should understand that there are different views and historical debates about these events, and you should be able to explain the different interpretations.

Summary activity

Copy the diagram below. Use the information in this chapter, and from other sources, to make brief notes under each heading.

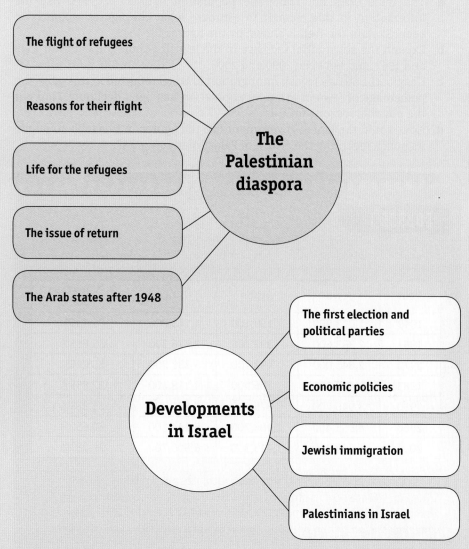

- The flight of refugees
- Reasons for their flight
- Life for the refugees
- The issue of return
- The Arab states after 1948

The Palestinian diaspora

Developments in Israel

- The first election and political parties
- Economic policies
- Jewish immigration
- Palestinians in Israel

Paper 1 exam practice

Question

Compare and contrast the views expressed in Sources A and B below on the role of the Israeli army in promoting nation-building.
[6 marks]

Skill

Cross-referencing

SOURCE A

Ben Gurion promoted the army as the essence of 'Israeliness'. It was perceived as a melting-pot for Ashkenazim and Sephardim, religious and secular, privileged and impoverished – a means of building an Israeli identity from over a hundred culturally disparate Jewish communities. The armed forces were increasingly venerated by a grateful public which could only see a continuing and sometimes unremitting hostility towards the state of Israel from one quarter or another.

Shindler, C. 2008. A History of Modern Israel. Cambridge, UK. Cambridge University Press. pp. 4–5.

Before you start

Cross-referencing questions require you to compare **and** contrast the information/content/nature of **two** sources. Before you attempt this question, refer to page 218 for advice on how to tackle these questions, and a simplified markscheme.

SOURCE B

The Israeli army spearheaded the effort to Westernize the Arab Jews. However, the general socio-economic divisions also applied inside the army, and Mizrachi Jews, often reluctant conscripts, were given logistical posts, a lasting stain on their prestige and later civilian careers in a society that revered commando fighters and air force pilots. Thus the army promoted militarization instead of acting as an agent of modernization or socialization.

Pappe, I. 2006. A History of Modern Palestine. (Second Edition). Cambridge, UK. Cambridge University Press. pp. 174–75.

Student answer

Source A states that the army was seen as a 'melting pot' in which Israelis of different cultural, religious and socio-economic backgrounds could merge and form a common Israeli identity. But Source A says that the Arab Jews were to be 'Westernised' in the army. In other words, they had to learn the customs of the Ashkenazi Jews. Source A does not explain whether this melting-pot idea was successful or not. Source B, however, suggests that the army did not succeed in modernising or socialising the Arab Jews, and instead it reinforced the divisions in society because Arab Jews were not given the kind of jobs that would make them heroes in the eyes of the Israeli public.

Examiner comments

This is a good answer that links the two sources and explains the differences between their views on the social function of the army. The answer also correctly shows another difference: Source A does not comment on how successful the policy was, whereas Source B suggests that it was not successful. However, the answer does not point out any similarities between the two sources regarding the views of Israeli society towards the army. The candidate has therefore done enough to get into Band 2, and be awarded 5 marks.

Activity

Look again at the two sources, the simplified markscheme on page 218, and the student answer on page 91. Now try to rewrite the answer, linking the two sources by pointing out the similarities as well as the differences between them.

Paper 2 practice questions

1   Account for the demographic shifts in the Middle East following the 1948–49 Arab–Israeli War.

2   Analyse the reasons for the flight of Palestinian refugees between 1947 and 1952.

3   Examine the impact of the 1948–49 War on the surrounding Arab countries.

4   Analyse the social and economic impact of immigration on Israel in the early 1950s.

5   Explain why the Palestinian refugee problem was so difficult to resolve.

6   To what extent is it accurate to say that Israel is not a model of democracy?

5 The Suez Crisis of 1956

Introduction

The Suez Crisis of 1956 was more than simply another conflict between Israel and the Arab states. It had far wider implications and significance. It was a clash between Arab nationalism and the colonial powers, Britain and France, who wanted to maintain their power and influence in the region. The Suez Crisis also extended the Cold War into the Middle East, when the USA and the USSR were drawn into the conflict. Egypt – under its new leader, Gamal Abdel Nasser – was at the centre of the power struggles.

Key questions

- What were the effects of the growth of Egyptian nationalism?
- What happened during the Suez Crisis and the Sinai War?
- What was the role of outside powers and their significance in the Suez Crisis?

Overview

- Egypt was a former British colony, where many Egyptians resented the continuing British influence over the corrupt and inefficient government of King Farouk. After the Second World War, Egyptian army officers formed the revolutionary Free Officers movement to bring about change.
- In 1952, the Free Officers ousted Farouk. The new government, under Nasser, negotiated a British withdrawal from the Suez Canal Zone and organised loans for an ambitious Aswan Dam project.
- Relations between Egypt and Israel remained tense because of Egyptian-backed incursions by Palestinians into Israel, and Israeli reprisals.
- Western countries were angered by Nasser's foreign policy, and suspicious of his links with the Soviet bloc. They withdrew their offers of loans for the Aswan Dam. Nasser nationalised the Suez Canal, intending to use the revenues to fund the dam project. Attempts to resolve the issue by diplomatic means failed.
- Britain, France and Israel drew up a secret plan to invade Egypt, seize the Suez Canal and force Nasser from power. The Israeli invasion and occupation of the Sinai Peninsula was followed by Anglo–French air strikes and a seaborne invasion, resulting in an international crisis.

Timeline

1952 **Jul:** Free Officers coup; Farouk overthrown

1954 Nasser replaces Neguib as leader of Egypt

1955 **Feb:** Baghdad Pact formed

1956 **May:** Egypt recognises Communist China

Jul: West withdraws promises of loans for building of Aswan Dam

26 Jul: Egypt nationalises Suez Canal; start of Suez Crisis

Oct: secret meetings between Britain, France and Israel

24 Oct: Sèvres Protocol

29 Oct: Israel invades Egypt; start of Sinai War

30 Oct: Anglo–French ultimatums to Egypt and Israel

31 Oct: British and French bomb Egyptian airfields

2 Nov: Israel defeats Egyptian forces in Sinai campaign

4 Nov: Egypt blocks Suez Canal; Soviet troops crush Hungarian uprising

5 Nov: Anglo–French paratrooper landings in Port Said; USSR threatens intervention

6 Nov: Anglo–French seaborne landings in Port Said; UN ceasefire; British and French troops start to withdraw

15 Nov: UNEF troops monitor ceasefire

22 Dec: evacuation of British and French forces completed

1957 **Jan:** evacuation of Israeli forces completed (except from Gaza and Sharm el-Sheikh); Eden resigns as prime minister

Mar: Eisenhower Doctrine

93

- The USA joined the USSR, the United Nations, the Commonwealth and the rest of the world in condemning the invasion. Britain, France and Israel were forced to withdraw from Egypt.
- As a result of its involvement, Britain lost its influence in the Middle East. It faced suspicion in the Arab world, and was forced to acknowledge the predominance of the USA in dictating foreign policy.
- The United Nations sent a peacekeeping force to monitor the border between Israel and Egypt. This enhanced the UN's role in world affairs.
- As a result of the Suez Crisis, the USA and the USSR became more involved in the Middle East. The two superpowers increased the tensions in the region by supplying arms, and the Cold War extended into the Middle East. The USA feared Soviet influence in the region, a factor which ensured future American support for Israel.
- The Suez Crisis was a triumph for Nasser, who gained increased prestige and influence in the Arab world.

Egyptians crowd around a British tank in a street in Port Said during the Suez Crisis, 12 November 1956

What were the effects of the growth of Egyptian nationalism?

Relations between Britain and Egypt

Egypt became a British 'protectorate' in 1882, when Britain invaded Egypt. Britain wanted to ensure stability in the country, to safeguard the operation of the **Suez Canal** and the flow of cotton exports from Egypt. In 1888, an international treaty was drawn up to guarantee freedom of passage through the canal for all states, in war as well as in peacetime. The Suez Canal Company owned, operated and profited from the canal, which was the major trading link between Europe and Asia (see map on page 24). The British and French governments were major shareholders in the Suez Canal Company.

Many Egyptians regarded the British as an alien presence, and resented their political and economic control. Britain formally recognised Egypt's independence in 1922, but the country remained under strong British influence. Britain still owned the majority of the shares in the Suez Canal Company, and maintained troops in Egypt to protect the canal. Britain confirmed the independence of Egypt in a 1936 treaty, but this treaty also gave Britain the right to station troops in the Canal Zone for a further 20 years. During the Second World War, Egypt became a base for 250,000 British and other Allied troops. These soldiers were involved in fighting the Italian and German armies in North Africa. For some Egyptian nationalists, resentment against the ongoing British military presence in their country caused them to favour the Axis side (Germany, Italy and Japan). Egypt remained officially neutral for most of the war, resisting British pressure to join the Allies until 1945.

After the Second World War, Britain continued to maintain a garrison (a military post) of 70,000 troops in the Canal Zone. Britain was the biggest user of the canal, and much of the oil on which Europe depended still came through the canal from the Persian Gulf. However, increasing amounts came overland by pipeline to oil terminals in the Mediterranean region. Despite this, the profits from the Suez Canal were worth $100 million annually by the 1950s.

Conditions in Egypt after the Second World War

King Farouk's government in Egypt represented the country's wealthy landowners, and Farouk had a reputation as a rich playboy who was out of touch with conditions in Egypt. Many Egyptians resented Farouk's willingness to allow the virtual occupation of the country by Britain during the war, when the British had effectively dictated policy to his government. For example, in 1942 Farouk had given in to pressure from Churchill to replace his prime minister with one more acceptable to the Allies. His willingness to co-operate with Britain continued after the war. Egyptians also blamed Farouk and his government for Egypt's humiliating defeat in the 1948–49 War against Israel.

Critics of Farouk's government accused it of incompetence and corruption. They also rejected King Farouk's lifestyle, and his ignorance of the economic and social problems that faced the vast majority of Egyptians. In the early 1950s, Egypt had a population of 39 million, about 80% of whom were illiterate and living in conditions of extreme poverty. Nearly 99% of the population lived in the Nile Valley and the Nile Delta. Nearly two-thirds of the land was owned by a small number of wealthy landowners, who made up only 6% of the Egyptian population. The poor peasant farmers (the *fellaheen*) owned very small plots, if they owned any land at all.

Suez Canal The Suez Canal (see map on page 98) was designed by a French engineer, and built with British and French funds between 1859 and 1869. An estimated 120,000 Egyptian workers died during the canal's construction. The canal linked the Mediterranean Sea with the Red Sea, and reduced the journey from Europe to India by 8200 km (5100 miles). After the discovery of oil in the Persian Gulf region, it became the main route for oil supplies to Europe.

King Farouk (1920–65)
Farouk became king of Egypt at the age of 16, following the death of his father. The young king was initially popular. However, his love of luxury, excess and extravagance put him totally out of touch with ordinary Egyptians, most of whom lived in poverty. Farouk was blamed for the corruption and inefficiency of his government, and was deposed in the Free Officers coup in 1952. He was succeeded briefly as king by his infant son, Fuad, until the Egyptian monarchy was abolished in 1953. Farouk lived in exile in Monaco and then Rome until his death.

fellaheen Also written as *fellahin*, this is the Arabic word for farmers, peasants, agricultural workers or anyone else who makes his or her living by working the land (as opposed to nomadic herders). The singular form of the word is *fellah*.

The rise of Egyptian nationalism

After the Second World War, there was growing support for a revolutionary form of nationalism in Egypt. This was partly due to general dissatisfaction with the corrupt and inefficient monarchy, and its indifference to the need for reform. There was also great resentment at Britain's continuing influence over Egypt. Revolutionary nationalism was also fuelled by anger at the failure of the Arab states to prevent the establishment of Israel, as well as Israel's victory in the 1948–49 War. These feelings were particularly strong among young army officers, some of whom formed a revolutionary movement called the Free Officers. The Free Officers secretly planned to overthrow the government and bring about changes to Egypt's domestic and foreign policies.

SOURCE A

It was not only the King's inability to remove British influence that outraged the Free Officers. His expensive appetite for pleasure and self-indulgence was well known. Scandal, corruption and incompetence were commonplace in the government and bureaucracy. All three contributed to Egypt's defeat by Israel in the 1948 war: money for arms and supplies was misapplied; soldiers were given obsolete or unserviceable weapons, and the military leaders wasted soldiers' lives through contradictory orders and impracticable objectives. Not surprisingly the Free Officers became convinced that it was necessary to remove the monarchy as well as the British if Egypt's honour was to be retrieved.

Kohler, J. and Taylor, J. 1985. Africa and the Middle East. London, UK. Edward Arnold. p. 104.

Questions

Why did the Free Officers blame Egypt's defeat by Israel in the 1948–49 War on the government of King Farouk? Was it valid to hold the government fully responsible for this defeat?

Gamal Abdel Nasser (1918–70) Nasser was educated at the Cairo Military Academy, and played an active role in the Egyptian nationalist movement early on. He and other army officers formed the Free Officers movement. Nasser fought in the 1948–49 War against Israel, played a leading role in the 1952 coup, and led Egypt from 1954 until his death from a heart attack in 1970. He became a hero in the Arab world for his resistance to Israel and the West.

Another source of opposition to Farouk's government was the Muslim Brotherhood (see page 76). This group was founded in Egypt in 1928, and was dedicated to establishing a society based on the teachings of Islam. The Muslim Brotherhood was opposed to Western institutions and cultural influences, and by 1950 it had become a powerful influence in Egypt.

In 1951, there were guerrilla attacks on the British garrison in the Canal Zone. The British reacted harshly, and 50 Egyptian policemen were killed in a raid on Ismailia. For a while, the Egyptian government cut off supplies of food and labour to the British bases. The tensions also resulted in attacks on British property in Cairo, led by the Muslim Brotherhood. Britain increased its garrison in the Canal Zone to 80,000. A succession of governments appointed by Farouk failed to suppress the unrest. This strengthened the determination of the Free Officers to overthrow the government and replace it with one that would tackle the problems facing Egypt.

The military coup and the role of Nasser

In July 1952, the Free Officers seized control of the Egyptian army headquarters, the airport and the communications centres in Cairo in a bloodless coup. Farouk was forced to abdicate, and was allowed to leave the country to go into exile. The popular and respected General Mohammed Neguib became president of Egypt, but he was little more than a figurehead. The most powerful member of the new government was Colonel **Gamal Abdel Nasser**.

The new government moved quickly to suppress opposition. It put down an attempt by workers to take over a textile mill in Alexandria, and imprisoned 200 communist leaders. After an assassination attempt on Nasser, the government also banned the Muslim Brotherhood, executed six of the group's members and sentenced its leader to life imprisonment. When Egypt formally became a republic in 1953, all political parties were banned. In 1954, Neguib resigned and Nasser took over the positions of president and prime minister. Nasser also became leader of the Free Officers, the police and the army.

Two of the aims of the Free Officers revolution were strongly nationalist: members of the movement wanted to free Egypt of what they saw as an alien monarchy, and to eliminate foreign power and influence. The first aim was achieved with the abdication of King Farouk. The Free Officers hoped to achieve the second aim by getting rid of the British garrison in the Canal Zone. In 1954, Nasser negotiated a new treaty in which Britain agreed to withdraw its troops within two years. At this stage, Britain was willing to negotiate with Nasser as he was the leader of the most powerful Arab nation. Both Britain and the USA wanted to maintain Arab support and reduce the possibility of increased Soviet influence in the Middle East. The Suez Canal was no longer of such vital strategic importance to Britain since India had become independent in 1947. By 1954, Britain had already moved the British Middle East Military Headquarters from Egypt to Cyprus. The evacuation of British troops from the Canal Zone was completed in March 1956, ending a 74-year British military presence in Egypt. The airfields and military equipment, including radar, at the former British bases became part of Egypt's military defences.

Another aim of the Free Officers revolution was to reform the economic and social structures in Egypt. The Free Officers wanted to destroy the power of the great landowners, redistribute the land among the *fellaheen*, and modernise Egypt. Nasser's most ambitious project was the construction of a high dam across the Nile River at Aswan. This scheme would control the floodwaters of the Nile by storing them in a great artificial lake (later called Lake Nasser). The water would be used for irrigation, to increase the amount of land that could be used for farming by 25%. This in turn would reduce the amount of food that had to be imported.

The dam would also provide hydro-electric power for industry, which was seen as the key to modernisation. The dam project was very important for Egypt's economy, as it held the promise of raising living standards and boosting economic development through industrialisation. The project was also of political significance to Nasser, as it had the potential to improve his popularity in Egypt and his prestige in the Arab world. Egypt secured promises of loans to fund the project from the USA, Britain and the **World Bank**.

Relations between Egypt and Israel 1949–56

Relations between Israel and the Arab states had remained hostile since the 1949 armistice agreements that ended the first Arab–Israeli war. The Arab states refused to recognise Israel or to trade with it, and would not allow Israeli aircraft to fly over Arab airspace. They closed the oil pipelines to Israel, and the Iraq Petroleum Company moved its headquarters from Haifa to Tripoli. Egypt would not allow Israeli ships, or indeed any ships trading with Israel, to use the Suez Canal. With the co-operation of Saudi Arabia, Egypt also blockaded the Straits of Tiran to Israeli shipping. All of these actions increased the tensions between Israel and the Arab states, especially Egypt.

97

Questions

Why would many Egyptians have welcomed the coup that brought Nasser to power? Who would *not* have welcomed it?

World Bank The World Bank and the International Monetary Fund (IMF) were formed in 1944. They were part of an attempt to stabilise the world economy after the problems of the Great Depression of the 1930s, and the destruction caused by the Second World War. The World Bank arranges long-term, low-interest loans for projects in developing countries, and the IMF approves loans to countries in financial difficulties. The World Bank and the IMF are dominated by the USA and other Western countries, and they promote free market capitalist economic policies. The headquarters of both institutions are in Washington, DC.

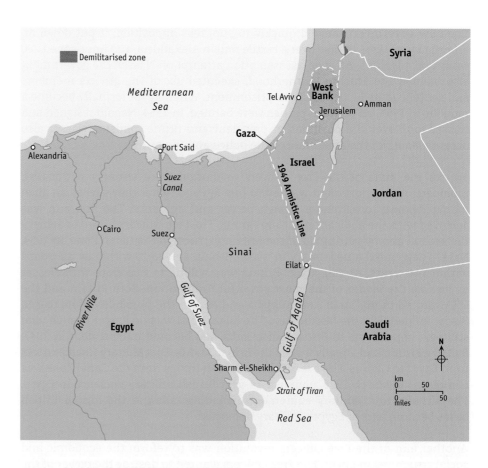

A map showing the Middle East in 1956

In the Gaza Strip, 300,000 Palestinians lived in a narrow coastal area under Egyptian military control. Frequent raids by Palestinians across the border into Israel brought harsh and instant reprisals from the Israeli Defence Force (IDF). Some – but certainly not all – of the raids from Gaza were attacks on Israeli settlements by Palestinian *fedayeen* fighters. Israel accused Egypt of supporting these *fedayeen* raids, and claimed that the Israeli reprisals were a justifiable response to them. A similar situation developed along Israel's long border with Jordan, and in the demilitarised zone between Israel and Syria. Israeli statistics show that between 1949 and 1956 there were 10,000–15,000 instances of infiltration each year. However, the number had fallen significantly by 1956 because of IDF reprisals. Sources B and C examine the causes and effects of the Palestinian infiltration into Israel during the 1949–56 period.

After Nasser came to power in Egypt in 1954, there were concerns in Israel about how this would affect relations between the two countries. Some Israeli political leaders such as Moshe Sharett (prime minister between 1953 and 1955, and then foreign minister) favoured moderation and negotiation, and there were secret contacts between Sharett and Nasser. However, military leaders such as Moshe Dayan, the chief of staff of the defence force, regarded Nasser as a threat to Israeli security. Dayan and Ben Gurion (the former prime minister, who was temporarily in retirement but emerged to become prime minister once again in 1955) wanted instant retaliation for any raids, as well as subversive action to discredit Nasser. In 1954, Israeli agents tried to damage Egypt's relations with the USA by attacking American-owned buildings in Cairo and blaming it on the Egyptians. Although this plot failed, it led to strained relations between Israel and Egypt after two of the Israeli agents were tried and executed.

fedayeen In Arabic, *fedayeen* literally means 'self-sacrificers'. The *fedayeen* were Palestinian guerrilla fighters who launched raids across the border into Israel.

SOURCE B

Following the signing of the armistice agreements in 1949, the Arab states maintained a policy of isolating Israel and of focusing their rhetoric on a 'second round' of war. There was an increase in attacks against Israel, leading in 1951 to more than 150 Israelis killed or wounded, the worst attacks originating in the Gaza Strip. Israel adopted an active strategy, including a campaign of reprisal raids. These raids had early failures, and reprisals helped little in reducing the threat of infiltrating terrorists. But planning continued, and the Israelis contemplated the occupation of Gaza, which would deny the Arabs a launching pad from which to attack Israeli population centres. The IDF created an elite group of paratroop commandos ... to launch a campaign of reprisal raids into enemy territory in an effort to halt the attacks on Israel ...

Tensions rose on Israel's borders as Palestinians, often accompanied by other Arabs, began infiltrating Israel from the West Bank and the Gaza Strip, and attacking people and property. Israel held the Arab governments responsible and launched retaliatory raids. The ensuing cycle of violence, in which Israeli and Arab civilians and soldiers were killed, escalated and encompassed Syria as well.

Reich, B. 2008. A Brief History of Israel (Second Edition). New York, USA. Checkmark Books. p. 64.

SOURCE C

But, though there were some terroristic and politically-motivated infiltrations, which increased over the early and mid-1950s, Israeli statistics and Arab evidence ... show that the vast bulk of the infiltration, 90 per cent and more, through 1949–56, was economically or socially motivated. Most of the infiltrators came to retrieve possessions and crops and, thereafter, to steal. A small proportion engaged in smuggling. More crossed the border to resettle in their former villages and towns or to visit relatives or just to look at their former homes and lands.

Apart from such 'civilian' infiltration, there was, throughout the years, a steady if small proportion of 'political' or terrorist infiltration – geared to sabotaging Israeli targets and killing and injuring Israelis. This infiltration was motivated by hatred, and in many cases, revenge – revenge for the national and personal wrongs and injuries inflicted during 1948 or during subsequent border incidents.

Morris, B. 1993. Israel's Border Wars 1949–1956: Arab Infiltration, Israeli Retaliation, and the Countdown to the Suez War. Oxford, UK. Clarendon Press. p. 428.

Historical debate

Compare the reasons given in Sources B and C for raids into Israel from Gaza. Use the information that you learnt in previous chapters about the historiography of Israeli history to explain these different perspectives.

On 28 February 1955, the IDF launched an attack against the Egyptian military headquarters in Gaza, destroying it and killing 35 Egyptian soldiers. The attack was intended to undermine Nasser's prestige in the Arab world, and to provoke a military response from Nasser. Although this did not happen, the Gaza Raid had significant repercussions. It fuelled Egypt's desire for revenge, and the Egyptians began in earnest to arm and train *fedayeen* fighters. It also caused Nasser to try almost immediately to strengthen Egypt's defences by seeking supplies of armaments, resulting in an arms deal with Czechoslovakia. According to Ilan Pappe, the raid destroyed the 'delicate edifice of trust that Sharett and Nasser had begun building in a series of secret negotiations exploring the chances for peace between Israel and Egypt'. Benny Morris notes that the raid resulted in a major policy switch by Egypt: its soldiers began to support a 'revenge-oriented campaign of revenge and murder' along the Gaza border with Israel.

When Egypt signed the arms deal with Czechoslovakia in September 1955, concerns mounted in Israel. Dayan and others hoped once again to provoke a confrontation with Egypt before the military balance between the two countries shifted in Egypt's favour. In November 1955, the IDF launched another attack against Egyptian military positions in Gaza, killing 50 Egyptian soldiers and capturing 50 more. It was the largest military operation by the IDF since the 1948–49 War. Although the attack further increased Egypt's desire for revenge and its support for the *fedayeen*, it did not lead to war.

SOURCE D

Ilan Pappe explains how the tension between Israel and the Arab states was aggravated by propaganda directed against Israel by Nasser and other Arab leaders.

However, the Arab leaders themselves were sending ambiguous messages of both peace and war to the Israeli leadership, of which Ben Gurion chose to see only the more hostile approaches. Many of the Arab leaders immediately after the 1948 war were much more committed to the peace process the UN had started and was nurturing, than was Ben Gurion. What explains Ben Gurion's intransigence was the emphasis the UN was still putting on the refugee question, more specifically on the need to repatriate them unconditionally. But the Arab world also presented another, more hostile, front which was broadcast in fiery public speeches and publicised through inflammatory articles in the local press, all employing warlike rhetoric and promising revenge for the 1948 defeat. The Egyptian and Syrian leaders went beyond words and struck large arms deals with the Eastern bloc, modernising their armies and preparing them for war. When they partly translated words into action by engaging in guerrilla warfare on the Jewish state's borders, the inevitable Israeli retaliation, often out of all proportion, sowed insecurity in the Arab regimes bordering Israel, and contributed much to creating an 'eve of war' atmosphere.

Pappe, I. 2006. A History of Modern Palestine (*Second Edition*). *Cambridge, UK. Cambridge University Press. p 161.*

Question

How did the Arab states contribute to the build-up of tension in the Middle East in the period between 1948 and 1956?

In December 1955, in what Israeli historian Avi Shlaim calls 'an unprovoked act of aggression by Israel', Israeli commandos launched a raid into Syria. The Israeli action was condemned by the United Nations, and resulted in a refusal by the USA to supply arms to Israel. Although Syria reacted with restraint, tensions rose and the potential for conflict between Israel and its Arab neighbours significantly increased.

The influence of the Cold War

Nasser, the Soviet leader Nikita Khrushchev and the presidents of Iraq and Yemen press a button to blast open a diversion canal for the Nile around the Aswan Dam on 14 May 1964

Events in the Middle East in the early 1950s must also be seen in a global context. The Cold War, which had started in Europe after 1945, had extended to Asia. The French were trying to re-establish colonial control over Indochina, and were fighting a losing battle against a Vietnamese nationalist group, the communist-led Viet Minh. The Chinese Communist Party came to power and established the People's Republic of China in 1949. Between 1950 and 1953, many Western countries became involved in the Korean War, as part of a United Nations operation to support non-communist South Korea against communist North Korea.

The USA and its allies were suspicious about Soviet intentions, and were determined to prevent the extension of communist influence into other parts of the world. For this reason they formed a military alliance, the North Atlantic Treaty Organisation (NATO), in 1949. The NATO countries were afraid that instability in the Arab states would make them vulnerable to Soviet intervention, so a similar alliance was formed in the Middle East in 1955. This was the Baghdad Pact, which was designed both to protect British interests in the region and to prevent the extension of Soviet influence. Baghdad Pact members were Britain, Turkey, Pakistan, Iran and Iraq. It had unofficial support from the USA, which later joined the pact when it was re-formed as the Central Treaty Organisation (CENTO) in 1959.

non-alignment This was a policy adopted by developing countries unwilling to take sides during the Cold War. These countries declared themselves to be the 'Third World', not allied to either the First World (the West) or the Second World (the Soviet bloc) in the Cold War. This decision was made at the Bandung Conference in Indonesia in 1955, a meeting of newly independent Asian and African nations. Nasser was present at this conference.

After 1954, Western countries became increasingly concerned about Nasser's actions. He refused to join the Baghdad Pact, calling it an instrument of imperialism in the Middle East. He actively opposed Iraq's membership, and persuaded the new king of Jordan, Hussein, not to join. Nasser also convinced Hussein to dismiss his military advisor, the British General Glubb, who was largely responsible for building up Jordan's Arab Legion into the strongest military force in the region. When Nasser attended the Bandung Conference in April 1955 and professed his support for **non-alignment**, Western countries became even more suspicious, associating non-alignment with communism. When Egypt signed an arms deal with Czechoslovakia in September 1955, Western fears about growing communist influence seemed to be confirmed.

SOURCE E

In the Anglo–American effort to establish a Cold War Middle East bulwark [fortification; protection; barricade], one country that was unwilling to co-operate was Egypt. Nasser opposed such pacts, interpreting them as further attempts to sustain Western control over the Middle East. His objective was pan-Arab independence, as he loathed British imperialism, which still maintained its presence in Egypt. With his support of Algeria's resistance to French occupation, contempt for Israel as an instance of Western colonialism, suspicion of US intervention, as well as hatred for Britain and imperialism in general, Nasser was needless to say unpopular in the West.

Harms, G. 2005. *The Palestine–Israel Conflict: A Basic Introduction.* London, UK. Pluto Press. p. 104.

Communist China When China became a communist state in 1949, Western countries refused to recognise the communist government and would not allow China to join the United Nations. The West claimed that Taiwan, which was non-communist, represented the Chinese people. Taiwan was the island off the coast of China where the nationalist dictator Jiang Jieshi had fled with his forces after their defeat by the Chinese communists in 1949. China was admitted to the UN in 1971, with the status of a permanent member of the Security Council along with the USA, USSR, Britain and France. The USA only formally recognised China in 1979.

Western attitudes towards Nasser must also be seen in the context of the post-war anti-colonial struggles in British and French colonies in Africa and Asia. Since 1952, Britain had been involved in suppressing a nationalist uprising (sometimes called the Mau Mau Rebellion) demanding independence in Kenya. In 1954, the French were forced to withdraw from Indochina after a humiliating defeat by Vietnamese nationalists.

In the same year, France became involved in a long and bitter war to maintain control of Algeria. The Front de Libération Nationale (FLN), the Algerian nationalist organisation committed to liberating Algeria from French control, was formed in Cairo in 1954. The FLN leaders organised the war against France from their headquarters in Cairo. Britain and France were angered by Nasser's open expressions of support for the anti-colonial movements in their colonies. The British were further antagonised by Nasser's support for EOKA, the National Organisation of Cypriot Fighters, which was formed in 1955 to fight to end British rule in Cyprus.

When Egypt formally recognised **Communist China** in May 1956, the USA withdrew its offer of loans for the Aswan project. Britain and the World Bank also withdrew their financial support for the project. They hoped to send a signal to Nasser that what they perceived to be anti-Western policies were not in Egypt's best interests.

Activities

1 Write a newspaper article from Cairo in July 1952, reporting on the Free Officers coup that has just occurred. Writing for Western readers, analyse why the coup happened and what changes are likely to follow.

2 Design a spider diagram to illustrate the build-up of tensions between Israel and the Arab states by 1956.

3 Divide into groups of five students. Each student should research one of the following topics, and give a short presentation to the rest of the group. In each case, you need to explain the significance of your information for understanding the situation in the Middle East by 1956.

- USSR: the death of Stalin and its impact on Soviet policy
- USA: McCarthyism and the Red Scare
- Britain: its declining status as a world power and as a colonial power
- The Korean War and the perceived communist threat in East Asia
- Anti-colonial nationalist movements in Africa.

4 Funding for the Aswan High Dam project played a central role in the events leading to the Suez Crisis. Find out how the project eventually went ahead, and whether it brought about the dramatic economic and social transformation that the Egyptian government hoped it would.

5 Explain how Nasser was at the centre of the tensions that were developing in the Middle East by 1956.

What happened during the Suez Crisis and the Sinai War?

The nationalisation of the Suez Canal

This poster from around 1930 advertises the Suez Canal as a peaceful shipping route; the advertisement was produced by the Empire Marketing Board, a body that promoted trade in the British Empire

Theory of knowledge

History and language

Source F is a short extract from a very long speech that Nasser made on this occasion. In the full speech, he repeated some phrases and ideas several times. What rhetorical devices does he use in this extract to convince and persuade his audience to support the government's decision? The original speech was made in Arabic. What problems should historians bear in mind when they are reading a speech that has been translated?

Fact

Nasser made the announcement in a 90-minute speech in Alexandria, Egypt's second largest city, to a crowd of 250,000 cheering people. In his speech he referred to the colonial exploitation of Egypt, and the heavy price paid by Egyptian workers in the building of the Suez Canal. During the course of the speech, he mentioned the name of the French engineer who built the canal – Ferdinand de Lesseps – 13 times. The name 'de Lesseps' was the code word to activate the takeover of the offices, communications centre and headquarters of the Suez Canal Company. By the time Nasser's speech was over, all of these were in Egyptian hands.

Nasser reacted quickly to the announcement that Western loans for the Aswan Dam project had been suspended. On 26 July 1956, he declared that Egypt would nationalise the Suez Canal Company. Egypt would pay compensation to the shareholders. The Canal revenues, worth about US$100 million annually, would be used by Egypt to finance the dam project.

SOURCE F

The Canal was dug by Egypt's sons and 120,000 of them died while working. The Suez Canal Company in Paris is an imposter company …

But history will never repeat itself. On the contrary, we shall build the High Dam. We shall restore our usurped rights. We shall build the High Dam as we want it. We are determined to do it … Thus, today, citizens, when we build the High Dam we are actually building the dam to defend our dignity, freedom, and pride, and to eradicate humiliation and submission.

Egypt … announces that it will fight to the last drop of its blood … for the sake of Egypt. We shall not let warmongers, imperialists, or those who trade in human beings dominate us. We shall depend on our hands and on our blood … We shall build a strong and dignified Egypt, the Arab Egypt …

Today, citizens, the Suez Canal Company has been nationalised … Today our wealth has been restored to us.

Extract from the speech by Nasser in which he announced the nationalisation of the Suez Canal on 26 July 1956. US Department of State Publication, 1956. Kallaway, P. (ed.). 1987. History Alive. Pietermaritzburg, South Africa. Shooter and Shuter. p. 281.

Britain and France reacted angrily to Nasser's announcement. Their economies depended on oil from the Middle East, much of which was shipped through the Suez Canal. The British prime minister, **Anthony Eden** (see page 105) stated that the two countries did not want to be at the mercy of Nasser. Britain began to consider taking military action. Eden explained his views in correspondence with the US president, but President Eisenhower indicated that the USA did not support the use of force.

Initially, there were attempts to settle the issue by diplomacy. A Suez Canal conference was held in London in August 1956, and was attended by the major maritime powers. Their proposal that the canal should be placed under international control was rejected by Nasser. As a compromise arrangement, the USA suggested the formation of a Canal Users' Association to control and operate the canal and pay Egypt for the use of it, but this was also rejected by Egypt.

Britain and France withdrew their pilots from the canal, thinking that this would make it unworkable and in this way demonstrate to Nasser that the Egyptians needed Western assistance to run the canal properly. But Egyptian pilots handled the crisis and actually increased the flow of shipping through the canal, showing that colonial-style fears of Egyptian incompetence were unfounded. Britain and France also tried to get United Nations support for a motion condemning Nasser's action and placing the control of the canal under an international body, but this failed because the USSR used its veto in the **United Nations Security Council** to block it.

The British government, and especially Eden, now came to the conclusion that all diplomatic channels had failed. They believed that military action would be necessary to force an outcome that suited British interests. Britain did not expect active support from the USA but assumed that, in the words of Eric Morris, it would be 'benevolently neutral'.

The secret alliance between Britain, France and Israel

At this stage it became apparent that British and French interests coincided with those of Israel. France had agreed to supply Israel with weapons, including aircraft and tanks, and also to provide the country with the materials necessary to start developing its own nuclear capability. There had been top-level meetings between the French and Israeli governments to discuss their concerns about Nasser. Although Britain was initially unwilling to risk Arab hostility by supporting Israel, in October 1956 it joined these secret discussions. Britain, France and Israel jointly agreed that Nasser should be forced from power.

The three countries all wanted to attack Egypt and humiliate Nasser, and each country believed this would have specific advantages for its own national interests. Britain saw such an attack as a means of maintaining British influence in the Middle East and control of the Canal Zone. France hoped that the anti-colonial uprising in Algeria would collapse without Egyptian support for the FLN. It also believed that Nasser's nationalisation of the Suez Canal was enough in itself to justify military action against Egypt. Both Britain and France were anxious not to be seen to 'appease' Nasser – the discredited policy that their two governments had adopted towards Hitler in the 1930s.

Israel had the most to gain, although initially the Israeli government was suspicious of Britain because of its links with Arab countries such as Jordan. Israel wanted to break the restrictions on its economy by forcing Egypt to lift its blockade of the Straits of Tiran, and to allow Israeli ships to use the Suez Canal. The Israelis also wanted to strike at Egypt, which they accused of encouraging *fedayeen* raids from Gaza into Israel. An invasion of Gaza and Sinai would give Israel the opportunity to destroy the *fedayeen* bases in those areas. Israel was also concerned about the growth of Egypt's military strength, especially after the Czech arms deal. Egypt, Syria and Jordan had placed their armies under joint command, and the Israelis wanted to assert the military dominance of the IDF before it was too late. They also hoped that British bombers would be able to destroy the Egyptian air force, and that a change of government in Egypt would be to their advantage – a new, less aggressive government might be forced to recognise Israel.

Anthony Eden (1897–1977)
Eden succeeded Winston Churchill as Britain's prime minister in 1955. He resigned in January 1957 when British policies and actions during the Suez Crisis were condemned both internationally and at home.

United Nations Security Council The Security Council is responsible for deciding what action the UN should take in any crisis that threatens world peace. Its decisions are legally binding and enforceable. At the time of the Suez Crisis, the five permanent members of the 11-member council (the USA, USSR, Britain, France and China) had the power to veto any decision by withholding their support for it. This meant that any one of them could prevent the UN from taking an action that it considered damaging to its national interests. The General Assembly of the UN, where all countries were represented and no country had the power of veto, was the forum where issues were discussed and recommendations were made. However, these resolutions were not legally binding.

SOURCE G

Benny Morris explains his view of the reasons why Israel decided to attack Egypt by launching the Sinai Campaign.

It was, in the long term, a pre-emptive war. It was not pre-emption in the immediate, narrow sense of destroying the Egyptian army before it became too strong, for that need no longer existed after the massive French arms shipments of spring and summer 1956. But it was pre-emptive in the sense that, between 1949 and 1956, Israelis believed that the Arab states would eventually launch a war to destroy the Jewish state. The Sinai Campaign aimed to thwart this, at least for some years, by destroying the Arab world's potentially strongest army and buying Israel time, during which, perhaps, the Arabs would abandon their destructive goal. The momentary coalescence of Israeli, French, and British antagonism towards Nasser's Egypt during the summer and autumn of 1956 enabled Ben Gurion to launch his war with Anglo-French political protection and aerial and sea cover, and with the prospect of minimal Israeli losses.

Israel's border policy and the plunge into the Sinai Campaign cannot be understood without taking into account the deep feeling of isolation and siege that prevailed between 1949 and 1956. The threat of a 'Second Round', Arab propaganda and political warfare, including the refusal to recognise the Jewish state's right to exist, the blockade of Israeli shipping and air traffic at the Straits of Tiran, and the closure of the Suez Canal to Israeli ships and goods, the US witholding of arms, and, above all, the constant infiltration, the attacks, and the border skirmishes, all contributed. The war of 1956 was a momentous release of pent-up, vengeful energies.

Morris, B. 1993. Israel's Border Wars, 1949–1956: Arab Infiltration, Israeli Retaliation, and the Countdown to the Suez War. Oxford, UK. Clarendon Press. pp. 444–45.

Questions

'Pre-emptive' means to take action to prevent something from happening. Why does Benny Morris say that the Sinai Campaign was a pre-emptive war? What was Israel trying to achieve? Do you think that Morris feels that the decision was justified?

At the final meeting held at Sèvres, France, on 24 October 1956, Ben Gurion and the British and French foreign ministers agreed on a plan that they hoped would bring about Nasser's downfall. They drew up a controversial document called the Sèvres Protocol, which was a detailed plan and a precise timetable of how they hoped to achieve this.

They planned a joint campaign against Egypt, based on the basis that a war between Israel and Egypt would present the Anglo–French forces with an opportunity to intervene. The agreement was that Israel would launch an attack into Egypt across the Sinai Peninsula, with the aim of reaching the Suez Canal as quickly as possible. Britain and France would then step in, to 'protect' the canal from both the Egyptians and the Israelis, by issuing an ultimatum calling on both sides to withdraw their troops from the canal. They knew that Nasser would certainly reject this demand, and this would be the pretext for armed Anglo–French intervention. This would take the form of air strikes, followed by a seaborne invasion. While British and French forces occupied key positions in the Canal Zone, Israel would have the opportunity to occupy the whole of Sinai and extend Israeli control as far as the Suez Canal.

Britain and France began preparing for this invasion by sending warships and transports to the eastern Mediterranean area, and transferring paratroopers and aircrews to bases in Malta and Cyprus.

The Sinai War and the Anglo–French invasion

A young Egyptian boy and a British tank amid the rubble of a war-torn street during the Suez Crisis

On 29 October 1956, Israel launched its attack – and, in doing so, began the Sinai War. Israeli paratroopers were dropped near the Suez Canal, while army units made their way across Sinai. Other army units moved southwards to capture Sharm el-Sheikh, the port that controlled the entrance to the Gulf of Aqaba. The following day, Britain and France issued an ultimatum calling for a ceasefire and demanding that both sides withdraw their troops to 16 km (10 miles) east and west of the canal. They threatened to use force if either side rejected the ultimatum. At that stage, Israeli forces were nowhere near the canal, but they accepted the terms of the ultimatum. As all three countries had expected, Nasser rejected it. He refused, understandably, to withdraw Egyptian troops from Egyptian territory. Using this as a pretext, Britain and France bombed Egyptian airfields and Port Said at the northern end of the canal.

Meanwhile, Israeli forces advanced a further 350 km (217 miles) across Sinai and reached the canal. They were able to do so without fear of air attacks, as the British and French air strikes had destroyed many Egyptian planes on the ground. On 5 November 1956, Britain and France dropped paratroopers into the Canal Zone. On the following day, these two countries launched a full-scale invasion. The Egyptians sank ships filled with concrete in the canal in an effort to slow the British and French advance.

However, Britain and France had not anticipated the international reaction to their actions. In the Arab countries, the direct pipelines carrying oil to the terminals on the Mediterranean were attacked, effectively cutting off Europe's oil supplies. The United Nations General Assembly proposed a resolution demanding an immediate end to the invasion, which was passed by 64 votes to 5. Only Australia and New Zealand supported Britain, France and Israel. To the surprise and resentment of Britain and France, the USA led the criticism of their actions. It joined the USSR, the Commonwealth and the rest of the world in denouncing such 'imperialist aggression'.

SOURCE H

The Israeli attack on Egypt was but the first step in carrying out the conspirators' carefully elaborated conspiracy. Following this attack came the Anglo-French ultimatum to Egypt and a hasty movement toward the Egyptian shores of England's and France's armed forces concentrated for a long time in the eastern Mediterranean …

In its statement on the armed aggression against Egypt, the Soviet government vigorously condemned the aggressive acts of the governments of England, France and Israel which are incompatible with the principles and aims of the United Nations …

The peoples of Africa and Asia have succeeded in recent years in achieving great success in the struggle for their national independence. Forced to retreat under pressure of the mighty national-liberating movement which triumphed in many countries of Asia and Africa, the colonisers have not abandoned the thought of revenge.

The Anglo-French colonisers do not conceal the fact that in committing aggression against Egypt they pursue much further aims. Their schemes are not limited to attempts to seize the Suez Canal and to occupy Egyptian territory. It is a matter of direct threat to all Arab states that strive to strengthen their national independence.

Extract from the Soviet newspaper Pravda, *2 November 1956. Quoted in Browne, H. 1971.* Flashpoints: Sinai and Suez. *London, UK. Longman. pp. 92–93.*

Questions

What evidence is there in Source H that the secret plot hatched at Sèvres was obvious to outsiders? How did the USSR seek to gain political advantage out of the Suez Crisis? How does the information in Source H help to explain why the USA was quick to condemn Britain and France?

Less than 24 hours after landing at Port Said, British and French troops began to be evacuated from Egypt. A week later, UN peacekeeping troops arrived to oversee the ceasefire. Under pressure from the USA, Israel reluctantly agreed to withdraw its forces from Sinai early in 1957. A total of 33 British and French troops, 171 Israelis and over 1000 Egyptians, mainly civilians, died in the Suez Crisis and Sinai War.

The Suez Crisis had ended, but there were immense diplomatic consequences for all countries involved. The crisis changed the balance of power in the region, and brought the superpowers into the Middle East. This would have long-term consequences for the region, and meant that the Arab–Israeli conflict now had wider Cold War implications.

Activities

1 Design a flowchart to illustrate the key events during the Suez Crisis. Use arrows to indicate the sequence of events, the links between them, and the cause-and-effect relationships.

2 In groups, discuss the following statement:

'Diplomatic attempts to solve the Suez Crisis were doomed to failure before they even started because none of the countries involved wanted a peaceful solution to the crisis. They had too much to gain from it.'

3 Find out the details about the top-secret negotiations between Israel, France, and Britain that culminated in the Sèvres Protocol.

4 Write a newspaper editorial, commenting on Nasser's announcement that Egypt has nationalised the Suez Canal. You may either criticise the action of the Egyptian government as irresponsible and illegal, or take the view that Egypt is justified in doing so as the canal is a symbol of economic imperialism.

What was the role of outside powers and their significance in the Suez Crisis?

The role of Britain and France

From the time that Nasser nationalised the Suez Canal in July 1956, some members of the British government favoured taking strong action to show Nasser that Britain was still a powerful force in the Middle East. Britain's prime minister, Anthony Eden, particularly supported this view. In letters to Eisenhower, Eden explained his conviction that Nasser needed to be taught a lesson. Although the British government took part in diplomatic attempts to solve the Suez Crisis, Eden never really abandoned this view.

This meant that when the French approached the British government about plotting with the Israelis, Eden was a willing partner. He overruled the recommendations of some of his advisors, who warned that such a plot would damage Britain's relations with its remaining allies in the Arab world, such as Iraq and Jordan. Eden sent his foreign minister to Paris to meet with the Israelis and the French. However, there is evidence that Eden realised the serious implications of what Britain was involved in, because he tried (unsuccessfully) to ensure that all copies of the Sèvres Protocol were destroyed immediately.

When the Anglo–French forces invaded Egypt, British actions were criticised by other members of the Commonwealth, especially former British colonies. They saw Britain's behaviour as an example of **gunboat diplomacy**. The British nation itself was divided. The opposition Labour Party loudly criticised the government's actions, demanding 'Law not War'. There were demonstrations in British cities demanding Eden's resignation. Eden also faced criticism from within his own cabinet, and eventually he was forced to resign as prime minister in January 1957. The Suez Crisis, and especially Britain's part in it, ended Eden's political career.

Fact
Eden's government – and later British governments – refused to admit that there had been a secret meeting, even though the French and Israeli governments later admitted that it had taken place. When the official documents relating to the Suez Crisis were declassified, no trace of the Sèvres Protocol was found among Eden's papers. It is assumed that he destroyed it. The French government claimed that it had been lost. The only surviving copy was found among Ben Gurion's papers, and is in the Israeli state archives. In 1996, special permission was given to photocopy it for a BBC documentary on the 40th anniversary of the Suez Crisis.

gunboat diplomacy This term describes the intimidating tactics used by European powers in the colonial era. It refers to the practice of subduing uprisings or opposition to colonial policies in other parts of the world by the threat of military action. This involved a display of superior military power to intimidate the weaker countries.

SOURCE 1

On the British side, Anthony Eden bore the ultimate responsibility and received most of the opprobrium [blame] for the collusion with France and Israel. Eden was desperate for a pretext to go to war in order to get rid of Nasser and the alliance with Israel was the price he reluctantly paid to procure such a pretext. The elaborate plot embodied in the protocol was so transparent that it is still difficult to understand how Eden could have believed that it would not be seen as such. What is clear is that having got embroiled in the war plot, Eden became desperate to hide the traces. His attempt to round up and destroy all the copies of the Protocol of Sèvres has to be seen in this light. He wanted to expunge the war plot, in which Britain had been a reluctant but a full and formal participant, from the historical record. What he embarked on was a massive attempt to deceive. This attempt ended in miserable failure, like all the expedients that Eden resorted to in his vendetta against the Egyptian leader whom he perceived, for no good reason, as another Hitler.

Shlaim, A. 1997. 'The Protocol of Sèvres, 1956: Anatomy of a War Plot'. International Affairs. 73:3. pp. 509–10.

Theory of knowledge

History and ethics

There is a saying that 'the end justifies the means'. What exactly does this mean? How does it relate to Eden's actions in the Suez Crisis? Is it acceptable for a government to use underhand methods to achieve what it perceives to be a justifiable and even noble end?

A demonstration against British action in the Suez Crisis, held in Manchester, UK, on 2 October 1956

The Suez Crisis also exposed Britain's weak economic situation. When the oil pipelines from the Persian Gulf to the Mediterranean region were attacked, there were expensive petrol shortages. Britain had to introduce petrol rationing.

As a means of putting pressure on Britain and France to withdraw their forces, Eisenhower refused to allow additional oil supplies from South America, the two countries' only remaining source of oil. Britain was in severe financial difficulty, and the USA refused to lend any money or to approve a loan to Britain from the International Monetary Fund (see page 97).

With growing international pressure, the oil crisis, and the imminent collapse of its currency, the British government gave in to pressure and agreed to withdraw its troops. This left France no option but to do the same, as its soldiers were under British command. This put a strain on Anglo–French relations, with France convinced that it had been let down by its ally. The crisis weakened the French government, contributing to its collapse two years later. The humiliating diplomatic defeat of Britain and France in favour of Nasser was an inspiration to nationalist movements, and increased demands for independence in the African colonies. In particular, the FLN – which had its headquarters in Cairo – increased its attempts to force the French to leave Algeria.

The Suez Crisis achieved exactly the opposite of what Britain and France had intended. They had not gained control of the canal, and had failed to overthrow Nasser. British and French companies and banks in Egypt were nationalised, and foreigners were expelled. The crisis improved Nasser's prestige in Egypt, the Arab world and among developing countries. He enjoyed a reputation as the man who had successfully stood up to imperialist aggression. Instead of protecting the Suez Canal and ensuring the uninterrupted flow of oil, British and French intervention had resulted in the canal's closure. This first occurred when a ship in the canal was hit in the air strikes, and then again when the Egyptians sank ships filled with concrete in order to stop the advance of the invading forces. Britain and France lost any remaining political or military influence in the Middle East. They were forced to recognise their relative weakness in the face of superpower opposition.

SOURCE J

For the French the 'Suez Affair' was a failure, nothing worse; their credibility in the Arab world had already been lost by arms shipments to Israel and oppression in Algeria. For the British, Suez was a catastrophe. Quite apart from the domestic repercussions and the damage to Anglo–American relations, it had soured moderate Arab opinion and discredited all the old and cherished pretensions to being the friend of the Arabs …

Worst of all from a British point of view, Suez vindicated the construction placed on the policies of the European powers by Nasser. Far from silencing him, it enhanced his reputation, exaggerated his revolutionary rhetoric, amplified its appeal. Already idolized, the president of Egypt was now idealized.

Keay, J. 2003. Sowing the Wind: The Mismanagement of the Middle East 1900–1960. London, UK. John Murray. p. 442.

The role of the USA and the USSR

Although it was not directly involved in the Suez Crisis, the USA played an important role behind the scenes. The Middle East supplied less than 10% of the oil requirements of the USA at that stage, and so the country's economic interests were not fundamentally affected by the nationalisation of the Suez Canal. Nevertheless, between August and October 1956 the USA used its influence to promote a diplomatic solution to the crisis. Correspondence between Eisenhower and Eden shows that the American government made it clear that it did not support military action. When Israel, Britain and France went ahead with their secretly planned invasion of Egypt, the USA was angered by the irresponsible actions of its allies, and was quick to lead the condemnation of their attacks.

There were several reasons why the USA could not approve of British and French actions. It did not want to risk alienating the Arab states, or the newly independent Asian and African nations, and driving them into an alliance with the USSR. At a critical time in the Cold War, the superpowers were in competition to win allies in the developing world, and both wanted to be seen to support anti-colonialism. Eisenhower later wrote that the USA could not afford to let the USSR take the lead in condemning the use of force against Egypt, and in this way win the support and confidence of the newly independent countries.

Another factor that influenced American policy was that 1956 was an election year in the USA, and Eisenhower was running for re-election. The Anglo–French invasion came just days before the election itself. Eisenhower did not want the USA to be involved in any world conflict that might influence his position with the voters. The USA was able to use its considerable economic power to force Britain and France to accept the United Nations' call for a ceasefire.

The USSR was also quick to condemn the British and French invasion (see Source H on page 108). It warned that it was willing to use military power, and even hinted at nuclear strikes on London and Paris, if British and French forces were not withdrawn. It was the first time in the Cold War that the USSR openly threatened to use force. For a few days, there were fears that the crisis might become a global one, and the USA placed its troops on standby. But the Soviet Union was preoccupied with crushing an anti-communist revolt in Hungary at the time, and so was not prepared to be drawn any further into the Middle East crisis. In fact, the Suez Crisis proved to be useful to the USSR at the time because it distracted world attention from the revolt in Hungary, which the Soviet army was repressing with great brutality.

The Suez Crisis created a power vacuum in the Middle East, which encouraged both superpowers to become more involved in the region. The USSR increased its influence in the Arab world by playing on fears of Western interference. It increased its aid to Egypt to rebuild its military forces, and for the Aswan High Dam project. However, Egypt maintained its non-aligned status and did not become a communist state. The USSR also gained prestige in African and Asian countries because it had stood up for Egypt against imperialist aggression. To many of these countries, the Aswan Dam became a symbol of Soviet support for the developing world.

In March 1957, the US Congress approved the **Eisenhower Doctrine**, to oppose what the Americans perceived as the Soviet threat in the Middle East. This offered economic and military aid, including troops, to any Middle Eastern country that believed it was threatened by 'communist aggression'.

Eisenhower Doctrine This refers to a speech by President Eisenhower to Congress in January 1957, in which he promised economic assistance or aid from US military forces to any country requesting help against 'armed aggression from any nation controlled by international communism'. It was part of the US policy of 'containment' during the Cold War, which aimed to prevent the extension of Soviet influence. It echoed the 1947 Truman Doctrine, which had committed the USA to military involvement to prevent the extension of communism in Europe.

Although Arab states such as Iraq, Jordan and Saudi Arabia took immediate advantage of this offer, Egypt and Syria stuck to their policy of non-alignment. The implication of the Eisenhower Doctrine was that the USA was taking over the role, previously assumed by Britain, of managing the affairs of the Middle East. It showed that Britain could no longer direct the defence, or police the internal affairs, of countries in the region. The balance of power in the Middle East had shifted.

SOURCE K

American and Soviet planners saw the nascent [emerging] Jewish state as a possible asset in their efforts to diminish the overwhelming influence of Great Britain in the Middle East. Both appreciated the vital strategic importance of the region, both were in search of local allies and clients, and both saw Britain as an obstacle to the enhancement of their own influence. Although we naturally tend to see the United States and the Soviet Union as the primary powers in the Middle East (as elsewhere) in the wake of World War II, in fact this only became true in the mid- to late 1950s. Their ascendance, and the eclipse of both of the formerly dominant great powers in the region, Britain and France, was only fully brought home during the Suez crisis of 1956, when the latter, acting in collusion with Israel, were humiliated by the United States and the Soviet Union, which turned back their tripartite invasion of Egypt.

Khalidi, R. 2006. The Iron Cage: The Story of the Palestinian Struggle for Statehood. Oxford, UK. Oneworld. p. 128.

The role of the United Nations

On the day after the Israeli attack on Egypt, the United Nations Security Council met to discuss a resolution condemning the action and demanding the immediate withdrawal of Israeli forces. However, Britain and France used their vetoes to defeat the resolution. On the following day, they launched their own attack on Egypt. To bypass the British and French use of the veto, the matter was then referred to the General Assembly (where no country held a veto). The General Assembly met in a special emergency session, and called for a ceasefire and the withdrawal of all forces from Egypt. In another resolution, the UN created a United Nations Emergency Force (UNEF) to be sent to the Middle East to oversee the ceasefire. This was the first time that a blue-helmeted UN peacekeeping force was created.

The 6000 troops that made up UNEF came from ten member countries that were considered neutral and impartial towards the crisis, and which were acceptable to the Egyptian government. The first aim of UNEF was to supervise the ceasefire and the withdrawal of the invading armies. It also aimed to position itself between the Israeli and Egyptian forces, so that negotiations for a settlement could take place in a less hostile atmosphere. The peacekeepers were only to use force in self-defence or as a last resort. The details of the peacekeeping operation were discussed at length between Nasser and the secretary-general of the UN, **Dag Hammarskjöld**. In these talks it was agreed that, in terms of the UN Charter, Egypt would have the right to demand the withdrawal of the UN force at any time in the future.

Question

What was the significance of the Suez Crisis for the superpowers? Use Source K and the information in the text to put together your answer.

Dag Hammarskjöld (1905–61) Hammarskjöld was a Swedish economist and diplomat who served as secretary-general of the United Nations from 1953 until his death in 1961. He worked tirelessly for peace in the Middle East by promoting armistice agreements between Israel and the Arab states, working to resolve the Suez Crisis by diplomatic means, organising the UN Emergency Force in 1956, and arranging the subsequent clearance of the Suez Canal. He died in a plane crash in 1961, while on a visit to the Congo to promote peacekeeping efforts. Hammarskjöld was posthumously awarded the Nobel Peace Prize.

After the British, French and Israeli forces were withdrawn, the UNEF force was stationed on the ceasefire lines for the next ten years. Its purpose was to prevent another conflict between Israel and Egypt, especially in the potential flashpoints of Gaza and Sharm el-Sheikh. The UN also supervised the clean-up of the Suez Canal, which was re-opened to shipping in April 1957.

This cartoon appeared in the November 1956 issue of Punch *magazine*

There are conflicting opinions about the effectiveness of UN actions. Some analysts argue that the UN was a clear winner in the Suez Crisis, gaining a greater role on the world stage. David Johnson argues that UNEF played a central role in maintaining peace between Israel and Egypt for the next ten years, until its withdrawal at the request of the Egyptian government in May 1967. Stewart Ross is more critical, however, pointing out that the UN could only pass resolutions in reaction to events that had happened, rather than preventing them from happening. He argues that the UN was also essentially powerless unless the USA and the USSR agreed on an issue.

114

Questions

In this cartoon, the stern schoolteacher is Dag Hammarskjöld – the secretary-general of the United Nations. The three schoolboys writing lines are Ben Gurion and the foreign ministers of Britain and France, while Nasser gloats on the left. Meanwhile, the bully in the background is Khrushchev, the Soviet leader, who is beating up Hungary while the teacher's back is turned. What is the intention of the cartoonist? In what ways does this cartoon reflect a British perspective of the Suez Crisis?

The significance of the Suez Crisis and the Sinai War for Israel

The Sinai War demonstrated Israeli military superiority against the Egyptian army. However, in spite of its military success, Israel did not make any long-term territorial or political gains. It was forced to withdraw from Sinai and Gaza, and to restore Israel's 1948–49 borders. Israel was still not recognised by the Arab governments, and the country's security situation was not permanently resolved. Furthermore, Israel's alliance with the former colonial powers confirmed Arab suspicions that Israel was, in the words of Geoffrey Warner, a 'springboard of Western imperialism in the Middle East'. Historian Colin Shindler observes that the 'political fruits of the collusion with Britain and France were minimal' and that Israeli actions had served to alienate the superpowers as well as the developing world.

However, the presence of UN peacekeeping forces in Gaza and in Sharm el-Sheikh (at the entrance to the Gulf of Aqaba) offered Israel some short-term security gains. The UN recognised Israel's right to freedom of navigation through the Straits of Tiran. This meant that Israel could import oil through the port of Eilat, and transport it via pipeline to refineries at Haifa.

The success of Israel's army strengthened the position of the Israeli politicians who supported intervention and reprisal, rather than moderation and negotiation, in Israel's dealings with the Arab states. According to Ilan Pappe, the militarisation of Israeli society that began with Israel's victory in the 1948–49 War was completed by Israel's success in the Sinai campaign.

The USA was angered by Israeli actions during the Sinai War, but the shifting power relations in the Middle East that resulted from the war led to significant and lasting changes in American policy towards Israel.

115

SOURCE L

Eisenhower won his election in America. The crisis affirmed the country's new status as the global superpower, challenged only by the USSR. Suez was also to be the last incident in which America was to take strong action against Israel. As Eisenhower had feared, the Russians moved into the Middle East to fill the gap left by the disorderly retreat of the British, so the Americans felt compelled to get in as well. Thus the cold war spread to north Africa and Egypt (the Russians duly stepped in to finance the Aswan dam, and much else), and Israel became ever more closely tied to the USA.

Before 1956, Israel had been militarily vulnerable, but, beyond the Arab world, morally and politically unassailable. The Israeli occupation of Sinai (and Gaza) in 1956 began the gradual inversion of this state of affairs, as it marked the first expansion of Israel beyond its original borders, with all the subsequent criticisms of its occupation of Arab or Palestinian land. In 1956 the Israelis were quickly forced to withdraw from Sinai by American (and Russian) pressure. Never again, however, would an American president face down Israel as Eisenhower had done at Suez.

'The Suez crisis: An affair to remember'. The Economist, 27 July 2006.
www.economist.com/node/7218678?story_id=7218678

Questions

How and why did American policy towards Israel change after the Suez Crisis? What does the writer of Source L mean by saying that before this Israel had been 'morally and politically unassailable'? Why did this change after Suez?

The significance of the Suez Crisis for Nasser and the Arab world

Although Egypt was defeated, the Suez affair was a triumph for Nasser and his popularity increased enormously. He was hailed as the hero of the Arab world, who had stood up to the bullying tactics of the former colonial powers. Under Nasser's leadership, Egypt now had complete control of the Suez Canal, as well as British military stores in the Canal Zone. The canal was cleared with American aid and under UN supervision, and re-opened for shipping in April 1957.

As a result of the Suez Crisis, many Arab states turned against the West. Britain and France had tried to use military force to dictate policy, had attempted to overthrow the government of one of the leading Arab states, and had worked with Israel. The Suez Crisis also heightened the tensions in the Middle East by increasing anti-Israeli sentiment in the Arab countries. It changed the outlook of the Palestinian refugees, too: according to Ilan Pappe, the crisis resulted in a 'revolution in strategy, tactics and structure in the political movement emerging in the refugee camps'. You will learn more about the role of Nasser and developments in the Arab world after the Suez Crisis in the next chapter.

Activities

1   Draw up a table to summarise the positive and negative results of the Suez Crisis and Sinai War for the countries directly and indirectly involved. Use a table such as this one for your summary:

	Positive results	Negative results
Egypt		
Israel		
Britain		
France		
USA		
USSR		

2   In an obituary written about Anthony Eden after his death in 1977, *The Times* wrote: 'Eden was the last prime minister to believe that Britain was a great power, and the first to confront a crisis that proved she was not.' Examine Britain's role in the Suez Crisis and write an article to support or challenge this view.

3   Read the article 'Suez: End of empire' by Paul Reynolds, which was published on 24 July 2006 as part of a BBC series analysing the significance of the Suez Crisis 50 years on. Find it at this website address:

http://news.bbc.co.uk/2/hi/middle_east/5199392.stm

Explain how the crisis influenced Anglo–French relations, and also the relationship between Britain and the USA. Comment, too, on the statement made towards the end of the article that 'Modern revisionist theories hold that the mistake was really made by President Eisenhower.'

4   Write a summary of the significance of the Suez Crisis and Sinai War in the context of the Arab–Israeli conflict.

End of chapter activities

Summary

You should now understand what happened in Egypt after the Second World War, and how it led to the Suez Crisis in 1956. You should be able to explain the wider context of the Cold War and relations between Israel and Egypt from 1949 to 1956. You should also be able to relate what happened during the Suez Crisis, and explain the role of each of the countries that were involved. You should especially be able to explain the significance of the crisis for each of these countries, and its impact on the balance of power in the Middle East.

Summary activity

Copy the diagram below. Use the information in this chapter, and from other sources, to make brief notes under each heading.

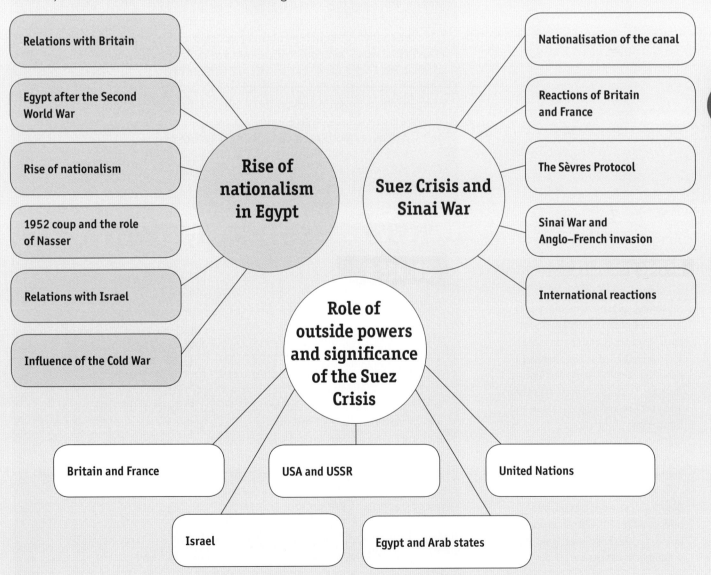

Paper 1 exam practice

Question

With reference to their origin and purpose, assess the value and limitations of Sources A and B below for historians investigating the Suez Crisis.
[6 marks]

Skill

Assessing the value and limitations (utility/reliability) of two sources

SOURCE A

An extract from an editorial from the Guardian, *a left-wing British newspaper that was critical of the actions of Eden's government, 2 November 1956.*

The Prime Minister rests his case on the belief that the Anglo-French action will have prevented a greater war in the Middle East. We must hope he is right. Only time can show. But our action will leave a legacy all over the world which temporary success can never obliterate. The British and French governments are guilty of aggression. They themselves have used war as an instrument of policy, in direct defiance of their promises in the United Nations Charter. In the process they may prove to have destroyed the United Nations – for it can hardly survive unless it takes strenuous action against them – and to have left themselves with no moral basis for future policy.

Quoted in Browne, H. 1971. Flashpoints: Suez and Sinai. *London, UK. Longman. p. 80.*

SOURCE B

Anthony Eden, writing in 1960, reflects on the Suez Crisis.

Much of the subsequent controversy over the Suez decision has been about the trees and not about the wood. The main question is whether inertia would have brought better results for the peace of the word than action. I think not. ... Suez was a short-term emergency operation which succeeded, and an attempt to halt a long-term deterioration, whose outcome is still unknown. A clash between Israel and Egypt was inevitable, given Nasser's declared intention. Whenever this took place, it could bring grave danger to the general peace. It was far better that it should not happen at a moment of Egypt's choosing, and the explosion could not have occurred in circumstances less damaging, given the speedy action of Britain and France.

Eden, A. 1960. Full Circle. *London, UK. Cassell. Quoted in Browne, H. 1971.* Flashpoints: Suez and Sinai. *London, UK. Longman. p. 80.*

Before you start

Value and limitations (utility/reliability) questions require you to assess **two** sources over a range of possible issues – and to comment on their value to historians studying a particular event or period of history. You need to consider both the **origin and purpose** and also the **value and limitations** of the sources. You should link these in your answer, showing how origin/purpose relate to value/limitations.

Before you attempt this question, refer to pages 219–20 for advice on how to tackle these questions, and a simplified markscheme.

Student answer

Source A is a newspaper editorial published at the time of the Suez Crisis in a newspaper that was critical of the government's decision to get involved in Suez. The purpose of the editorial is to draw the attention of the British public to the fact that their government is guilty of aggression that may threaten the future peace of the world, and that it has left itself 'no moral basis' for any future action.

Source B is written by Anthony Eden, who was prime minister at the time and the man who made the decision to plot with France and Israel to invade Egypt. He is trying to justify the actions of the government and the decisions that he made, and says that the 'speedy action of Britain and France' prevented a worse conflict from happening.

Examiner comments

The student has examined the origin and purpose of both the sources well, explaining why the views they express of the Suez Crisis differ considerably. However, the answer does not say anything about the value and limitations about either source, and so is not good enough to get into Band 1.

Activity

Look again at the two sources, the student answer above, and the simplified markscheme on page 220. Now try to write a paragraph or two to push the answer up into Band 1, and so obtain the full 6 marks. Remember that you need to examine the value and limitations of both sources, as well as their origin and purpose.

Paper 2 practice questions

1 To what extent can the Suez Crisis be blamed on the rise of nationalism in Egypt after the Second World War?

2 Assess the impact of the Sèvres Protocol and its aftermath on international relations in 1956.

3 Account for the increasing hostility between Israel and Egypt from their 1949 armistice until the end of the Sinai War in 1956.

4 Discuss the origins of the Suez Crisis and its consequences for Britain.

5 Analyse the role of the superpowers in the Suez Crisis and the impact of the crisis on the Cold War.

6 Arabism, Zionism and Palestinian nationalism

Timeline

1897 Aug: First Zionist Congress held in Basel

1916 Jun: start of Arab Revolt against Ottoman Empire

1917 Nov: Balfour Declaration

1920 Aug: British and French mandates imposed over much of Middle East

1928 Mar: formation of Muslim Brotherhood

1952 Jul: Free Officers coup in Egypt

1954 Feb: Nasser comes to power

1956 Oct–Nov: Suez Crisis and Sinai War

1958 Feb: formation of United Arab Republic

1959 Oct: formation of Fatah

1961 Sep: dissolution of United Arab Republic

1962 Oct: Egyptian intervention in Yemen

1964 Feb: formation of Palestine Liberation Organisation

1967 Jun: Arab defeat in war against Israel; Israel occupies West Bank, Gaza, Sinai and Golan Heights

Aug: formation of Popular Front for the Liberation of Palestine (PFLP)

1968 Mar: Battle of Karameh

1969 Feb: Yasser Arafat becomes leader of PLO

1970 Sep: Black September; death of Nasser

1972 Sep: Munich Olympics massacre

1974 Nov: UN accepts PLO as representative of Palestinians

1975 Apr: civil war in Lebanon

1978 Mar: Israel invades Lebanon

Introduction

Three nationalist movements had significant effects on developments in the Middle East. These were Arabism, Zionism and Palestinian nationalism. Arabism refers to the idea of a common Arab identity and a desire for union and social justice among Arabs. The Arabist movement emerged strongly in the 1950s, but actually began in earlier decades. Zionism was a political movement that sought to establish a permanent 'national home' for Jewish people in Palestine. Palestinian nationalism arose out of the displacement of the Palestinian people, which was a result of the establishment of this Jewish 'national home'.

Key questions

- What was the impact of Arabism in the 1950s and 1960s?
- How did Zionism affect the history of the Middle East?
- What role did the Palestine Liberation Organisation play?

Overview

- Arab nationalism had its roots in the 1916 Arab Revolt against Ottoman rule, and was stimulated by the establishment of Israel and the subsequent Arab–Israeli conflict.
- During the 1950s and 1960s, Egypt under Nasser became the centre of the Arabist movement. The aims of Arabism were a closer political union (pan-Arabism) and social reform (Arab socialism).
- The union of Egypt and Syria in 1958 to form the United Arab Republic was short-lived. By the time of Nasser's death in 1970, the dream of Arab unity had not been realised.
- Zionism developed as a response to the anti-Semitism that Jews encountered in late 19th-century Europe. The Balfour Declaration showed the British government's support for the Zionist movement, and raised Zionists' hopes that they would achieve their aim of a national home in Palestine.
- During the period of the British mandate in Palestine, Zionists worked to increase Jewish immigration and set up the administrative structures of a future state. It became obvious, however, that the realisation of Zionist ambitions would result in conflict with the Palestinian Arabs.

- The establishment of Israel in 1948 did not satisfy revisionist Zionists, who believed that Zionist goals were incomplete while part of Jerusalem and the West Bank remained under Arab control. They promoted the expansion of Jewish settlements into these areas after Israel's victory in the 1967 War.

- By the late 1950s, many Palestinians began to believe that the restoration of their homeland would depend on their own efforts, rather than those of Arab governments. The emergence of Palestinian nationalism led to the establishment of Fatah and the Palestine Liberation Organisation (PLO).

- After the 1967 War, the PLO intensified its armed struggle against Israel. It wanted to raise world awareness of the situation of the Palestinians through hijackings and other acts of violence on an international scale.

- The presence of the PLO contributed to political instability and civil war in neighbouring Arab countries, which became the targets of Israeli reprisals. The PLO was expelled from Jordan in 1970, and then also from Lebanon in 1982.

A map showing Arab countries in 2012; pan-Arabists hoped to unite all Arabs, from Morocco to Oman, in a single state

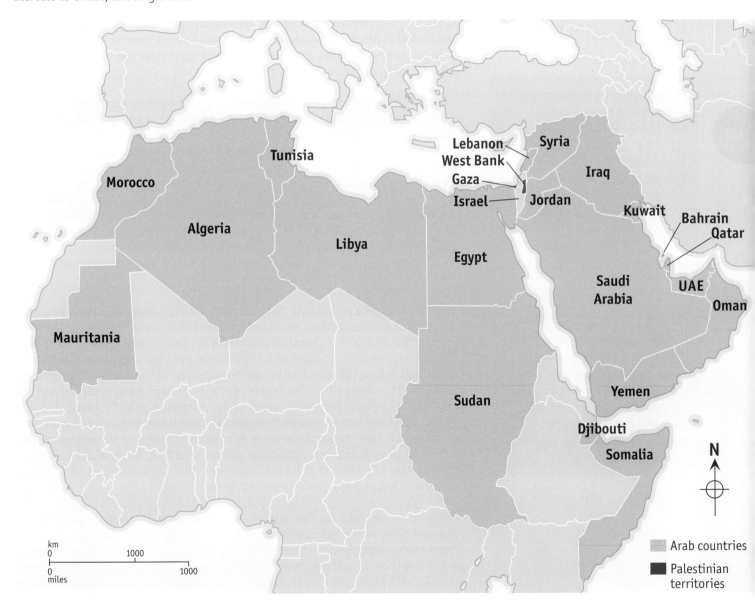

What was the impact of Arabism in the 1950s and 1960s?

Historians use different terms to describe the heightened political awareness and the growth of popular nationalism that emerged in Arab countries in the 1950s and 1960s. Some refer to it as 'Arabism', and focus on the emergence of a sense of common identity based on a shared language, culture and heritage. Others speak of 'pan-Arabism', and stress the attempts to forge links and political unity between Arab states. Others focus on 'Arab socialism' – the idea of governments controlling resources to ensure a more equal distribution of wealth and services, in the interests of Arab society as a whole. Egypt, under its leader Gamal Abdel Nasser, was at the centre of Arab nationalism in the 1950s. However, the origins of Arab nationalism lay in an earlier period.

The origins of Arab nationalism

During the 16th century, the Arab countries of North Africa and the Middle East became part of the Ottoman (or Turkish) empire. In the 19th century, the power of the Ottoman rulers over this vast empire declined. Britain and France took advantage of Ottoman weakness to establish European colonies in the Arab countries of North Africa. Algeria, Morocco and Tunisia became French colonies, while the British declared a 'protectorate' over Egypt. The rest of the Arab lands of the Middle East remained under Ottoman control.

Arab Revolt There were two Arab Revolts. The 1916 revolt was an Arab uprising against Ottoman rule, supported by British forces (including 'Lawrence of Arabia' – see page 26). The Arab Revolt of 1936–39 was directed at the British administration in the mandate of Palestine. This second revolt was a response to increasing Jewish immigration and land sales.

From the 1880s onwards, nationalist movements began to emerge in the areas of the Middle East under Ottoman control. They demanded greater autonomy for the Arabs. One of these movements was The League of the Arab Fatherland, which proposed the creation of a separate Arab state. However, at this stage the nationalist movement did not have wide support. When the First World War broke out in 1914, the Ottoman Empire allied itself with Germany. The Arab nationalists saw this as an opportunity to achieve their goals. The **Arab Revolt** of 1916 was inspired by their dream of an independent and united Arab nation. With British support, Arab forces defeated the Turkish army in Palestine and Syria. However, their hopes of British support for the creation of an Arab state after the war were destroyed by the assurances that the British government made to the Zionists in the Balfour Declaration.

Re-read pages 26–27 in Chapter 2 to remind yourself of the details of Britain's contradictory promises of support to the Arabs and the Zionists during the First World War, and of the secret agreement between Britain and France to divide the Ottoman Empire between them after the First World War.

After the First World War, the Ottoman Empire was dissolved. However, only Saudi Arabia was recognised as an independent Arab state. The rest of the Arab lands in the Middle East became mandates of the colonial powers. Syria and Lebanon were given to France, and Britain took Iraq, Transjordan and Palestine. French and British officials and troops moved in to administer and control the mandates. This meant that the whole of the Arabic-speaking world, except for parts of the Arabian Peninsula, were under European rule. To many Arabs it seemed that they had simply exchanged Ottoman rulers for Western ones, and the hopes of Arab nationalists were frustrated. There was strong resistance to the European mandates, especially in Syria and Iraq. In an effort to control this resistance, France and Britain separated the administration of Lebanon and Kuwait respectively from the rest of Syria and Iraq.

Foreign rule resulted in the growth of nationalism, especially among the educated élite, in the mandates as well as in the European colonies in North Africa. Nationalism was particularly strong in Egypt, where Britain maintained an economic and military presence despite recognising Egypt's independent status in 1922. During the 1920s, France split the administration of Lebanon from that of Syria, to make it easier to suppress nationalist opposition to French rule.

In Algeria, too, the 1920s and 1930s saw the rise of an Algerian nationalist movement demanding greater autonomy from France. However, there was no broad nationalist movement linking the anti-colonial resistance in different Arab states. Egyptian nationalists wanted to rid Egypt of British influence, while Algerian nationalists wanted independence from France.

The Muslim Brotherhood, which was founded in Egypt in 1928 by a schoolteacher, **Hasan al-Banna**, was an Islamic rather than an Arabist movement. It wanted to promote traditional Islamic values and practices. However, according to historian Albert Hourani, the Muslim Brothers believed that contact with the West had brought 'alien values, immorality, missionary activity and imperial domination'. In this sense, they shared certain aims with the nationalist movements. The Muslim Brotherhood in Egypt later served as a model for similar movements in other countries. Between 1936 and 1939, the Muslim Brotherhood played a role in supporting the Arab Revolt in Palestine, which was directed at both the British administration in the mandate and the increasing population of Jewish immigrants in Palestine.

During the 1930s, a wider form of national consciousness began to emerge in the Arab world, as historian Albert Hourani explains in Source A.

> ### SOURCE A
>
> The idea that a group of people form a nation, and that the nation should be independent, is a simple one, too simple by itself to provide guidance for the way in which social life should be organised. In this period, however, it served as a focus for a cluster of other ideas. In general, the nationalism of the period was secularist, believing in a bond which could embrace people of different schools or faiths, and a policy based upon the interests of state and society, and it was constitutionalist, holding that the will of the nation should be expressed by elected governments responsible to elected assemblies. It placed great emphasis on the need for popular education, which would enable the nation to participate more fully in its collective life. It stood for the development of national industries, since industrialisation seemed to be the source of strength.
>
> *Hourani, A. 1991. A History of the Arab Peoples.* London, UK. Faber and Faber. *p. 343.*

During the 1930s, too, a more radical form of nationalism – called the Ba'ath movement – developed in Syria. Ba'ath means 'renaissance' or 'resurrection' in Arabic, and the Ba'athists had socialist as well as nationalist goals. They called for an end to French rule and for pan-Arab unity. They also supported the redistribution of wealth in Arab society for the common good. Unlike the Muslim Brotherhood, the Ba'athist movement was a secular one. It was established by French-educated Syrian intellectuals, one of the most influential of whom was **Michel Aflaq**. They formed the Arab Ba'ath Movement in the early 1940s. Ba'athist political parties later formed in several Arab countries, notably Syria and Iraq. By the time the Second World War broke out in 1939, Britain had recognised the independence of Iraq, although there was still a strong British military and economic presence in this former mandate. The other mandates, however, remained under European rule, as did the French colonies in North Africa.

Hasan al-Banna (1906–49)
Al-Banna was the founder of the Muslim Brotherhood. He believed that contact with Western secularism was weakening and corrupting the Muslim world. Although Al-Banna did not promote violence, the Muslim Brotherhood later established a secret military branch that was involved in the assassination of the Egyptian prime minister in 1948. Al-Banna was himself assassinated in 1949.

123

Question
What would the aims of a 'secularist' and 'constitutionalist' nationalist movement be?

Michel Aflaq (1910–89) Aflaq formed the Ba'athist movement, together with Salah al-Din al-Bitar. Ba'athism was a secular, non-violent form of Arab nationalism that aimed to establish a single socialist Arab state. Aflaq supported free speech, human rights and democratic ideals. However, the Ba'athist regimes that later came to power in Syria and Iraq used Ba'athist ideology as a pretence for dictatorship.

During the war, support for Arab nationalism grew and there was a wave of hostility towards Britain and France. Arab nationalists saw the war as an opportunity to advance their cause, and some believed that support for the Axis powers would be in their interests. Sustained anti-French resistance in Syria and Lebanon forced the French to agree to end the mandates, a move that was formalised in 1946.

After the war, the main focus of Arab nationalists was on Palestine, and on opposing the creation of a Jewish state in what had been Arab Palestine. However, Arab opposition to the partition of Palestine in 1947 was ignored as there was overwhelming international support for the establishment of Israel. When the Arab states attempted to prevent this in the 1948–49 War, their military defeat by Israel – and the flight of 760,000 refugees from Palestine into surrounding Arab countries – were major setbacks for the Arab cause. However, the Arab–Israeli conflict that developed out of this war further stimulated Arab nationalism.

Nasser and pan-Arab nationalism

After Egypt's defeat by Israel in the 1948–49 War, dissatisfied Egyptian army officers staged the Free Officers coup in 1952, which brought Nasser to power. Under Nasser, the Arab nationalist movement became a powerful political force during the 1950s and 1960s. Egypt became the centre of the movement, which had broad aims for a closer union of states, non-alignment in the struggle between the superpowers, and social reforms.

Many people throughout the Arab world believed Nasser could achieve these goals, especially after his success against the British in the Suez Crisis in 1956 (covered in detail in Chapter 5). Nasser became the symbol of Arab nationalism: in many countries, Arab nationalism and 'Nasserism' became synonymous, and 'Nasserist' parties were established in several of these countries. Historian Martin Meredith notes that it was the Suez invasion that propelled Nasser to a 'pinnacle of prestige and influence' throughout the Arab world, where he was 'acclaimed and idolised' as the leader who had successfully resisted imperialism.

In Egypt, Nasser's government applied policies that came to be called 'Arab socialism'. It used land from wealthy landlords and foreign landowners to redistribute to the rural poor; it advanced the position of women by granting them the vote in 1956; and it provided free education. Thousands of schools were built, and Egypt's illiteracy rate fell from 80% to 50%. The government also extended state control over the economy: the main banks, the cotton export trade and nearly 300 companies were nationalised. Under Nasser, there were significant improvements in Egypt's social and economic developments, However, Guy Arnold points out that the continuing hostility between Egypt and Israel was a constant economic burden on Egypt, and that the military requirements were a 'handicap to development'.

At the same time as introducing progressive social and economic reforms, the Nasser regime suppressed opposition movements. All parties were banned except the Arab Socialist Union. The Muslim Brotherhood was also outlawed, and its leaders were imprisoned or exiled. Nasser saw Arab socialism as pro-socialist but anti-Marxist, and he resisted attempts by the USSR to influence Egyptian policy. He knew that many Egyptians would be alienated by the Marxist rejection of religion. At the same time, however, Nasserism was not an Islamist movement.

SOURCE B

Historian Ali Mazrui explains Nasser's view of the relationship between Arabism and Islam.

The Egyptian revolution of 1952 established a different kind of linkage with Islam. Gamal 'Abd al-Nasser, the leader of the revolution, interpreted Egypt as the centre of three circles – the circles of Islam, the Arab world and Africa. The struggle against imperialism was therefore to be seen in the context of the three forces of Islamic resistance, Arab nationalism and pan-Africanism.

And yet Nasser was cautious about what he regarded as the more 'extreme' forms of Islamic fundamentalism – especially the movement known as the Muslim Brotherhood. He outlawed the movement and imprisoned some of its leaders. In an age of increasingly competitive ideologies, Islam was indeed a potential ally in the struggle against imperialism – but also a potential danger to political stability among Egyptians themselves.

Gamal 'Abd al-Nasser's own preference was for the political mobilization of pan-Arabism against both Zionism and Western imperialism. Although his pan-Arabism had a military arm in the struggle against Israel, the central force of the Egyptian revolution lay in non-violent mass mobilization.

Mazrui, A. (ed.). 2003. *General History of Africa: Volume 8: Africa since 1935.* Cape Town, South Africa. New Africa Education/UNESCO. pp. 115–16.

Question

How could Islam be considered both a 'potential ally' and a 'potential danger' to Nasser?

125

Nasser appealed to ordinary Arab people across national borders, bypassing their rulers by using the new medium of transistor radio. The Egyptian radio station, the 'Voice of the Arabs', spread the rhetoric of Arab unity, progress and anti-colonialism into the most remote corners of the region. Nasser's radio broadcasts were heard by millions. They were used as a means of strengthening Egypt's position in the Arab world and Nasser's leadership of pan-Arabism. Nasser actively aided the Algerian nationalist movement, the FLN, in their war against the French. He also denounced colonialism elsewhere, and his ideas were popular and influential in the wave of anti-colonial nationalist movements that emerged at this time. Nasser was also a prominent supporter of 'non-alignment', and was a founder of the Non-Aligned Movement that was established in 1955. Egypt was also a founder member of the Organisation of African Unity, which was formed in 1963. Nasser was a moderating influence in this organisation, urging unity and agreement rather than polarisation between radicals and moderates.

Nasser speaks in Damascus, Syria, in 1960, at ceremonies marking the second anniversary of the United Arab Republic; this union between Egypt and Syria ended the following year

SOURCE C

Basking in the adulation, Nasser set out to impose Egypt's leadership on the Arab world. He became a master of propaganda, the most successful communicator with the Arab masses in modern times, discovering that he could sway and manipulate crowds with oratory that sent them into paroxysms of applause. Once renowned as a tedious, shy and awkward speaker, sticking to prepared texts written in neo-classical Arabic, he now captivated audiences on radio and television and at huge rallies using the language of the streets, mocking Western politicians and denouncing 'imperialism' and 'reactionaries' at every opportunity. The Nasser cult soon took hold, both in Egypt and in the rest of the Arab world. It made Cairo the fountainhead of the new nationalism, spreading the message of an Arab 'revolution' across the region.

Meredith, M. 2005. The State of Africa: A History of Fifty Years of Independence. Johannesburg, South Africa. Jonathan Ball Publishers. p. 43.

SOURCE D

In other Arab countries ... 'Nasirism' met with a vast and continuing public acceptance. The personality of 'Abd al-Nasir, the successes of his regime – the political victory of the Suez crisis of 1956, the building of the High Dam, the measures of social reform – and the promise of strong leadership in defence of the Palestinian cause; all these seemed to hold out the hope of a different world, of a united Arab nation rejuvenated by genuine social revolution and taking its rightful place in the world. Such hopes were encouraged by skilful use of the press and radio, which appealed above the heads of other governments to the 'Arab people'. These appeals deepened conflicts between Arab governments, but Nasirism remained a potent symbol of unity and revolution, and embodied itself in political movements of wide scope, such as the Movement of Arab Nationalists which was founded in Beirut and was popular among Palestinian refugees.

Hourani, A. 1991. A History of the Arab Peoples. London, UK. Faber and Faber. p. 407.

Activity

Compare and contrast the views of the two historians in Sources C and D on the reasons for the appeal of Nasserism, and of the role it played in strengthening Arab nationalism.

Arab unity and disunity

The first tentative step towards Arab unity had been the formation of the Arab League in Cairo in 1945 by Egypt, Syria, Iraq, Lebanon, Transjordan and Saudi Arabia. The Arab League's purpose was to establish closer relations between the Arab states, and to co-ordinate collaboration between them. It had voiced its opposition to the United Nations plan to partition Palestine, and the member states had jointly decided to attack the newly established state of Israel in 1948. However, the Arab League had not taken any further steps to establish closer union between the Arab states.

After his success in the Suez Crisis, some Arab leaders looked to Nasser to create a new pan-Arab movement that would achieve unity. These feelings were especially strong in Syria, where there was popular support for the idea of a union between Syria and Egypt. This was encouraged by the Ba'athist Party, which was concerned about the growing strength of the Syrian Communist Party and saw union with Egypt as a means of controlling its growth.

The advantage to Nasser of a union with Syria was both symbolic and strategic. Firstly, it would improve his image as the leader of Arab nationalism. Secondly, it would provide a link for Egypt – which was geographically isolated and lacking in resources – with other Arab states. In 1958, Egypt and Syria announced the establishment of the United Arab Republic (UAR), a unitary state ruled from Cairo. Nasser was the head of state of the UAR, and Egypt was without doubt the dominant partner in the union.

Syria had to bring its banks and major industries under state control, in line with the economic policies that had been applied in Egypt. At Nasser's insistence, all political parties were disbanded, including the Ba'ath Party which had supported the union. Arab nationalists hailed the formation of the UAR as the first concrete step towards pan-Arab unity, although Guy Arnold suggests that it was 'little more than an expression of Arab solidarity'. Later in the year, the UAR formed the United Arab States with North Yemen.

Conservative Arab leaders were alarmed by the union of what they perceived to be two radical states – Egypt and Syria – to form the UAR. In response, the kingdoms of Iraq and Jordan formed the Arab Federation in February 1958. King Faisal II of Iraq was the head of state, and his cousin Hussein of Jordan was the deputy. They were the great-grandsons of Sharif Hussayn of Mecca, who had led the Arab Revolt against the Turks in 1916. Theoretically, the two countries formed a strong union: oil-rich Iraq with the military strength of Jordan.

Both Faisal and Hussein had maintained links with Britain, and consequently were seen by more radical Arab nationalists as being pawns of the colonial powers. The establishment of the UAR also created problems for Lebanon: there was support among the Muslim and Druze communities in Lebanon for the nation to join the UAR, but the Christian president and the Christian half of the population were strongly opposed to this. By May 1958, there was civil war in Lebanon over the issue, and the government appealed for American aid to suppress the rebels and restore order.

In July 1958, King Faisal II of Iraq and his family and advisors were overthrown and killed in a bloody military coup in Baghdad. Iraq became a republic, and immediately withdrew from the Western-dominated Baghdad Pact. Many members of the Iraqi Revolutionary Command Council that seized control of the country favoured union with the UAR. It seemed to many Arab nationalists that they had taken a step closer to the dream of pan-Arab unity. Concerned that pro-Nasser groups might try to seize power in Lebanon and Jordan as well, the USA and Britain respectively sent troops to support the 'moderate' Arab governments in power in these two countries.

However, the new military leader of Iraq, Abdul Kassim, was an Iraqi nationalist rather than a pan-Arabist, and Iraq did not join the UAR. The UAR itself lasted for only three years. The Syrian middle class was suspicious of Nasser's Arab socialism: landowners opposed the land-reform programme, and business leaders opposed moves to nationalise banks and major industries. The Syrian army and bureaucracy resented Syria's second-class status in the union, where the army and government were dominated by Egyptians. In 1961, the UAR broke up after a military coup in Damascus brought a Syrian nationalist group to power, and Syria left the union. The collapse of the UAR was a blow to the ideals of Arab nationalists. Egypt continued to call itself the United Arab Republic, but it was clear that the experiment of a pan-Arab state dominated by Egypt had failed.

> **Fact**
> Lebanon had greater religious and cultural diversity than other Arab countries, and had a Christian population almost equal in number to Muslims. There was also a substantial Druze minority. Under Ottoman rule, and then under the French mandate, religious differences had been emphasised to create divisions. However, independent Lebanon hoped to maintain unity and stability by granting the presidency to the Christian community and the premiership to the Muslims. The delicate balance in Lebanese politics was disrupted by the arrival of hundreds of thousands of Palestinian refugees. During the 1970s and 1980s, divisive civil wars – aggravated by Syrian and Israeli intervention – destroyed the economy and the stability of Lebanon.

Another factor that ruined prospects for Arab unity was Nasser's intervention in Yemen. In 1962, a group of pro-Egyptian army officers seized power in Yemen, and Nasser sent troops to support them against the deposed hereditary ruler who had the support of rural tribes and clans. The intervention turned into a long guerrilla campaign, lasting five years, which was costly for Egypt both in casualties and military expenses. Nasser later referred to it as 'my Vietnam'. The presence of Egyptian troops in the south of the Arabian Peninsula alarmed the Saudi government to such an extent that it sent military support to the opposition royalist forces. Nasser's intervention in Yemen alienated the more conservative members of the Arab League, and widened the gulf between Nasser and the traditional Arab monarchies.

SOURCE E

To the Kings of Saudi Arabia and Jordan, Nasserism was anathema. Feisal [king of Saudi Arabia] was suspected of plotting the assassination of the Egyptian upstart, and Hussein [king of Jordan] called him a 'political trapeze artist.' Both feared his ambition as leader of the Arab world and felt threatened by the blaring propaganda beamed from Cairo radio to their subjects. The 'imperialists', whom Nasser denounced, bought the Saudis' oil and made them rich; they also provided their defence systems. In 1965, King Feisal of Saudi Arabia sought to create an Islamic anti-Nasser front, so fearful was the threat of Nasser's socialism with its confiscations and its republicanism.

Kohler, J. and Taylor, J. 1985. Africa and the Middle East. London, UK. Edward Arnold. p. 108.

Question

Why would conservative Arab monarchies such as Saudi Arabia and Jordan be opposed to Nasser?

In 1963, there were further signs of disunity and instability in the Arab world. In Iraq in February 1963, Abdul Kassim was overthrown in a successful Ba'athist coup. The following month, another coup restored the Ba'athists to power in Syria. There were talks about forming a second United Arab Republic of Egypt, Syria and Iraq. However, this never went ahead, partly because the Ba'athists would not accept Nasser as the leader of such a union.

During the 1960s, the countries with major oil reserves – at that stage Saudi Arabia, Iraq and Kuwait – began to receive increasing revenues. This gave these nations greater economic independence. As a result, there was less incentive for Iraq to form a union with its poorer Arab neighbours.

As well as Arab socialism and pan-Arab unity, another issue that dominated Arab politics in the Nasser era was the struggle against Israel. In the end, this contributed to the decline of Nasser's power and popularity. The defeat of Egypt, Syria and Jordan by Israel in the 1967 War was a blow to Arab nationalism and unity. (You will learn about the 1967 War in Chapter 7.) The Arab defeat exposed the weakness of the Arab armies compared to Israel, as well as the internal conflicts between their leaders. Nasser's prestige was severely damaged. He offered to resign, but was persuaded to remain in office by his supporters in Egypt.

SOURCE F

The devastating defeat of Egypt by Israel in 1967 was a deep humiliation for Nasser and brought to an end his position of primacy in the Arab world. For the last three years of his rule he had to rebuild his armed forces, whose losses of military hardware had been extensive and collapse of morale even worse, and still more important rebuild the national confidence. Isolated at home and only just surviving politically ... condemned by other Arab leaders for his spectacular failure to make any showing at all against Israel, and in ill-health, Nasser, nevertheless, set about the mammoth task of reconstruction and recovery.

Arnold, G. 2006. Africa: A Modern History. London, UK. Atlantic Books. p. 173.

Nasser sits with King Hussein of Jordan (right) and Yasser Arafat (left), leader of the Palestine Liberation Organisation, after mediating a truce in the war between Jordan and Palestinian guerrillas, on 27 September 1970; Nasser died the following day

Nasser died of a heart attack in 1970 at the age of 52. His funeral caused a mass outpouring of Egyptian and Arab grief. He had brought a degree of unity to the Arab world and, under his leadership, the living standards of ordinary Egyptians had improved substantially. According to historians Kohler and Taylor, Nasser's achievements included ridding Egypt of foreign influences, giving hope to the *fellaheen*, and instilling a feeling of pride among Egyptians through his modernisation programme – especially the Aswan Dam project. He was succeeded by Anwar Sadat, who reversed many of Nasser's policies – his social and economic programmes, Egypt's relations with the USA, and the nation's relationship with Israel. You will learn more about Sadat's Egypt in Chapter 8.

After the Arab defeat in 1967 and the death of Nasser in 1970, there was a move away from Arab nationalism to radical Islamism. Many disillusioned young people in Egypt and throughout the Arab world began to look for meaning and motivation in a politicised form of Islam, using it as a political ideology to achieve both political and economic goals.

Activities

1   Design a spider diagram to illustrate the origins of Arab nationalism before the 1950s.

2   Read the article called 'How Suez made Nasser into an Arab icon', published by the BBC on 26 July 2006 on this website:

http://news.bbc.co.uk/2/hi/middle_east/5204490.stm

Explain the writer's views on the links between Nasser and Arabism.

3   Draw up a table to list and evaluate the success of Nasser's policies. You can use this table as an example:

	What were his aims?	How were they implemented?	How successful were they?
Arab socialism			
Pan-Arab unity			
Foreign policy			

4   Write an argument to support or oppose this statement:

'The aims of Arab nationalism were fundamentally unrealistic, and Nasser's attempts to put them into action were flawed from the outset.'

How did Zionism affect the history of the Middle East?

Zionism refers to the movement to establish a Jewish state, which started in Europe in the late 19th century. Although several possible locations for this state were suggested, by the 1890s the Zionist movement had decided that it should be in Palestine. This was because of the region's biblical and historical links to the Jewish people. However, there were many different interpretations of Zionism, and debates about how this goal should be achieved. In the early decades, there were divisions between 'political' and 'practical' Zionists (see pages 132–33). During the period of the British mandate in Palestine, there were differences between 'revisionist' and 'labour' Zionists (see pages 134–35). After the Second World War, there were conflicting views about tactics between 'militant' and 'diplomatic' Zionists (see page 136).

The establishment of the state of Israel in 1948 fulfilled the Zionist dream, but this did not mean the end of Zionism as a movement. Zionism continued to play a key role, with 'religious Zionism' and 'neo-Zionism' (see page 137) both having a significant influence on Israeli politics and society. In the 1990s, many academics, writers, journalists and film-makers became part of a 'post Zionist' debate, in which they questioned some of the assumptions and actions of the Zionist movement. The Revisionist, or New, Historians are part of this debate.

It is important to remember that not all Jews are Zionists. Many Orthodox Jews, both in Israel and the Diaspora, reject Zionism as a secular movement that conflicts with biblical teachings. Many secular – as well as religious – Jews in the Diaspora sympathise with Israel, but do not wish to live there. More than half of the Jewish people in the world choose to live in countries other than Israel. Some Jews are highly critical of the actions of the Israeli government. Not all Jews in Israel support Zionist policies regarding settlements and relations with the Palestinian Arabs.

It is also important to remember that not all Zionists are Jews. There is significant support for militant Zionist policies from conservative Christian groups, especially in the USA where they are associated with right-wing Republicanism. These Christian pro-Zionists have had a strong influence on US foreign policy in the Middle East.

The origins of Zionism

As you read in Chapter 2, Zionism developed as an idea among Jewish intellectuals in Europe in the late 19th century. Although the term 'Zion' was a biblical name for Jerusalem, Zionism was a secular movement with a political agenda. Its aim was the creation of a Jewish state in Palestine, which at that time was part of the Ottoman Empire.

The historical roots of Zionism lay in three sets of circumstances that affected Jewish communities in Europe in the late 19th century. Firstly, most Jews had not become assimilated into European society, and instead were often regarded as an isolated minority. Secondly, there was an increase in anti-Semitism in the late 19th century, which resulted in violent attacks on Jewish communities in Eastern Europe. Such discrimination was also evident in supposedly liberal Western European countries such as France. The worst violence was in Tsarist Russia, and at that time more than half of the 8 million Jews in the world lived in areas ruled by the tsar. A third factor was the rise of nationalism in Europe, which intensified the view that the Jews were an alien element in the nation. In the new national consciousness, Jews were seen as outsiders and foreigners rather than as loyal citizens. In some places they were regarded as a threat because they were in economic competition with the rest of the 'nation'.

However, the concept of nationalism also inspired a solution to the 'Jewish question' from the Austro-Hungarian Jewish writer Theodor Herzl. Herzl is regarded as the founder of the Zionist movement (see page 23). In his book, *Der Judenstaat* ('The Jewish State'), published in 1896, Herzl set out a detailed plan for the creation of a state for the Jewish nation. Source G (on page 132) discusses the impact of Herzl's book, and Source H explains Herzl's view that the concept of nationalism posed both a problem and a solution for the Jews.

SOURCE G

This small pamphlet electrified Jews across Europe with a vision of the future, but particularly among the downtrodden masses of Eastern Europe. It argued that anti-Semitism showed no sign of fading away and assimilation was no protection. Jews would still be considered as aliens in the societies in which they lived – no matter how much they contributed to it. Religious antagonism, economic rivalry and social difference would worsen – and the Jews would suffer. The solution, Herzl maintained, was mass emigration and settlement in a new land where a Jewish state could be established.

Shindler, C. 2007. What Do Zionists Believe? London, UK. Granta Books. p. 39.

SOURCE H

If nationalism posed a problem to the Jews by identifying them as an alien and unwanted minority, it also suggested a solution: self-determination for the Jews in a state of their own in which they would constitute a majority. Zionism, however, embodied the urge to create not merely a new Jewish state in Palestine, but also a new society, based on the universal values of freedom, democracy, and social justice …

[Herzl] concluded that assimilation and emancipation would not work, because the Jews were a nation. Their problem was not economic or social or religious but national. It followed rationally from these premises that the only solution was for the Jews to leave the diaspora and acquire a territory over which they would exercise sovereignty and establish a state of their own.

Shlaim, A. 2000. The Iron Wall: Israel and the Arab World. London, UK. Penguin. p. 2.

Activity

Geographers and economists use the term 'push and pull' factors to describe reasons for human migration. 'Push' factors refer to the forces that drive people away from a place, and 'pull' factors are those that attract them to a new location. Read Sources G and H and list the 'push and pull' factors that drove Jewish migrants to move to Palestine.

Political Zionism

In 1897, Herzl organised the First Zionist Congress, which was held in Basel in Switzerland. The Congress defined the aim of Zionism as the desire 'to create for the Jewish people a home in Palestine secured by public law'. This was the fundamental goal and strategy of what came to be called 'political Zionism'. It saw the issue as a political one with international implications, which needed to be addressed using diplomacy and negotiation. In other words, it aimed to get international political support for the Zionist ideal. After the Congress, Herzl focused his efforts on trying (unsuccessfully) to persuade the Ottoman ruler to grant a special charter to allow Jewish settlement and the creation of a homeland in Palestine. He also met with other world leaders – such as the pope, the German kaiser, the king of Italy and the British colonial secretary – to try to persuade them to support the project. Shlaim points out that a fundamental feature of the political Zionist movement, and one that was continued by other leaders after Herzl, was to win the support of the dominant power in the region for the establishment of a Jewish homeland in the Middle East. Before the First World War, this dominant power was the Ottoman Empire; between the wars it was Britain; and after the Second World War it was the USA.

After Herzl's death, the next significant leader of political Zionism was Chaim Weizmann (see page 26). It was largely due to Weizmann's efforts that the British government issued the Balfour Declaration in 1917, which announced

British support for the establishment of a 'national home for the Jewish people in Palestine' (see pages 26–27). After the British mandate in Palestine was established in 1920, Weizmann continued to believe that co-operation with Britain was the key to upholding Zionist interests.

Practical Zionism

Another early form of Zionism was 'practical Zionism'. In contrast to the idea of securing political and diplomatic support first, practical Zionists simply moved to Palestine. They believed that Jewish immigration to Palestine, the purchase of land from Arab landlords and the establishment of settlements were the key to implementing the Zionist dream. Foremost among the first practical Zionists was Hovevi Zion (the Lovers of Zion), a movement established in Russia in 1881 to promote settlement in Palestine as a way of escaping the persecution facing Russian Jews. Between 1882 and 1903, 25,000 Jews from Russia and Eastern Europe moved in small groups to Palestine, to start agricultural settlements in what Zionists referred to as the first *Aliyah* (emigration).

This 1912 photograph shows 84-year-old Jewish settler Baruch Alter working on a kibbutz in Palestine; Alter saved for ten years to leave his home in Minsk, Russia

Sharing a similar commitment to the practical occupation of the land, the Marxist Zionists had another vision of Zionism. They believed that the creation of a Jewish state would correct what Shindler describes as the 'abnormal socio-economic structure of Jews in the diaspora' by settling them on the land. For centuries, discriminatory laws had prohibited Jewish access to land in many European countries, as well as banning Jews from certain professions. This meant that very few Jews owned farms or worked the land. The second *Aliyah*, between 1903 and 1914, brought many Marxist Zionists to Palestine. A great number of them were refugees from the failed 1905 Revolution in Russia. Their Marxist vision was put into practice in the establishment of *kibbutzim*, where work, decisions and income were shared collectively. Sources I and J (on page 134) show that historians have different views about the vision and methods of the early Zionist settlers in Palestine.

SOURCE I

Many early Zionists at the end of the nineteenth century ... advocated a Jewish national home within Palestine – the geographical location of ancient Israel. It was to be a homeland guaranteed by the international community, with land purchased from local notables. Zionist pioneers in Palestine saw themselves as colonizers not colonialists. They argued that they were there by historic right and not on the sufferance of others. Unlike European imperialists, they did not come with armies, ready to expropriate the land and dispossess its inhabitants, but with hoes and pitchforks to cultivate the soil. They perceived Zionism as the return of the Jews to the Land of Israel and the construction of a just society in their ancient homeland.

Shindler, C. 2007. What Do Zionists Believe? London, UK. Granta Books. p. 7.

SOURCE J

However, nothing could compare to the colonizing energy brought by the Zionists, evident already in that early period of modernization. Although their number was small, it was with hindsight a colonising immigration. It was not a proper colonization, as Palestine was not occupied by a European power. But like colonialism elsewhere, it was a European movement, with people entering Palestine for the sake of European interests, not local ones. The locals were seen as a commodity or an asset to be exploited for the benefit of the newcomers or an obstacle to be removed ... For the early Zionists, the indigenous people were cheap labourers or producers of cash crops.

Pappe, I. 2006. A History of Modern Palestine. (Second Edition). Cambridge, UK. Cambridge University Press. pp. 41–42.

Activity

Sources I and J distinguish between colonisation and colonialism. What is the difference? Compare the views expressed in Sources I and J about the links between Zionist settlements and colonialism.

Developments in Zionism under the British mandate

Revisionist Zionism

The World Zionist Organisation established a 'Jewish Agency' to encourage immigration and administer the *yishuv* (the Jewish community in Palestine). The aim of the Zionists was to create a Jewish majority in Palestine. However, as more land came under Jewish occupation, Arab opposition to Jewish immigration grew increasingly militant. As a result, British policy moved from supporting Zionism towards a more even-handed approach, in an effort to appease Arab opinion. In response, a more radical – and nationalist – form of Zionism emerged: revisionist Zionism.

The man who developed the ideas that became known as revisionist Zionism was **Ze'ev Jabotinsky**. He rejected the Zionist Organisation's official policy of co-operation with the British, and broke away to form the New Zionist Organisation in 1925. A fundamental principle of revisionist Zionism was that the whole of *Eretz Israel* (the Land of Israel), as it had been in biblical times, rightfully belonged to the Jews.

Jabotinsky acknowledged that the Arabs would not willingly allow Palestine to be turned into a Jewish state, and argued that the Jews would only succeed in doing so from a position of strength. He firmly believed that the Arabs would be forced to compromise only if the Jews created an 'Iron Wall' to demonstrate their superior military strength. Jabotinsky first used this term in an article he wrote in 1923 entitled 'On the Iron Wall (We and the Arabs)'.

Jabotinsky saw the 'Iron Wall' as a means of breaking Arab resistance to the establishment of a Jewish state. Only then, he believed, should the Jews negotiate with the Arabs and offer them civil and national rights, although he did not specify what he meant by this. When moderate Zionists criticised Jabotinsky's views as immoral, he responded by claiming that Zionism was a positive force that had justice on its side, and that the Jews had a moral right to return to Palestine.

During the 1920s and 1930s, many Jewish immigrants in Palestine became disillusioned about the perceived lack of progress towards the achievement of a Jewish state. They were attracted to the views of revisionist Zionism. Jabotinsky's ideas influenced the Zionist movement as a whole, and some of his supporters went on to form the militant groups Irgun and Lehi (see page 34).

Labour Zionism

However, there were other Zionist viewpoints – such as that of the 'Labour Zionists' – who believed that the Jewish state could be achieved through immigration and settlement, rather than by building up a military force. In 1920 the Labour Zionists formed a trade union, the *Histradut*, which used a slogan of 'Jewish land, Jewish labour, Jewish produce'. They wanted to build a Zionist economy and a workers' society. Members of the labour movement played a prominent role in the leadership of the *yishuv*, building up the structures of a future Jewish state.

The most prominent of these leaders was David Ben Gurion (see page 29), who led the Jewish Agency from 1935 onwards. Like Weizmann, Ben Gurion believed in the importance of co-operating with the British in order to achieve Zionist objectives. However, the Arab Revolt of 1936–39 made him realise the strength of Arab opposition to the establishment of a Jewish state.

Ben Gurion came to the conclusion that building military strength was important if the Zionists were going to achieve their goals. He did not, however, adopt Jabotinsky's terminology of the 'Iron Wall'. When the British government's 1939 White Paper placed limits on Jewish immigration, Ben Gurion and others in the Zionist movement turned to the USA as a more sympathetic supporter of the Zionist cause.

Ze'ev Jabotinsky (1880–1940)
Jabotinsky was born in Russia, and studied law at university. While working as a journalist in Western Europe, he became devoted to the Zionist cause. He was a founder of the Haganah, and an early advocate of the use of force against Palestinian Arab nationalism. He broke with the mainstream Zionists over differences in ideology and tactics. Irgun was the military branch of the Jabotinsky movement, and he became its commander. He is regarded as the ideological father of the right wing in Israeli politics. Jabotinsky also wrote poetry, novels and short stories, was fluent in many languages, and translated several classics of world literature into Hebrew.

135

Zionism after the Second World War

After the Second World War, many Holocaust survivors came to settle in Palestine; the Jewish orphans in this picture, whose parents died in German concentration camps, were allowed to enter Palestine in August 1947 as part of the legal immigration quota

The Holocaust strengthened the determination of the Zionist movement. In the words of Avi Shlaim, 'the tragedy of European Jewry became a source of strength for Zionism'. After the Second World War, the 1945 Zionist Conference decided on a policy of active opposition to British rule. Jewish military groups launched an armed uprising to force the British to leave Palestine. Ben Gurion supported this move towards 'militant Zionism' as an alternative to the 'diplomatic Zionism' that Weizmann still advocated.

The Zionist movement was divided in its attitude towards the UN Partition Plan of 1947. Ben Gurion and the Jewish Agency officially welcomed the plan as a tangible symbol of international acceptance for the creation of a Jewish state. Revisionist Zionists rejected it. The leader of Irgun, Menachem Begin, stated that the group would never accept partition, and that *Eretz Israel* – with Jerusalem as its capital – remained its goal.

Zionism as a political force in Israel

Zionism achieved its primary objective when the state of Israel was established in 1948. However, this did not mean the end of Zionism as a movement. Many revisionist Zionists believed that the Zionist vision was incomplete while part of Jerusalem and the West Bank remained under Arab control. Israel's victory in the 1967 War (which you will read about in Chapter 7) gave rise to a new form of 'religious Zionism', which actively and militantly supported the expansion of Jewish settlements in the territories that Israel had occupied during this war.

SOURCE K

The conquest of the West Bank, which as Judea and Samaria had formed part of the biblical Jewish kingdom, convinced many Orthodox Jewish rabbis and teachers that they were living in a messianic era and that salvation was at hand … Almost immediately these rabbis began to sanctify the land of their ancestors and to make it an object of religious passion. They made the sanctity of the land a central tenet of religious Zionism. From this it followed that anyone who was prepared to give away parts of the sacred land was perceived as a traitor and an enemy of the Jewish people …

Gush Emunim, the Bloc of the Faithful, and the settlements it set up in Judea and Samaria were the most palpable expression of the new wave of messianism that swept though considerable segments of Israeli society. Gush Emunim settlers effectively turned the Palestinians into aliens on their own soil. While the Labour Party sponsored settlements in the hope of increasing Israel's share of the disputed land, the parties of the right, both secular and religious, used ideological reasons to support settlements in the entire Land of Israel

Shlaim, A. 2000. *The Iron Wall: Israel and the Arab World.* London, UK. Penguin. pp. 549–50.

Gush Emunim The Gush Emunim movement combines religious fundamentalism and secular Zionism. It was founded after the 1967 War to promote the establishment of Jewish settlements in areas occupied by Israel during that conflict. As a political movement, Gush Emunim is opposed to any territorial concessions to the Arab states, and promotes the establishment of settlements in all of *Eretz Israel*.

Another form of Zionism that emerged in the 1970s, according to Ilan Pappe, was a form of 'neo-Zionist fundamentalism'. This began among Mizrachi Jews and was aimed at 'turning Israel into a theocracy', a state subject to religious authority. This development was partly explained by the frustration the Mizrachi Jews felt at their inferior economic and social position in Israeli society. The increase in support for Zionism coincided with a swing to the right in Israeli politics in the 1970s. Many Mizrachi Jews gave their support to the right-wing Herut Party led by Menachem Begin.

Activities

1 Read through the information in this chapter on the impact of Zionism. List the names of the different interpretations of Zionism that are mentioned, and write a brief definition of each one.

2 Design a spider diagram to explain the origins of Zionism.

3 Divide into two groups. One group should prepare an argument to support the Zionist viewpoint, and the other to support the Arab viewpoint, of the Zionist aim to establish a 'national home for the Jewish people in Palestine'.

4 In 1975, the General Assembly of the United Nations passed Resolution 3379, which condemned Zionism as a form of racism and racial discrimination. Find out the circumstances under which this resolution was adopted, Israel's reaction to it, and the attitudes of the superpowers. Why was this resolution repealed in 1991?

What role did the Palestine Liberation Organisation play?

The formation of the Palestine Liberation Organisation

By the late 1950s, many of the refugees who had left Palestine in 1948 had lost faith in the commitment of the Arab governments to their cause. They began to believe that the only way they would ever regain Palestine would be to fight for it themselves. In the words of Shindler, the Palestinians 'began to define themselves as a nation and not merely as part of a wider Arab world'. Rashid Khalidi attributes this change in outlook to the emergence of a new generation in the Palestinian diaspora.

> **Fatah** This was the acronym – in reverse – of Harakat al-Tahrir al-Filistin. This means the Movement for the Liberation of Palestine. *Al-Fatah* also means 'victory' or 'the conquest' in Arabic.

Yasser Arafat (1929–2004)

Arafat was born in Cairo to Palestinian parents. He fought in the 1948–49 War against Israel, and studied engineering at Cairo University. Arafat was a founder of Fatah, and he served as chairman of the PLO from 1969 until his death in 2004. He was the international representative and symbol of the Palestinian people. Although Arafat initially supported an armed struggle to achieve Palestinian demands, he was later prepared to negotiate a solution, resulting in the 1993 Oslo Peace Accords. In 1994, he was a joint winner of the Nobel Peace Prize. Arafat became leader of the Palestinian Authority in 1996, when the Palestinians were granted limited self-government in the West Bank and Gaza.

SOURCE 1

This new generation of Palestinian activists was rooted in a major change in the social basis of political power, which deeply influenced the politics of the subsequent decades. The entire stratum of leaders drawn from the notable [élite] class who had dominated Palestinian politics until 1948 had been swept away by the tidal wave of the nakba that had engulfed Palestinian society … it meant the eclipse of the old political class and the rise of an entirely new generation of activists from new social strata, and with a different worldview, and entirely different solutions to the problems of Palestine and the Palestinian people … This new generation operated in the conditions of extreme dispersion and fragmentation that characterized Palestinian society after 1948 … Nevertheless there was more of an even playing field in this brave new world, where education and skills were vital, and where a newly educated generation, trained in the newly established schools of the UN Relief and Works Agency (UNRWA), created to minister to the needs of the Palestinian refugees, were able to find jobs all over the Arab world.

It was the Palestinians of this new diaspora, in Cairo, Beirut, and Kuwait, who in the subsequent decades were to revive Palestinian identity and a Palestinian national movement on a new basis … In time, they came up against the constraints placed on Palestinian activism by the Arab regimes, and had to decide how they related to the Arab governments that, since their first intervention in Palestinian politics in 1936, had played an ambiguous role at best, and often a negative one as far as the Palestinians were concerned.

Khalidi, R. 2006. The Iron Cage: The Story of the Palestinian Struggle for Statehood. Oxford, UK. Oneworld Publications. pp. 136–38.

In 1959, a group of Palestinian students living in Kuwait formed **Fatah**, under the leadership of **Yasser Arafat**. They saw their group as a national liberation movement that was fighting to regain its homeland. Fatah spread its message by publishing a newspaper, *Filastinuna* ('Our Palestine').

SOURCE M

Ilan Pappe compares the membership and leadership of Fatah with the older and more élitist Palestinian leadership before 1948, and comments on the ideology of Fatah.

The most striking phenomenon of Fatah in those early years was its young membership, made up of both students and workers, some of whom quickly made their way to the top. This made Fatah significantly different in composition and orientation from the traditional political parties of the Mandate period. No less unusual was the absence of an articulated ideology: Palestine has to be liberated, Israel destroyed, and there was no room for the Jews who had come after the First World War. Beyond that, however, this programme could not be easily located on the political spectrum between left and right, or included in any dictionary of post-colonial ideologies.

Pappe, I. 2006. A History of Modern Palestine (Second Edition). Cambridge, UK. Cambridge University Press. p. 164.

Activity

Use the information in Sources L and M to explain the emergence and the nature of new leadership in the Palestinian diaspora. Explain Khalidi's implied criticism of the Arab governments. What does Pappe mean by the absence of an 'articulated ideology' in Fatah?

Fatah armed and trained groups of *fedayeen* to carry out guerrilla raids into Israel from Gaza, Jordan and Syria. The Israelis responded to this by sending IDF units on reprisal raids. The guerrilla attacks and the military response had the same effects: civilians on both sides of the Israeli border became the targets and victims of violence.

A group of Palestinian women receiving rifle instruction as part of their training as fedayeen *guerrillas*

Until this time, Arab nationalists had rejected the idea of a separate Palestinian identity. They had viewed the conflict with Israel as an Arab struggle, rather than a specifically Palestinian one. However, with the formation and actions of Fatah, the Arab leaders decided that they needed to adapt this view of the Palestinians as a separate group. At a meeting in Cairo in 1964, they proposed the formation of the Palestine Liberation Organisation. The chairman of the PLO would represent the Palestinians in the Arab League. Arab governments believed this would channel Palestinian grievances into a less militant form and, more importantly, keep the Palestinians under their control.

SOURCE N

The idea of the fedayeen, willing to give up their lives in a people's war, threatened not only Israel, but the established Arab leaders as well. These leaders had always used the Palestinian cause for their own ends, competing with each other in verbal claims of support for the Palestinians. None of them wanted to see an independent Palestinian movement. The Arab leaders called a summit conference in 1964 to try to regain their slipping control of the Palestinians. At Nasser's request, they created a Palestinian organization – the Palestine Liberation Organization (PLO) – to control the guerrilla groups ... Fatah attended the first conference of the PLO in May 1964, but maintained its organizational independence. Other guerrilla groups refused even to attend the conference.

Peoples Press Palestine Book Project. 1981. Our Roots are Still Alive: The Story of the Palestinian People. *New York, USA. Institute for Independent Social Journalism. p. 101.*

The PLO was an umbrella organisation, representing all regions and groupings among the Palestinians. It held its first meeting in Jerusalem in 1964, where it declared its determination to create a 'democratic and secular' Palestinian state to replace Israel in all of Palestine. However, the different factions within the PLO did not agree on how this should be achieved. Some believed in using diplomatic means and working through the UN; others felt that only an armed struggle would achieve their goal. Not all members of the PLO were guerrilla fighters: there were also professional people who did administrative and relief work. The PLO had its own welfare service, Samed, which was originally established to assist the families of *fedayeen* who had been killed in action. However, it later assumed wider responsibilities, such as dealing with the problem of unemployment among the Palestinian refugees. The PLO also set up its own Red Crescent society, which provided not only first aid and medical services but also employment in workshops that produced household commodities, such as furniture, utensils and clothing.

During 1966, Fatah stepped up its guerrilla raids into Israel. The response from Israel was to stage military reprisals into Jordan, from where many of the attacks had come. In March 1968, the Israel Defence Force (IDF) attacked the Jordanian town of Karameh, the site of a PLO guerrilla camp and Fatah headquarters. It used 15,000 troops, as well as tanks and aircraft, in the attack. This action was in response to an attack on an Israeli bus which had been blown up by a mine.

The 300 Palestinian guerrillas at Karameh were eventually defeated, but they put up a strong defence and inflicted relatively heavy casualties on the IDF. The battle of Karameh became a legend among the Palestinians, and thousands more joined the guerrilla forces as a direct result of it.

After Karameh, the PLO revised its charter and adopted a more uncompromising line. It declared that armed struggle was the only way to liberate Palestine. The charter also described Zionism as 'racist and fanatic in its nature, aggressive, expansionist and colonial in its aims, and fascist in its methods'. In 1969, Yasser Arafat became the chairman of the PLO. Fatah was the largest organisation within the PLO but smaller, more extremist groups formed revolutionary movements, such as the Popular Front for the Liberation of Palestine (PFLP) and the Popular Democratic Front for the Liberation of Palestine (PDFLP). These movements wanted to bring about revolutionary change in the Arab world, as well as destroy Israel and establish a Marxist state in Palestine. The increase in guerrilla activities and reprisal raids added to the tensions that were building, and were a direct cause of Israel's decision to attack the Arab states, and the subsequent 1967 War.

During this war, Israel defeated the Arab armies and occupied large areas of Arab territory. These areas included the West Bank and Gaza, where many of the Palestinian refugees from the 1948–49 War lived. Another 590,000 Palestinians in the West Bank and 380,000 more in Gaza were now under Israeli military control in the **'occupied territories'**. Many Palestinians fled once again, some becoming refugees for a second time. Although the UN passed Resolution 242, calling on Israel to withdraw from these territories, Israel ignored it and instead started to build Jewish settlements there. This increased the determination of the Palestinian guerrilla groups to hit back at Israel.

The PLO in Jordan

Thousands more Palestinian refugees moved to Jordan, where they now made up over half of the population. Many of them were still living in refugee camps, with their own administrative structures that acted independently of the Jordanian government. They had in effect established a state-within-a-state. Heavily armed Palestinian commandos controlled the camps, and set up roadblocks at will. They also patrolled the streets of Amman, the capital of Jordan, which became a virtual Palestinian stronghold. Hussein, the Jordanian king, increasingly viewed the Palestinians as a threat to his life and the monarchy. The government of Jordan felt the refugees were a threat to stability in the country.

The PLO continued to launch guerrilla raids into Israel, which led to inevitable reprisal raids into Jordan by the IDF. The raids and counter-attacks increased the tensions in Jordan, and there were clashes between Palestinian commandos and the Jordanian army.

Arafat and many other leaders in the PLO wanted to avoid an open confrontation with the stronger Jordanian army. They tried, therefore, to avoid actions that would provoke Jordan's authorities. However, more radical elements within the PLO regarded Hussein as a reactionary. These groups wanted to overthrow Hussein's government, and use Jordan as a base from which to attack Israel and regain Palestine. Some members of the Popular Front for the Liberation of Palestine, such as **Leila Khaled**, began to use high-profile hijackings of international airlines as a way of raising awareness of their cause.

George Habash (1926–2008)

Habash was a Palestinian Christian, who left Palestine with his family in the mass flight in 1948. After 1967, Habash believed that only armed struggle and revolutionary violence could liberate Palestine. Under his leadership, the radical PFLP pioneered the use of high-profile hijackings to raise international awareness of their cause. Many in the West regarded him as a notorious and dangerous terrorist. However, in an obituary published at the time of his death in 2008, the *Guardian* referred to him as 'the conscience of the revolution'.

Fact

The most notorious attack carried out by Black September was the murder of 11 Israeli athletes at the 1972 Olympic Games in Munich. Members of Black September killed two of the athletes and held nine others hostage, demanding the release of more than 200 Palestinians held in Israeli jails. A failed rescue attempt by the German police resulted in the deaths of the hostages as well as five of the kidnappers. The incident created worldwide publicity for the Palestinian cause, but also outrage and condemnation of their actions.

In September 1970, the PFLP – which was led by **George Habash** – hijacked three large passenger planes (one British, one Swiss and one American) and flew them to Jordan. The 600 passengers were held as hostages, but were later released. The planes were blown up when the PFLP's demands for the release of Palestinian prisoners in Israel were not met.

The government of Jordan felt that it was losing control, and Hussein decided to use force to expel the PLO. In September 1970, the Jordanian army attacked the guerrilla bases. Thousands of Palestinians were killed, most of them civilians. When the Syrian army sent tanks as an indication of support for the Palestinians, Israel and Western powers were concerned that the war would escalate. The Israeli government, supported by the USA, considered intervening if it seemed likely that the Jordanian army might be defeated. It was the efforts of Nasser that stopped the bloodshed in Jordan. Shortly before his death, he put pressure on both sides to agree to a ceasefire at a meeting of Arab states in Cairo. However, the Jordanian army attacked the Palestinian camps again in 1971. The PLO guerrillas were defeated and forced to flee, and their political and military presence in Jordan was destroyed. More than 30,000 Palestinians were killed in this bitter conflict between the PLO and the Jordanian security forces. Many Palestinians felt that they had been betrayed by Hussein's actions. Other Arab states condemned the war and called for peace negotiations, but did not intervene directly or come to the assistance of the Palestinians.

The PLO in Lebanon

After the expulsion of the PLO from Jordan, many Palestinians fled to Lebanon, which became the main centre of PLO resistance. They had become increasingly disillusioned by the lack of support from Arab governments, and many believed a more radical approach was needed. They had seen the international reaction to the PFLP hijackings, and decided to use similar tactics to force the world to recognise their situation. A small extremist group, calling itself Black September after the start of the civil war in Jordan in 1970, conducted a campaign of extreme violence. This included the assassination of the Jordanian prime minister, and the shooting of passengers at Lod Airport outside Tel Aviv in Israel (where most of the victims were Christian pilgrims from Puerto Rico). These actions were condemned by moderate factions within the PLO.

Armed police move in on the Black September extremists holding members of the Israeli Olympic team hostage at the 1972 Munich Olympic Games

From its headquarters in Lebanon, Yasser Arafat tried to steer the PLO towards a more moderate path. During the 1970s, the PLO and the Palestinian cause gained greater international recognition. In 1974, at a summit meeting held in Morocco, the Arab states declared their support for the right of the Palestinian people to establish an 'independent national authority'. Later the same year, Arafat was invited to address the General Assembly of the United Nations. This body later passed resolutions, one recognising the rights of the Palestinians to self-determination and return to Palestine, and the other granting the PLO 'observer status' at the UN. Several countries went on to recognise the PLO as the representative of the Palestinian people.

SOURCE O

The roots of the Palestinian question do not stem from any conflict between two religions or two nationalisms. Neither is it a border war between two neighbouring states. It is the cause of a people deprived of its homeland, dispersed and uprooted, living mostly in exile and in refugee camps … Today I have come bearing an olive branch and a freedom fighter's gun. Do not let the olive branch fall from my hand.

Extract from Arafat's address to the UN General Assembly, 13 November 1974. Quoted in Rea, T. and Wright, J. 1997. The Arab–Israeli Conflict. Oxford, UK. Oxford University Press. p. 46.

The presence of the PLO in Lebanon upset the delicate balance between the Christian and Muslim communities there, each of which was already split into moderate and militant factions. The arrival of large numbers of Palestinians from Jordan increased the tensions and a civil war broke out in 1975. Ilan Pappe believes that the PLO was substantially weakened by its involvement in the politics of Lebanon.

SOURCE P

In many ways, Arafat was his own worst enemy. His greatest failure was his inability to keep the PLO out of the Lebanese civil war, which erupted in 1975. An exaggerated sense of self-esteem and a false appreciation of his importance and that of his organization within Lebanon led him to try to play a leading role there. Against the advice of some of his closest associates, he involved the PLO in the Muslim-Christian strife, openly taking the Muslim side. In 1970, the Lebanese government had not wanted the PLO on its soil, but had been too weak to reject Egyptian and Jordanian pressure, but resented the interference in its internal affairs. The PLO could have remained neutral, but felt that its position in Lebanon depended on a Muslim victory.

Pappe, I. 2006. A History of Modern Palestine (Second Edition). Cambridge, UK. Cambridge University Press. p. 218.

Theory of knowledge

History and ethics
In retaliation for the PFLP hijacking of an Israeli passenger plane at Athens airport, during which one passenger was killed, an Israeli commando unit attacked Beirut airport and destroyed 13 planes. Are terrorism and violence ever justified? Is it acceptable to use violence in retaliation, or to save lives, or to intervene to prevent a greater evil from happening? What problems do such issues create for historians writing about these events?

Questions

What is the tone of Arafat's speech in Source O – is it conciliatory or threatening? How effective do you think it would have been at the time?

143

In a complex web of political alliances, both Syria and Israel became involved in the civil war in Lebanon as well. A fragile ceasefire was arranged in 1976. However, from their bases in Lebanon, PLO guerrillas continued to launch raids into Israel. In an attempt to destroy the PLO, Israel gave support to a Lebanese militia – the South Lebanese Army (SLA). It hoped that the SLA would destroy the PLO, and the IDF could avoid becoming directly involved. However, in March 1978, Palestinian guerrillas hijacked a bus near Tel Aviv. In the ensuing shootout, 34 Israeli civilians were killed, and in response the Israeli army invaded Lebanon.

After a three-month occupation, during which between 100,000 and 200,000 civilians were forced to flee the fighting and shelling, Israeli forces withdrew from Lebanon. The UN, which had called for the withdrawal, sent a peacekeeping force to patrol the border. In spite of the UN presence, clashes and attacks between Israel and the PLO continued along the Lebanese border. In 1982, the Israeli army invaded Lebanon once again. Its aim was to destroy the PLO camps, but thousands of Lebanese and Palestinian civilians were also killed. As the cities and countryside of Lebanon were destroyed, many people around the world (and in Israel itself) criticised the actions of the Israeli army. A ceasefire was eventually arranged, and international forces transported the PLO survivors to other countries. The headquarters of the PLO moved to Tunisia, and – under Arafat's leadership – the organisation continued its efforts to gain support for the Palestinian cause.

SOURCE Q

Rashid Khalidi assesses Arafat's contribution to the Palestinian cause.

Yasser Arafat dominated the Palestinian political scene for over two generations. However, if he deserved much of the credit for returning to centre stage a people who momentarily appeared to have disappeared from the Middle East scene after 1948, to him also belonged a share of the blame for the problems with which his people were saddled at his death. This is particularly true of the flaws in the political structures that developed during Arafat's era of dominance of Palestinian politics. Yasser Arafat, an easily caricatured figure who did not arouse sympathy in most Western, and many Arab observers, readily lent himself to the personification of everything relating to Palestine. Indeed, in some measure he encouraged it. He was egocentric, revelled in attention, and was jealous of rivals. He worked tirelessly to keep all the strings controlling Palestinian politics, particularly the financial ones, in his hands alone. He lived single-mindedly for his political work, and he worked incessantly, putting in longer hours than his colleagues in the Palestinian leadership. He had few distractions, took little recreation, and never vacationed. In everything he did, he exploited to the full his capacious memory, his relentless drive, and his powerful, domineering personality.

Khalidi, R. 2006. The Iron Cage: The Story of the Palestinian Struggle for Statehood. Oxford, UK. Oneworld Publications. pp. 142–43.

Activity

Read Sources P (on page 143) and Q. Compare the views of these two historians on the strengths and weaknesses of Yasser Arafat's leadership of the PLO.

Activities

1 Draw up a table like the one below to summarise the positive and negative implications of the establishment of the PLO, from the perspectives of the people, governments or organisations listed:

	Positive implications of the founding of the PLO	Negative implications of the founding of the PLO
Israeli government		
Arab governments (e.g. Egypt and Jordan)		
Palestinian refugees in camps		
Fatah		
United Nations		
USA and USSR		

2 Divide into two groups to debate the tactics used by radical groups within the PLO. One group should prepare an argument to support the view that tactics such as hijacking, kidnapping and bombing were morally unacceptable, and also counter-productive as they alienated international sympathy for the Palestinian cause.

The other group should prepare an argument to support the view that the world had ignored the Palestinians and actions committed against them for over 20 years, and so radical groups were forced to use violent methods that grabbed world headlines.

3 Yasser Arafat, the founder of Fatah and leader of the PLO from 1968 onwards, died in 2004. Work out a list of questions that you would like to have asked him before his death, and write the answers you think he may have given. You can start by examining the information about him in the picture essay about his life on this website:

http://news.bbc.co.uk/2/shared/spl/hi/picture_gallery/04/middle_east_yasser_arafat0s_life/html/1.stm

4 'The PLO was also entangled in an international web encompassing anarchist, terrorist, guerrilla and liberation movements all around the world, including the IRA, the Red Brigades in Italy, the Baader-Meinhof gang in Germany, the Red Army from Japan, and the Viet Cong.'
(Ilan Pappe, *A History of Modern Palestine*, pp. 217–18)

Divide into groups of five. Each student should research one of the movements mentioned in this quotation, and do a short presentation to the rest of the group. In each case, explain briefly what the organisation was and what its links were to the PLO.

5 Using the information you have learned in Question 4 as a background, explain the changing aims and methods used by the PLO.

End of chapter activities

Summary

You should now understand the origins of the three forces of nationalism in the Middle East – pan-Arabism, Zionism and Palestinian nationalism – and the impact that each had on the Arab–Israeli conflict. You should be able to analyse how each of the three contributed to this conflict. You should also be aware of the different interpretations about goals and tactics within each movement, and be able to show that none of the three was a single united movement. You should understand the role and contribution of key figures to each movement.

Summary activity

Copy this diagram, and use the information in this chapter and from other sources to make brief notes under each heading.

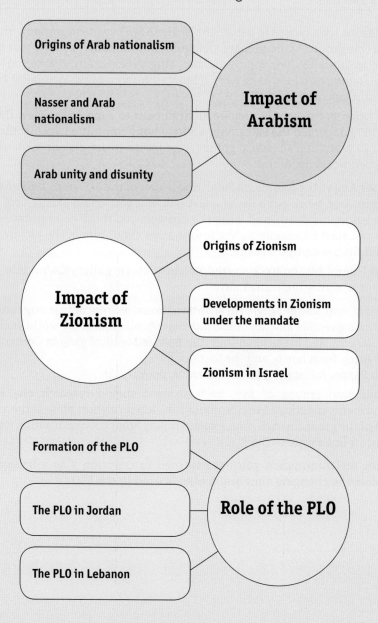

- Origins of Arab nationalism
- Nasser and Arab nationalism
- Arab unity and disunity

Impact of Arabism

Impact of Zionism

- Origins of Zionism
- Developments in Zionism under the mandate
- Zionism in Israel

- Formation of the PLO
- The PLO in Jordan
- The PLO in Lebanon

Role of the PLO

146

Paper 1 exam practice

Question

With reference to their origin and purpose, assess the value and limitations of Sources A and B below for historians investigating the origins of the Arab–Israeli conflict.

[6 marks]

Skill

Assessing the value and limitations (utility/reliability) of two sources

SOURCE A

Nahum Goldman, an early Zionist from Germany, describes his feelings after his first visit to Palestine in 1913.

When I left Palestine my Zionism had been enriched by a momentous factor, the country itself. Until then Zionism had been an abstract idea to me, and I had no real conception of what the return of the Jews meant in any concrete sense. My visit gave me that feeling for the soil without which Zionism is bound to remain quite unsubstantial. From then on I began to understand what it means, not merely negatively in terms of leaving the Diaspora, but also positively, as a new beginning in a Jewish homeland.

Goldman, N. 1969. The Autobiography of Nahum Goldman: Sixty Years of a Jewish Life. *New York, USA. Holt, Rinehart and Winston. p. 44.*

SOURCE B

A Palestinian refugee, Fawaz Turki, who fled with his family in 1948 to live in exile in Lebanon, reflects on his feelings about Palestine.

Our Palestinian consciousness, instead of dissipating, was enhanced and acquired a subtle nuance and a new dimension. It was buoyed by two concepts: the preservation of our memory of Palestine and our acquisition of education. We persisted in refusing the houses and monetary compensation offered by the UN to settle us in our host countries. We wanted nothing short of returning to our homeland. And from Syria, Lebanon, and Jordan, we would see, a few miles, a few yards, across the border, a land where we had been born, where we had lived, and where we felt the earth. 'This is my land,' we would shout, or cry, or sing, or plead, or reason. And to that land a people had come, a foreign community of colonizers, aided by a Western world in a hurry to rid itself of guilt and shame, demanding independence from history, from heaven, and from us.

Turki, F. 1972. The Disinherited: Journal of a Palestinian Exile. *New York, USA. Monthly Review Press. p. 54.*

Before you start

Value and limitations (utility/reliability) questions require you to assess **two** sources over a range of possible issues, and to comment on the value of these sources to historians studying a particular event or period of history. You need to consider both the **origin and purpose** and also the **value and limitations** of the sources. You should link these in your answer, showing how origin/purpose relate to value/limitations. Before you attempt this question, refer to pages 219–20 for advice on how to tackle these questions, and a simplified markscheme.

Student answer

Source A expresses the Zionist viewpoint about wanting to establish a 'Jewish homeland' in Palestine. Source B is written by a Palestinian man who was forced to flee with his family when Israel was established. It is written as a journal to record his feelings about the experiences of the refugees. It is obviously also written to evoke sympathy and understanding for the Palestinian cause.

It is valuable to historians exploring the origins of the Arab–Israeli conflict as it describes, in emotive terms, the circumstances and feelings of the Palestinian refugees, which is at the basis of the conflict. However, historians should also question whether the writer has political motives, because he expresses criticism of the Western world for supporting the establishment of Israel.

Examiner comments

The student has done well in examining the origin and purpose, as well as the value and limitations, of Source B. But other than saying that Source A is a Zionist viewpoint, the answer does not say anything else about its origin and purpose. There is nothing at all about the value and limitations of Source A. The answer is not good enough to get into Band 1, as there is explicit consideration of the origins, purpose, value and limitations of one source only.

Activity

Look again at the two sources, the simplified markscheme on page 220, and the student answer above. Now try to write a paragraph or two to push the answer up into Band 1, and so obtain the full 6 marks. Remember that you need to examine all four aspects of both sources to get into the top band.

Paper 2 practice questions

1   To what extent were the aims of Arab nationalism, Zionism and Palestinian nationalism incompatible?

2   Analyse the role of Nasser as the hero of Arab nationalism.

3   Assess the impact of Zionism on the history of the Middle East.

4   Examine the role of the Palestine Liberation Organisation between 1964 and 1979.

Introduction

After 1956, the hostility between Israel and the Arab states continued. This resulted in two more wars – in 1967 and 1973 – neither of which resolved the conflict, or solved the situation of the Palestinian refugees. The Israeli victory in the 1967 War changed the map of the Middle East dramatically, and added significantly to the problems of the Palestinians. The realisation by the Arab states during the 1973 War of their potential power over Western economies, through their control of oil supplies and prices, contributed to a change in international attitudes towards the conflict. During this period, the superpowers became more involved in the Middle East, as suppliers of arms to – and sources of pressure on – their respective allies.

Key questions

- What were the causes, events and consequences of the 1967 War?
- What were the causes, events and consequences of the 1973 War?

Overview

- Tensions between Israel and the Arab states increased for several reasons after the 1956 Suez Crisis. These included a massive arms build-up on both sides, *fedayeen* raids and Israeli reprisals, and disputes over water. Superpower interest in the Middle East region added to the volatile situation.
- This tension became a crisis in May 1967, after Nasser demanded the withdrawal of UN forces from Sinai and closed the Straits of Tiran to Israeli shipping. Propaganda in the Arab media increased Israeli fears of an imminent attack, and the Israeli government sought confirmation of American support.
- In June 1967, Israel attacked Egypt, Jordan and Syria. In six days, it destroyed their air forces and defeated their armies. In the process, Israel occupied vast areas of Arab territory – including the Gaza Strip, the Sinai Peninsula, the West Bank of the Jordan River, East Jerusalem and the Golan Heights.
- The UN passed Resolution 242, which called on Israel to withdraw from the land it had occupied, and for the Arab states to recognise Israel. This resolution became the basis for UN attempts to reach a negotiated settlement of the ongoing Arab–Israeli conflict.
- The 1967 War had mixed results. Despite its victory, Israel faced growing pressure because of the larger numbers of Palestinians now under Israeli control. Also, the Arab states were more determined than ever to avenge their defeat.

Timeline

1964 May: establishment of Palestine Liberation Organisation (PLO)

1966 Nov: defence agreement between Egypt and Syria; IDF attack on Jordanian village of Samu

1967 Apr: clash between Israeli and Syrian air forces

May: Egyptian troops move into Sinai; UNEF forces withdrawn from Egypt; Straits of Tiran closed to Israeli shipping; defence agreement between Egypt and Jordan

Jun: 1967 War (Six Day War)

Nov: UN Resolution 242

1969 17 Mar: Golda Meir becomes prime minister of Israel

Mar: start of War of Attrition

Dec: Rogers Plan

1970 Aug: end of War of Attrition

Sep: death of Nasser; Sadat becomes president of Egypt

Nov: Hafez Al-Assad comes to power after military coup in Syria

1971 Mar: alliance between Egypt, Syria and Libya

1972 Jul: Egypt expels Soviet advisors

1973 Jan: military alliance between Egypt and Syria

Oct: 1973 War (Yom Kippur War); OPEC oil embargo; UN Resolution 338

149

- The potential for conflict grew as the superpowers increased arms supplies to their respective allies. During 1969 and 1970, Egypt and Israel fought a destructive and inconclusive War of Attrition across the Suez Canal. In 1970, the conflict in Jordan between the PLO and the Jordanian army briefly threatened to become a wider Middle East war.

- After 1970, Egypt's new leader – Anwar Sadat – wanted to resolve the stalemate in the Middle East and regain the Sinai Peninsula. He aimed to do this by strengthening Egypt's military and diplomatic position, and making secret preparations for war.

- In October 1973, Egypt and Syria attacked Israel in a well-planned and co-ordinated campaign. During this fourth Arab–Israeli war, the Arab states used their 'oil weapon' by cutting off supplies, which put considerable pressure on Western economies. Diplomatic pressure by the superpowers forced the warring sides to accept a UN-sponsored ceasefire.

- The 1973 War had important political and economical repercussions for Israel. It changed the international attitude towards the Arab–Israeli conflict, and it gave the Arab leaders – especially Sadat – greater confidence.

Israeli soldiers dance in celebration at the sacred Wailing Wall in Old Jerusalem on 7 June 1967, after conquering this area during the 1967 War

What were the causes, events and consequences of the 1967 War?

The Middle East between 1956 and 1967

After 1956, both Israel and Egypt built up their armed forces, obtaining most of their arms from the superpowers. In this way, superpower involvement in the Middle East increased substantially. The USSR replaced the Egyptian military equipment destroyed by Britain and France in the Suez campaign and by Israel during the Sinai War. The Soviets also supplied Iraq and Syria, and regarded Syria as its closest ally in the region. However, although these Arab states accepted Soviet military aid, they resisted direct political influence. Nasser continued his policy of non-alignment, and in Egypt the Communist Party was banned.

The main objective of American foreign policy in the Middle East after 1956 was to limit Soviet influence in the region. This was the undisputed aim of the 1957 Eisenhower Doctrine (see page 112). The US Sixth Fleet patrolled the eastern Mediterranean area, a factor that aided American intervention in Lebanon in 1958. However, superpower support was not clear-cut along Arab–Israeli lines. The United States was prepared to supply weapons to the more conservative Arab states – such as Jordan, Saudi Arabia, Iran and Lebanon – as well as to Israel, in order to strengthen American influence in the region. Although the American public largely supported Israel, and Arab propaganda claimed that the main concern of the USA was to protect Israel, it is clear that American foreign policy was influenced by other factors as well. One key concern was the increasing dependence of Western economies on oil from the Middle East. As well as arms from the USA, Israel received weapons from France. The French also helped Israel to establish a nuclear programme to develop weapons, based at a nuclear facility at Dimona.

151

SOURCE A

Ilan Pappe explains the wider economic, social and political dimensions of the arms race in the Middle East.

No sooner had the Sinai campaign [of 1956] ended than war rhetoric on both sides of the divide heralded the imminence of another violent round of fighting between Israel and the Arab world. Unlike during the previous phase in the conflict, 1948 to 1956, the rhetoric was not balanced by peace efforts. On the contrary, it was accompanied by an arms race that for Israel included the acquisition of nuclear capability. On the Arab side it was highlighted by a massive build-up of modern armies with new weapons and inflated security budgets. On both sides, investment in weapons of mass destruction took priority over social and economic needs. Governments on both sides abandoned their welfare responsibilities, and some of them would pay dearly for this prioritization. The absence of sound social and economic policies created a vacuum that was eagerly filled by political Islam on the Palestinian side and Jewish fundamentalism on the Israeli side.

Pappe, I. 2006. *A History of Modern Palestine (Second Edition)*. Cambridge, UK. Cambridge University Press. p. 184.

Question

What were the local and international implications of the arms build-up in the Middle East in the 1960s?

By the mid 1960s, both the USSR and the USA had spent significant sums of money to arm their allies in the Middle East. To a certain extent, their prestige in the Cold War was linked to this arms provision. This meant that any regional war in the Middle East might escalate into a wider conflict with superpower involvement.

During the 1960s, there were increasing tensions between Israel and its Arab neighbours. These were caused partly by Fatah raids into Israel and reprisals by the Israeli Defence Force (IDF). Such activities were prevented along the border between Israel and Egypt by the presence of a UN peacekeeping force, which had been stationed there since the 1956 Sinai War.

However, along the border between Israel and Syria these actions were common. A particular source of conflict was the disagreement over who had the right to control the demilitarised zone, or DMZ, that the 1949 armistice agreement had defined as a no-man's-land. In February 1966, when a radical Ba'ath government came to power in Syria, it increased the country's support for the PLO and put pressure on Nasser to play a more active role in supporting the Palestinian cause.

Nasser was in a difficult situation: he wanted to retain his position as the perceived leader of the Arab world, but at the same time he had a more realistic assessment of the strength of the Arab military forces in comparison with those of Israel. In November 1966, he signed a defence pact with Syria, which provided for the establishment of a joint command over the armed forces of the two countries. Each agreed to come to the aid of its ally in case of war with Israel. In this way, Nasser hoped that he would be able to use his influence to restrain the ambitions of those in the Syrian government who wanted to pursue military action.

Although the Jordanian government discouraged PLO guerrilla raids into Israel, another area of tension was the border between Israel and Jordan. After a border incident in which three Israeli soldiers were killed by a mine planted by Fatah guerrillas, the IDF launched a massive raid into Jordan in November 1966, targeting the village of Samu. In the attack, a number of Jordanian troops and civilians were killed, and over 100 houses and public buildings were destroyed. The raid triggered unrest and protests among the Palestinians in Jordan, who demanded that Hussein's government do more to protect them. The Samu raid was condemned by the UN and the USA. The United States feared that the event would destabilise Jordan and undermine the government of King Hussein, a key American ally in the region. Many politicians in Israel criticised the raid, and questioned why the IDF had struck at Jordan – with whom the Israelis had less cause for concern – rather than at Syria, with whom relations were far more hostile.

Historical debate

Historians have different interpretations of the significance and implications of the Samu raid. Michael Oren claims that the Americans were 'appalled at Israel's apparent recklessness, its willingness to undermine the only Arab leader with whom it enjoyed a *modus vivendi*, a pro-Western moderate struggling against a radical sea'. Avi Shlaim states that the raid was a 'terrible blunder, and the IDF leaders knew it. Thereafter they reverted to targeting Syria'.

Question

Think of other wars that you have studied. Apart from water, what other resources have people and nations fought over in history?

SOURCE B

As Israel put its National Water Carrier into operation in 1964, and began to divert water from the Jordan River for use by the growing population in its heartland, the situation deteriorated. Syria responded with efforts to divert the Jordan River to reduce its flow to Israel. Tensions between Israel and Syria over water and the use of the DMZs [demilitarised zones] between them led to numerous border incidents. This war over water had its origins in the Arab summit in Cairo in 1964, when the Arab leaders made it a matter of policy to divert the waters of the Jordan River. Funds were allocated for this purpose, and both Syria and Lebanon began work on projects to shunt the waters of the Hasbani and Banias rivers away from the Jordan River, where Israel could not utilize it. Israel noted that such actions would be considered acts of war. Israel used artillery and tank fire and aircraft to stop these projects. The Israelis proved successful and the Arab efforts were halted.

Reich, B. 2005. A Brief History of Israel *(Second Edition)*. New York, USA. Checkmark Books. p. 77.

The causes of the 1967 War

Tensions along the borders mounted steadily during the early months of 1967. In April, a confrontation between Israel and Syria culminated in a clash between their air forces. Six Syrian planes were shot down, two of them over Damascus, the capital of Syria. Some historians regard this air battle as the first step in a chain of events that led directly to the outbreak of war in June 1967.

By May 1967, relations between Israel and Syria had reached a critical stage. Israel was angered by ongoing Syrian support for PLO raids, and the Syrian government was convinced that Israel was planning an attack. The crisis intensified when Syria's ally, the Soviet Union, stepped in. The USSR warned Egypt that it had evidence that an Israeli attack on its Syrian ally was imminent. Historians have since established that there is no convincing evidence that Israel was in fact planning an attack at this stage, so there are debates about the reasons for Soviet diplomatic intervention at this critical point.

SOURCE C

The reasons for the Russians' warning would remain obscure, leaving room for a gamut of theories as to why they had tendered it at that particular juncture and what they sought to gain. Some speculated that Moscow had invented the crisis in order to bolster Nasser's stature and to cement the Soviet-Syrian alliance. Other hypotheses held that the Soviets sought to lure Nasser into a war with Israel, to destroy him and so clear the field for Syrian preeminence and the penetration of Soviet cadres. The time was right to exploit America's distraction in Vietnam, many experts postulated, to curb rising Chinese influence in the area, and to deal a smashing blow to Zionism …

Lost in this conjecturing is the fact that there was little new in this Soviet warning to Sadat [Nasser's deputy], that reports of intended Israeli aggression against Syria had been issued repeatedly over the past year. These admonitions, it was noted, reflected deep rifts in the Kremlin leadership and differing perceptions of Soviet interests in the Middle East – a middle road between avoiding all clashes in the region and plunging it into war. Fully expecting an Israeli retaliation against Syria, the Soviets were keen to prevent a battle that was liable to result in Arab defeat and superpower confrontation. Yet, at the same time, they wanted to maintain a heightened level of tension in the area, a reminder of the Arabs' need for Soviet aid.

Oren, M. 2002. Six Days of War: June 1967 and the Making of the Modern Middle East. New York, USA. Ballantyne Books. pp. 54–55.

After the warning from the USSR, the pressure was once again on Nasser to demonstrate his leadership of the Arab world. He embarked on a risky exercise in **brinkmanship**, designed to demonstrate to the other Arab governments that he was willing to act decisively towards Israel. At the same time, Nasser was aware that any war that resulted would certainly not be in the best interests of the Arab states.

Historical debate

Historian Avi Shlaim suggests that it was not Syrian aggression, but 'Israel's strategy of escalation on the Syrian front which was probably the single most important factor in dragging the Middle East to war in June 1967'. He refers to a 1976 interview with Moshe Dayan (the Israeli minister of defence at the time of the 1967 War), which was published in 1997. In this interview, Dayan estimated that at least 80% of the border clashes with Syria were initiated by the Israelis. Dayan explained that he and some of his fellow officers did not accept the 1949 armistice lines as final, and hoped to extend Israel's border by 'snatching bits of territory and holding on to it until the enemy despairs and gives it to us'.

153

Question

Source C sums up some of the theories that have been suggested to explain the Soviet warning to Syria. If historians wanted to find out what prompted the Soviet action, what sources would they need to consult?

brinkmanship This term means testing the strength of an opponent by pressing a dangerous situation to the limit of safety and peace (the 'brink') before pulling back, in order to gain some advantage; this was an aggressive and risky practice in foreign policy that is often associated with the Cold War.

Some analysts think that it was Nasser's success in the 1956 Suez Crisis (see Chapter 5) that led him to act in this way. They suggest that he believed the USA would come to his rescue, as it had done in 1956 when it condemned the Anglo–French–Israeli invasion of Egypt and forced the three countries to withdraw.

SOURCE D

Avi Shlaim explains the dilemma that faced Nasser after he received the report from the USSR about an impending Israeli attack on Syria.

The report was untrue and Nasser knew that it was untrue, but he was in a quandary. His army was bogged down in an inconclusive war in Yemen, and he knew that Israel was militarily stronger than all the Arab confrontation states taken together. Yet, politically, he could not afford to remain inactive, because his leadership of the Arab world was being challenged. Since the Samu raid the Jordanians had been accusing him of cowardice and of hiding from the Israelis behind the skirts of the UN Emergency Force in Sinai. Syria had a defence pact with Egypt that compelled it to go to Syria's aid in the event of an Israeli attack. Clearly, Nasser had to do something, both to preserve his own credibility as an ally and to restrain the hotheads in Damascus. There is general agreement among commentators that Nasser neither wanted nor planned to go to war with Israel. What he did was to embark on an exercise in brinkmanship that was to carry him over the brink.

Shlaim, A. 2000. The Iron Wall: Israel and the Arab World. London, UK. Penguin. p. 237.

U Thant (1909–74) Thant was a Burmese diplomat who succeeded Dag Hammarskjöld as secretary-general of the United Nations (1962–71). His decision to withdraw UN forces from the Middle East at Nasser's request in 1967 was highly controversial at the time.

In May 1967, Nasser moved 100,000 Egyptian troops into the Sinai Peninsula, bringing them closer to the Israeli border. He then demanded the withdrawal of UN peacekeeping forces from Egyptian territory, a move intended to demonstrate Egyptian sovereignty. To the surprise of many governments, the UN secretary-general **U Thant** promptly agreed, and withdrew the UN forces. In doing so, he removed the buffer between the Egyptian and Israeli armies. On 22 May, Nasser closed the Straits of Tiran to Israeli shipping, denying Israel access to the Gulf of Aqaba and the port of Eilat. Israel considered this move to be an act of aggression, and called on the USA, Britain and France to act to uphold their guarantee of free passage into the gulf – an agreement that had been reached following the Suez Crisis.

Although there were growing concerns among the Israeli public, Israeli military leaders were confident that an Arab attack was unlikely. Some historians believe that many of them saw an opportunity to wage a war in which they were confident of an Israeli victory, and in which they could win useful territorial gains. Pappe suggests that Nasser's actions 'provided significant sections of the Israeli political élite with a perfect opportunity to realise their dream of a Greater Israel'. This desire for expanded Israeli territory was partly strategic, as an extension of Israel to the River Jordan in the east would give the country more defensible borders. There was also a nationalist motivation, as an extension of Israeli rule over the West Bank would mean that parts of the ancient biblical kingdom of Israel – Judea and Samaria – would come under Jewish control.

An Israeli bomber flies over a line-up of Israeli tanks in the southern frontier area of Israel on 23 May 1967

SOURCE E

As the tensions mounted, the Arab media forecast the imminent destruction of the Jewish state. On 29 May Nasser echoed these views in a speech to the Egyptian parliament.

Preparations have already been made. We are now ready to confront Israel. They have claimed many things about the 1956 Suez war, but no one believed them after the secrets of the 1956 collusion were uncovered – that mean collusion in which Israel took part. Now we are ready for the confrontation. We are now ready to deal with the entire Palestine question.

The issue now at hand is not the Gulf of Aqaba, the Straits of Tiran, or the withdrawal of UNEF, but the rights of the Palestine people. It is the aggression which took place in Palestine in 1948 with the collaboration of Britain and the United States. It is the expulsion of the Arabs from Palestine, the usurpation of their rights, and the plunder of their property. It is the disavowal of all the UN resolutions in favour of the Palestinian people ...

We demand the full rights of the Palestinian people. We say this out of our belief that Arab rights cannot be squandered because the Arabs throughout the Arab world are demanding these Arab rights.

Extract from Nasser's speech to the Egyptian National Assembly, 29 May 1967. Quoted in Laqueur, W. and Rubin, B. 1969. The Israel–Arab Reader. London, UK. Weidenfeld and Nicolson. p. 187.

Moshe Dayan (1915–81) Dayan was an Israeli general and politician. He was seen in Israel as a hero of the 1948–49 War. He served as minister of defence during and after the 1967 War. Dayan resigned in 1974 after criticism over Israel's lack of preparedness in the 1973 War. He returned to government in 1977 as foreign minister in Begin's government, and resigned in 1979 over Begin's refusal to negotiate with the Palestinians.

Yitzhak Rabin (1922–95)
Rabin was an Israeli military leader and politician. He was chief of staff of the IDF in the 1967 War, and was the Israeli ambassador to the USA from 1968. Rabin served as prime minister of Israel between 1974 and 1977, and again between 1992 and 1995. His participation in the 1993 Oslo Accords made him a joint winner of the 1994 Nobel Peace Prize. He was assassinated by a right-wing religious Zionist.

In Jordan, where more than half of the population was Palestinian, there was pressure on King Hussein to support Egypt and Syria in the impending confrontation with Israel. On 30 May, Jordan and Egypt signed a defence pact, which Iraq joined five days later.

As the pressure increased, there were growing fears and feelings of isolation among the Israeli population. Many began to believe that Israel faced imminent destruction, and that they were involved in a struggle for survival. There were growing pressures on the Israeli government. The prime minister, Levi Eshkol, formed a government of national unity to cope with the crisis. It included the right-wing Menachem Begin (see page 34), with **Moshe Dayan** as minister of defence.

Dayan was widely admired in Israel for his role in establishing IDF commando units, and for the part he had played in the 1956 Sinai campaign. He felt that the best response to the threat that Israel faced was military rather than political. According to historian Bernard Reich, the inclusion of Dayan in the government as minister of defence indicated that 'the time left for diplomacy to prevent war was short'. **Yitzhak Rabin** became chief of staff of the IDF.

However, Israel's government was concerned about the American response to any Israeli decision to take action. Previously, President Johnson had made it clear to the Israeli foreign minister that the US favoured a diplomatic solution, and would not support Israeli military action. Now another Israeli delegation went to Washington to ask the USA to put pressure on the Egyptians to re-open the Straits of Tiran. Israel also wanted to know whether, in the event of war, it would have American support if the Soviet Union became involved; and, if necessary, whether the USA would aid the replacement of Israeli arms lost in a conflict. This time, the American position had shifted. The USA gave tacit support for Israel to take action against Egypt. Two days later – on 5 June 1967 – the Israelis decided on a pre-emptive strike on the Arab states. The third Arab–Israeli war had begun.

SOURCE F

The long-range causes of the 1967 war were the continued inability of the Arabs to recognize and accept the political sovereignty of the Jews in Israel; the antagonism and desire for revenge that had been fuelled by defeats and humiliation in the previous wars, as well as by Israel's excessive retaliations; Arab fear of Israeli aggressiveness and expansionism; and Israeli '**hawkishness**' and the determination to maintain military superiority. The inability to find a solution for the plight of the Palestinian refugees, because of intransigence on both sides, provided the raison d'être [justification] and rallying point for the Arab crusade against Israel. The short-term and more proximate causes were the arms build-up on both sides in the previous decade; superpower interference and especially Soviet meddling; the volatile situation in Syria; Nasser's brinkmanship; the defense pacts that linked together Egypt, Syria and Jordan; and the failure of the international community to prevent war through diplomacy. All sides thus must share the blame for the outbreak of hostilities and for the consequences that followed.

Bickerton, I. and Klausner, C. 2001. A Concise History of the Arab–Israeli Conflict (Fourth Edition). New Jersey, USA. Prentice Hall. p. 154.

The events of the 1967 War

On 5 June 1967, Israeli planes launched devastating air attacks on Egypt, Jordan and Syria, and virtually destroyed these countries' air forces on the ground. With control of the air, Israeli forces moved quickly: on the Egyptian front, they captured the Gaza Strip and Sinai Peninsula and reached the east bank of the Suez Canal. A large part of the Egyptian army was surrounded and captured at the Mitla Pass. Once the Israeli army had captured Sharm el-Sheikh at the southern tip of the Sinai Peninsula, the closure of the Straits of Tiran was lifted, and Israel could gain access to the Gulf of Aqaba. After four days, with its air force destroyed and army defeated, Egypt accepted the UN call for a ceasefire.

There was heavy fighting between Jordan and Israel for control of the Old City of East Jerusalem, before it was captured by the Israelis. This outcome placed the western wall of the Temple complex (the Wailing Wall) and the Temple Mount, sites of special significance to Judaism, in Israeli hands. By the time that Jordan accepted the UN ceasefire on the third day of the war, all of the territory west of the Jordan River (the West Bank) was in Israeli hands. While the war in Sinai and Jordan was going on, there was limited shelling by the Syrian army into northern Israel from the Golan Heights. After the fighting against Egypt and Jordan ended, the IDF turned its attention northwards. It attacked and captured the Golan Heights, before accepting the UN-sponsored ceasefire.

A map showing Israeli conquests in the 1967 War; the red areas became known as the 'occupied territories'

hawkishness This term is used to describe policies that favour strong, militant or hardline policies, or even aggressiveness. The term 'dovishness' is used for policies that favour the peaceful resolution of conflict, through negotiation or diplomacy.

[Map showing: Occupied territories legend; Lebanon, Golan Heights, Syria, Haifa, Jordan River, Mediterranean Sea, West Bank, Tel Aviv, Jerusalem, Gaza, Beersheba, Jordan, Israel, Suez Canal, Egypt, Sinai, Saudi Arabia, Strait of Tiran, Gulf of Aqaba, Sharm el-Sheikh, Red Sea; scale 0–50 km, 0–50 miles; N compass]

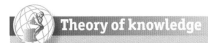 **Theory of knowledge**

Historical truth
Consider this extract from a news report from the *Cape Times*, 20 October 2010: 'Israel's former dovish education minister, Yuli Tamir, sparked controversy in December 2006 when she said that textbooks should show Israel's borders prior to the 1967 Six Day War, during which it conquered Sinai, the Gaza Strip, the Golan Heights and the West Bank, including East Jerusalem.'

What are the implications of this report? Why would a statement about a map be controversial? Is a map a representation of a 'fact'? Can a map show bias?

The victorious Israelis referred to their overwhelming success as the 'Six Day War'. The uneven nature of the victory was reflected in the losses on both sides. As many as 20,000 Arab soldiers died, compared to fewer than 1000 Israelis, and thousands of Arab soldiers were taken prisoner. The swift Israeli victory has been attributed above all to the pre-emptive strike, which gave them the element of surprise and enabled them to gain air superiority in a matter of hours on the first day.

Israel's Western arms supplies included French fighter aircraft and tanks, and advanced American electronic equipment that enabled the IDF to monitor Arab communications. This equipment was far more effective than the Eastern bloc military supplies used by the Arab armies. Another factor responsible for Israel's victory was the lack of unity among the Arab armies. Despite their joint defence pacts, the three countries failed to co-ordinate their military forces and in this way force Israel to fight a war on three fronts simultaneously.

The consequences of the 1967 War

Israel

The 1967 War brought substantial territorial gains for Israel, as well as increased security. Israel was now, without any doubt, the dominant power in the Middle East. The areas taken by Israel were placed under military occupation, and became known as the 'occupied territories' (see page 141). Control of these areas made Israel's borders considerably more secure. For example, Israeli settlements in northern Israel were no longer in range of Syrian shelling from the Golan Heights. Israel's control of Sinai also provided a barrier between the Israeli and Egyptian armies.

Israel had taken over the eastern half of the city of Jerusalem, which brought the sites sacred to Muslims and Christians – as well as those sacred to Judaism – under Israeli control. In addition to this, 135 Arab homes were demolished and 650 Arabs in the Maghrabi district were evicted to make way for a Jewish prayer area in front of the wall of the Temple.

The capture of Jerusalem was of great symbolic importance to the Jews. Their decision to annex the whole of Jerusalem and make it the capital of Israel was bitterly resented by the Palestinian Arabs. Yitzhak Rabin, who was Israeli chief of staff during the 1967 War, later defended this decision in an interview that he gave in 1975 (see Source H on page 159).

SOURCE G

Historian Michael Oren explains the benefits of the 1967 victory for Israel.

Israel had conquered 42 000 square miles [nearly 109 000 square km] and was now three and a half times its original size. Exceedingly vulnerable before the war, its major cities all within range of Arab guns, the Jewish state now threatened Damascus, Cairo, and Amman. Its own capital, Jerusalem, was united. Though ties had been severed with the Soviet Union and permanent strains left in its relations with France … Israel had earned the solid respect of the United States …

Moribund before the war, Israel's economy suddenly flourished as tourists and donations flooded the country, and oil was extracted from Sinai wells. Emigration all but ceased, and thousands of new immigrants hastened to partake of the glory.

Israel indeed basked in that glory as its press for weeks afterward praised the army's audacity, its ingenuity and power. Ha'aretz [an Israeli newspaper] informed its readers of the minting of a new victory coin, and supplied a recipe for 'victory cakes' to be baked for homecoming soldiers. 'From the podium of the UN, I proclaimed the glorious triumph of the IDF and the redemption of Jerusalem,' Abba Eban [the foreign minister] told a riveted audience in Lod. 'Never before has Israel stood more honored and revered by the nations of the world.'

Oren, M. 2002. *Six Days of War: June 1967 and the Making of the Modern Middle East. New York, USA. Ballantyne Books. pp. 307–9.*

SOURCE H

I believe that Jerusalem should remain a united city and the capital of Israel. Jerusalem is a living city of about 330 000 people, out of which about 75% are Jews, the others are non-Jews.

For 2000 years whenever a Jew was praying, and is praying, he turns his face to Jerusalem. For the Muslims, Jerusalem comes third, after Mecca and Medina. When a Muslim prays he turns his face to Mecca … You cannot just divide [Jerusalem] from the body of the Jewish state – for us, it is the heart of the Jewish state.

Extract from an interview given by Yitzhak Rabin in The Listener, *25 June 1975. Kallaway, P. (ed.). 1987.* History Alive. *Pietermaritzburg, South Africa. Shuter and Shooter. p. 290.*

However, although the Israeli victory had been swift and complete, the war aggravated existing problems. Nearly a million more Palestinians were now living under Israeli control, altering the population balance of the Jewish state. Another 300,000 displaced and embittered refugees had been created, heightening the existing grievances of the Palestinians in the diaspora. In spite of the convincing Israeli victory, the Arab governments still refused to recognise Israel, and so there was no clear prospect for future peace. The speed and decisiveness of the Israeli victory gave rise to a myth of invincibility in some parts of Israeli society, creating a sense of complacency that was put to the test six years later.

According to Avi Shlaim, the war marked the beginning of a new 'era of uncertainty' in Israel's history. The central question was what to do about the occupied territories. Moderate opinion in Israel warned against continued occupation, believing that this would make a negotiated settlement between Israel and the Arab governments impossible. Others, however, including religious Zionists and nationalists, welcomed the new opportunities for expansion. The debate created political divisions in Israel.

SOURCE I

Religious Zionists, impassioned nationalists and security specialists now all argued for a Greater Israel. All of a sudden, a besieged state now experienced the freedom of space, but the price was a fragmentation of its unity. Holding the territories now became the status quo. A stunning military victory had laid the foundations for the advance of the Israeli Right after decades in the political wilderness.

Shindler, C. 2008. A History of Modern Israel. *Cambridge, UK. Cambridge University Press. p. 125.*

159

Question

What were the advantages and disadvantages to Israel of its victory in the 1967 War?

Israel's decision to hold on to the occupied territories increased Arab hostility and international criticism. This was especially true when it involved the destruction of Arab homes and villages and the building of new Jewish settlements, especially on the West Bank. Some of those who criticised this decision suggested that the occupation of these territories had been the motivation behind Israel's pre-emptive strike at the beginning of the war. This viewpoint is reflected in the cartoon below.

*A cartoon by Zapiro (**Jonathan Shapiro**); it appeared in the Mail and Guardian, a South African newspaper, on 7 June 2007 – the 40th anniversary of the 1967 War*

The Palestinians

The 1967 War had a significant impact on the numbers of refugees in the region. As the Israeli army occupied parts of Jordan, between 200,000 and 300,000 Palestinians fled from the West Bank, many of them becoming refugees for the second time. A large number of these refugees fled eastwards into Jordan, putting additional strains on the country's economy and political structures. Tens of thousands of Syrians fled from the Golan Heights.

After the 1967 War, the entire area that had been the mandate of Palestine was now part of Israel. Another 590,000 Palestinians in the West Bank, and 380,000 in Gaza, were under Israeli military control in these occupied territories. As you read in Chapter 6, the 1967 War increased the determination of radical elements among the Palestinians to strike at Israel.

However, the defeat of the Arab armies and the new realities of the situation after the 1967 War also caused some groups to think differently about the future of the Middle East.

Questions

What is the message of this cartoon? How does the cartoonist use the biblical story of David and Goliath to comment satirically on the issue?

Jonathan Shapiro (b. 1958)

Known as Zapiro, Jonathan Shapiro is a Jewish South African political cartoonist who has published cartoons that criticise the Israeli government and Zionism. For this, he has been condemned by the South African Zionist Federation. In June 2010, this body wrote on its website, 'Over the years Zapiro has constantly vilified Israel, comparing its actions and those of its leaders … to the most extreme Nazism and even distorting history in his efforts to slander Israel.'

Look back at Chapter 6 to remind yourself of the impact of the Arab defeat in the 1967 War on the Palestinians.

SOURCE J

The first fresh thinking among Palestinians about the form to be taken by a new **polity** in Palestine was the proposal put forward at the end of the 1960s, following the June 1967 war ... This proposal originated with the Democratic Front for the Liberation of Palestine (DFLP). It was discreetly but effectively backed by leaders of the dominant, mainstream Fatah movement, who by now had wrested control of the PLO away from Egypt and the other Arab states that had originally sponsored its formation. This proposal called for a single, secular, democratic state in Palestine, in which citizens of all faiths would be equal. The democratic secular model eventually became the official position of the PLO, although the nature of this proposed state was never fully fleshed out ...

While addressing Palestinian aspirations for the 'restoration' of Arab Palestine, this new approach also postulated the equal citizenship rights of Israeli Jews and Palestinian Arabs. In this it marked a significant change from the provisions of the Palestinian National Charter of 1964, and the first acceptance by Palestinians after 1948 that Israelis had full and equal political rights in Palestine alongside Palestinian Arabs.

Khalidi, R. 2006. The Iron Cage: The Story of the Palestinian Struggle for Statehood. Oneworld. Oxford, UK. pp. 191–92.

polity This is the form of government or political structure of a state or society.

Questions

How does Source J suggest that there were changing power relations between the Palestinians and the Arab states after the 1967 War? In what ways does the source reflect a radical shift in thinking?

161

The Arab states

Even before the war had ended, Nasser resigned as president of Egypt. He was reinstated shortly afterwards, however, after popular protests demanded his return. Nasser's prestige had suffered, though, and his power and influence in the Arab world began to decline. In spite of the crushing defeat of the Arab armies, there was no lasting peace. At a conference of Arab states held in Khartoum in Sudan in August–September 1967, the leaders clearly stated their opposition to peace with Israel in the Khartoum Declaration.

SOURCE K

The Arab heads of state have agreed to unite their political efforts on the international and diplomatic level to eliminate the effects of the aggression and to ensure the withdrawal of the aggressive Israeli forces from the Arab lands which have been occupied since the 5 June aggression. This will be done within the framework of the main principle to which the Arab states adhere, namely: no peace with Israel, no recognition of Israel, no negotiations with it, and adherence to the rights of the Palestinian people in their country.

Extract from the Khartoum Arab Summit Communiqué, 1 September 1967. Quoted in Reich, B. 2005. A Brief History of Israel (Second Edition). New York, USA. Checkmark Books. p. 89.

The USSR agreed to replace the weapons lost by Egypt and Syria. The oil-rich states of Libya, Saudi Arabia and Kuwait offered to pay large sums to Egypt and Jordan to repair the damage that they had suffered during the war.

The international community

The speed of the Israeli victory meant that the superpowers were not directly involved in the war, and both of them supported the UN calls for a ceasefire. After the war, the arms race in the Middle East intensified. As well as replacing the weapons destroyed during the war, the USSR provided surface-to-air missiles to Egypt and Syria, in order to prevent a repetition of the destruction of their air forces on the ground. The USA became more firmly committed to supporting Israel, and remained its main arms supplier.

In November 1967, the United Nations Security Council drew up Resolution 242, which was signed by Israel, Egypt and Jordan (but not Syria). This Resolution was adopted unanimously by the Security Council on 22 November 1967.

SOURCE 1

The Security Council,

1. *Affirms* that the fulfilment of Charter principles requires the establishment of a just and lasting peace in the Middle East which should include the application of both the following principles:
(i) Withdrawal of Israeli armed forces from territories occupied in the recent conflict;
(ii) Termination of all claims or states of belligerency and respect for and acknowledgment of the sovereignty, territorial integrity and political independence of every State in the area and their right to live in peace within secure and recognized boundaries free from threats or acts of force;

2. *Affirms further* the necessity
(a) For guaranteeing freedom of navigation through international waterways in the area;
(b) For achieving a just settlement of the refugee problem;
(c) For guaranteeing the territorial inviolability and political independence of every State in the area, through measures including the establishment of demilitarized zones.

Extract from UN Resolution 242, which was adopted unanimously by the Security Council on 22 November 1967. UN Information System on the Question of Palestine (UNISPAL). http://unispal.un.org/unispal.nsf/0/7D35E1F 729DF491C85256EE700686136

Questions

What similarities does Goldschmidt imply between the Hussein-McMahon letters, the Balfour Declaration and Resolution 242? How appropriate is his assessment of them?

Gregory Harms suggests that, under the influence of the USA and the USSR, the UN produced a document that was loosely worded enough to satisfy both sides. However, he points out that the wording was ambiguous: it called for an Israeli withdrawal 'from territories occupied', which the Israelis took to mean *some* of the territories, and the Arabs interpreted as *all* of the territories. Harms quotes the words of historian Arthur Goldschmidt, who wrote that Resolution 242 'joined the Hussein-McMahon Correspondence and the Balfour Declaration in that gallery of ambiguous documents complicating the Arab–Israeli conflict'.

The essence of Resolution 242 was a 'land-for-peace' agreement: Israel should withdraw from the territory it had occupied, and in return the Arab states should recognise Israel. No solution to the situation of the Palestinians was suggested – other than urging a 'just settlement of the refugee problem'. Resolution 242 became the basis for all future peace negotiations between Israel and the Arab states. However, although they had signed the agreement, the Arab states still refused to recognise Israel. Israel in turn refused to withdraw from the occupied territories. As a result, Israel began to lose some international sympathy and support for what was perceived as stubbornness in refusing to return these territories.

The closure of the Suez Canal by an Egyptian blockade affected international trade for years following the war. The canal was only reopened in 1975, as part of an Egyptian attempt to restore its economy and improve relations with the West. Fourteen cargo ships that had been trapped in the canal for eight years were finally released.

> **Fact**
> During the closure of the Suez Canal between 1967 and 1975, shipping between Asia and Europe was forced to make the longer journey around the Cape of Good Hope. Even after the Suez Canal was reopened, large supertankers continued to use the Cape sea route because they were too big to use the canal. In recent years, some other shipping has also reverted to using the longer route because of the dangers of piracy off the Somali coast.

Activities

1 Historians sometimes categorise the causes of wars into these three types:

long-term causes: the background to the war; the pre-existing situation that made conflict likely; how events in the past contributed to later tensions
short-term causes: more recent events
immediate causes: the events that triggered the conflict; the sparks that led to the outbreak of war

Analyse the causes of the 1967 War and divide them into the three categories shown in this table:

The 1967 War		
Long-term causes	Short-term causes	Immediate causes

2 Write an argument either to support or to oppose this statement: 'Israel was justified in launching a pre-emptive strike on 5 June 1967. All the signs pointed to an impending attack by the Arab states'.

3 Write a newspaper headline that might have appeared in each of these newspapers during the series of crises (in May–June 1967) that led to the outbreak of war. Your headlines should reflect the appropriate bias.

- *Al Ahram* (Cairo)
- *Ha'aretz* (Jerusalem)
- *Pravda* (Moscow)
- *The New York Times*
- The *Guardian* (London)
- *The Times of India* (Delhi)

Then write a short paragraph to explain which of these newspapers you think would be most useful to a historian studying the causes of the 1967 War.

5 Read these quotations from two revisionist historians about the outcome of the 1967 War. Explain what each quotation is suggesting about the links between Israel's victory and Zionism. How do you think a Zionist historian would respond to these statements?

- 'The victory re-opened the old question about the territorial aims of Zionism.' (Avi Shlaim)
- 'Large areas of new territory were now in the hands of an ideological movement obsessed with space and land.' (Ilan Pappe)

163

Gunnar Jarring (1907–2002)

Jarring was a Swedish diplomat, who served as the special envoy of the UN secretary-general in the Middle East between the 1967 and 1973 Wars. He tried unsuccessfully to persuade the Israeli and Arab governments to implement UN Resolution 242.

Hafez al-Assad (1930–2000)

Al-Assad was a pilot in the Syrian air force, and a member of the Ba'ath Party. He served as minister of defence before seizing power in a bloodless coup in 1970. His government was recognised for bringing stability to Syria, but also for increasing authoritarian control. Al-Assad served as president of Syria from 1970 until his death in 2000, after which he was succeeded by his son, Bashar al-Assad.

What were the causes, events and consequences of the 1973 War?

The Middle East between 1967 and 1973

After the passing of Resolution 242, the United Nations secretary-general – U Thant – appointed a special representative, **Gunnar Jarring** of Sweden, to promote diplomatic negotiation in the Middle East. Jarring was based in Cyprus, and from there he flew to meet with the Israeli and Arab governments. According to Gregory Harms, Jarring encountered an 'openness to talks' from the Jordanian and Egyptian governments, while 'Israel stood inflexibly on its position and resisted Gunnar Jarring's peace mission to the region'.

In spite of the UN peace mission, and in opposition to its aims, the arms race in the Middle East intensified after 1967. France applied an arms embargo against Israel after the 1967 War, so the USA replaced France as the chief supplier of arms to Israel. The USSR provided the latest weapons, as well as technicians and training, to the Egyptian army. However, Nasser resisted Soviet attempts to establish a naval base in Egypt. In 1970, after **Hafez al-Assad** – the former defence minister – seized power in Syria, he strengthened Syria's links with the USSR and obtained financial and military aid to rebuild and strengthen Syria's army.

The Arab defeat in the 1967 War led to a change in the attitude of the Arab governments towards the Palestinians. Until then they had believed that the combined force of the Arab armies could defeat Israel and liberate Palestine, but the overwhelming success of the IDF in the war forced them to accept that this was unlikely. The Arab states had previously been hesitant to support the creation of a separate Palestinian authority. However, they were now prepared to accept the need for an armed struggle by the Palestinians themselves, in order to achieve the goal of liberating Palestine.

This view gained more support after Yasser Arafat became leader of the PLO in 1969. During this period, Nasser continued his support for the Palestinian cause, training and equipping Fatah guerrillas. However, with the Israeli occupation of Sinai, *fedayeen* raids into Israel came mainly from Jordan, Lebanon and Syria, rather than Egypt.

After the 1967 War and the Israeli occupation of vast areas of land, including the biblical areas of Judea and Samaria, some political and religious groups in Israel demanded expansion of Jewish settlements into the newly occupied territories. The Land of Israel Movement, founded in August 1967, firmly believed that Israel should retain all of the land occupied in the war. It promoted the establishment and extension of Jewish settlements into these areas.

The movement was encouraged by right-wing politicians, such as Menachem Begin and his Herut Party. The first settlement of this type was made in 1968 at Hebron. This was a site of great symbolic significance, where Jewish settlers had been attacked and killed by Palestinian Arabs in 1929, in the days of the British mandate. The Israeli government was initially uncertain about its attitude towards the new settlement at Hebron. However, the strength of popular support for the move forced it to accept the development, and subsequently support the establishment of further settlements.

These postage stamps demonstrate Egypt's support for the Palestinian cause; in spite of the break-up of the United Arab Republic between Egypt and Syria in 1961, Egypt continued to call itself the UAR

165

Questions

What is the symbolism used in these stamps? What emotions and actions do these designs hope to evoke?

SOURCE M

Colin Shindler explains the significance of the Hebron settlement.

Although many Jews – mainly ultra-Orthodox anti-Zionists – had been slaughtered there in 1929, the resettlement of Hebron was more than a nationalist goal. It symbolized the desire of religious Zionists to settle in Biblical Judea and Samaria. It marked the genesis of the religious settler movement and the colonization of the West Bank and Gaza. They embellished the zeal of the socialist Zionists of the past, but unlike the colonization of Israel, the settlement of the territories was coloured by all the trappings of a colonial enterprise.

Shindler, C. 2008. A History of Modern Israel. Cambridge, UK. Cambridge University Press. p. 141.

Questions

What was the significance of the settlement at Hebron in 1968?
In Source M, how does Shindler distinguish between this settlement and those made by socialist Zionists in the past?

In spite of the determination of certain groups to build new settlements, there were debates within Israel after 1967 about the occupation of Arab lands – and about the form that this occupation should take. Some people initially assumed that it would be a temporary measure, until an agreement could be reached with the Arab governments. Others questioned the morality of even a temporary occupation. There were different views among Israelis about the effects of the situation on the large number of Palestinians now living under Israeli occupation. Some felt that this would bring certain benefits to the Palestinians. Others were outspoken in their criticism of the treatment of the Palestinians in the occupied territories.

SOURCE N

In the immediate aftermath of the Six Day War, the Palestinian population behaved as if in a state of shock. It seemed amenable and cooperative to its new rulers, and there was a general feeling among Israelis that theirs was indeed an enlightened and benign occupation. Israelis were shocked to find how restrictive Jordanian rule had been, and how the Jordanians had very much relegated the West Bank to subordinate status within the Hashemite kingdom, neglecting its economy and failing to encourage its local institutions and aspirations.

If Jordan had not been a particularly forward-looking power, despite its Arab, Muslim and even Palestinian affinities, Israel had confidence that it could be a benign occupier, capable of enhancing the prosperity of the whole region …

Whether occupiers could ever be respected, whether occupation could ever be benign, was a question seldom asked in Israel during the early days of occupation. But even in those early days there were those who asked it, and who were worried at the effect of occupation, both on the anger of the ruled, and the arrogance of the rulers.

Gilbert, M. 1998. Israel: A History. London, UK. Black Swan. pp. 397–98.

SOURCE O

For years Israeli leaders tended to talk about 'an enlightened occupation' when assessing the first decade of Israeli rule in the West Bank and the Gaza Strip. From its beginning, however, when 590 000 Palestinians in the West Bank and 380 000 in the Gaza Strip fell under Israeli **hegemony**, there was little that could be described as 'enlightened' about the harsh and brutal occupation. The first blow inflicted on the population was the Israeli expulsion policy. The pragmatic leadership of the Jewish state, although exhilarated by its sudden acquisition of the whole of ex-Mandate Palestine, was nonetheless nervous about absorbing such a large number of Palestinians. Expulsion was neither an alien concept nor an unfamiliar practice to the Zionist movement …

[T]he threat of expulsion and relocation was one of the many burdens imposed by the occupation on the local population. It is difficult to describe its worst aspects. While mass expulsions took place at long intervals, passive bystanders and activists alike were subjected to military harassment in the form of house searches, curfews and abusive interrogation at checkpoints on a daily basis.

Pappe, I. 2006. A History of Modern Palestine (Second Edition). Cambridge, UK. Cambridge University Press. pp. 194–95.

166

hegemony The dominant influence of one region or country over others in political affairs. It can also refer to the power and influence of some social classes over others.

Activity

Compare and contrast the views of the two historians in Source N and O on the treatment of the Palestinians living under Israeli occupation after 1967.

The War of Attrition 1969–70

After the 1967 War, relations between Israel and the Arab states remained hostile. This was especially evident along the Suez Canal, where Israeli and Egyptian forces faced each other from the east and west banks respectively. After March 1969 this hostility developed into the War of Attrition, when the Egyptian army launched a large-scale offensive and Nasser renounced the UN ceasefire that had ended the 1967 War. Nasser's immediate objective was to force the Israelis back from the Suez Canal. His longer-term objective was to force Israel to withdraw to the pre-1967 border with Egypt. During this **war of attrition**, both sides shelled enemy positions along the canal, sent commando raids across it, and fought aerial battles between their two air forces. Israeli commando units attacked bridges over the Nile and electricity plants in Upper Egypt. They also captured the Egyptian island of Shadwan off the Red Sea coast, where they destroyed radar equipment. The Egyptians attacked the Bar Lev line of fortifications that the Israelis had built on the eastern side of the Suez Canal, and also sank an Israeli destroyer off the Sinai coast. The fighting intensified after 1970 when the USSR supplied Egypt with more armaments, as well as Soviet pilots to fly the aircraft they had supplied.

In the USA, there was greater awareness of – and more public sympathy for – the situation of the Palestinian refugees after the 1967 War. However, **Golda Meir**, who succeeded Levi Eshkol as prime minister of Israel in 1969, managed to convince the newly elected American president – **Richard Nixon** – to continue support for Israel. However, the Nixon government did not want to be drawn into a full-scale war in the Middle East. As a result of this concern, Nixon's secretary of state, William Rogers, put forward a plan in December 1969, and a revised version in June 1970. The Rogers Plan proposed resuming the UN diplomatic efforts to reach agreement about an Israeli withdrawal, the recognition of Israel, and the refugee issue. Egypt and Israel eventually accepted the plan, and agreed to a 90-day ceasefire along the canal, but hostilities began again soon afterwards. The War of Attrition continued, with high costs in casualties and military expenditure to both sides. It finally ended inconclusively in August 1970.

SOURCE P

Unlike the three wars that preceded it, the War of Attrition ended without anything that might be called a victory for one side or defeat for the other. In effect, the seventeen-month-long war ended in a draw. Israel's political and military leaders differed in their assessment of the outcome. Some, including the minister of defense, the chief of staff, and other generals, pointed out that Egypt failed to make any territorial gains in the course of the war. Others, for different reasons, considered that Egypt was the real victor in the war. A candid study of the position of the two sides before and after the war led Abba Eban [the Israeli foreign minister] to the conclusion that the psychological and international balance changed to Egypt's advantage …

The War of Attrition, waged at great economic cost and with heavy casualties, was the longest war in Israel's history. After it came to an end, Meir resorted to a diplomacy of attrition in defense of the status quo, and the eventual result was another full-scale Arab–Israeli war.

Shlaim, A. 2000. The Iron Wall: Israel and the Arab World. London, UK. Penguin. pp. 296–97.

war of attrition This term describes a conflict in which powers slowly destroy the enemy through constant attacks.

Golda Meir (1898–1978) Meir was born in Russia, and emigrated to the USA in 1906 and then to Palestine in 1921. She served as Israeli prime minister from 1969 to 1974, when she resigned following criticism of her government's failure to anticipate the Arab attack in the 1973 War.

Richard Nixon (1913–94) Nixon was Republican president of the USA from 1969 to 1974. As president, he was responsible for the American withdrawal from Vietnam and also for promoting stronger American support for Israel. He was re-elected as president in 1972, but forced to resign following the Watergate scandal in 1974 (see page 172).

Anwar Sadat (1918–81)

Sadat was one of the Free Officers who overthrew King Farouk in the 1952 Egyptian Revolution. He succeeded Nasser as president, and restored Egyptian morale with the success of the Arab armies in the 1973 War. He broke with other Arab countries by pursuing peace negotiations with Israel, visiting Jerusalem in 1977, and signing the 1978 Camp David Accord with the Israeli government. This last act made him a joint winner of the 1978 Nobel Peace Prize. He was assassinated in 1981 by fundamentalist army officers, associated with the Muslim Brotherhood, who were opposed to the peace process.

The situation in Jordan and the death of Nasser

As you read in Chapter 6, the 1967 War had a major impact on the position of the Palestinian refugees. Thousands more refugees moved to Jordan, where their presence added to mounting tensions between the Palestinians and the Jordanian authorities. It also led to an increasing radicalisation among factions of the PLO, and the formation of groups such as the Popular Front for the Liberation of Palestine (PFLP) (see page 141). Western awareness of the Palestinian issue increased substantially after the PFLP hijacked and blew up three Western airliners at Dawson's Field, outside Amman, in September 1970. Although this action did not win Western sympathisers to the Palestinian cause, it did raise awareness of the refugee problem.

In the same month, King Hussein of Jordan ordered his army to attack the PLO bases in Jordan. Both the USA and the USSR were acutely aware that if Israel and Syria became involved, there was a very real danger of another war in the Middle East. Both superpowers put pressure on their allies to act with restraint, although the United States made it clear to Hussein that they supported his actions. According to Ritchie Ovendale, the USA wanted to demonstrate to other Arab states that friendship with the West and a moderate foreign policy would be rewarded with American support. When Syrian tanks entered Jordan to demonstrate support for the PLO, the IDF was ready to intervene – with the USA's backing. In the event, however, Hussein's Jordanian army dealt with the Syrian threat on its own.

In the conflict between Jordan and the PLO, Nasser acted as peacemaker and managed to get the two sides to agree to a ceasefire. However, the tensions affected his health and within 24 hours of the signing of the agreement between King Hussein and Yasser Arafat, Nasser died of a heart attack in 1970. He was succeeded by the vice president, **Anwar Sadat**.

During his presidency, Sadat looked to the USA rather than the USSR for support for the Arab cause in the Middle East; this picture of Sadat and Kissinger was taken during the 1975 Sinai II Accord negotiations in Alexandria, Egypt

Sadat in power

An urgent problem facing the new president was the economic situation in Egypt. The War of Attrition had drained the Egyptian economy. While it continued, the Suez Canal could not be used for shipping, depriving Egypt of badly needed revenues. The cost of maintaining the army in a state of constant readiness for an Israeli attack across the canal was also a drain on resources. Sadat also badly needed a diplomatic victory against Israel to consolidate his position in Egypt and the Arab world. An obvious means of achieving this would be to regain the Sinai Peninsula, which had been under Israeli occupation since the 1967 War. Sadat was willing to recognise Israel in return for this land, but Israel was not prepared to negotiate. The government of Golda Meir was strongly opposed to any move that could be interpreted as weakness on Israel's part. Sadat realised that he needed the support of the USA to put pressure on the Israeli government. This was something that Egypt's ally, the USSR, could not do.

By 1972, Sadat had become increasingly disillusioned with Egypt's alliance with the Soviet Union. He believed that the USSR did not provide Egypt with the same degree of support that the USA gave to Israel. In July 1972, there was an abrupt change in Egyptian policy. Sadat expelled the 15,000 Soviet advisors and technicians who were in Egypt, and the Soviet military equipment and installations set up there after the 1967 War became Egyptian property. The move was popular in Egypt, where there was resentment at Soviet interference – especially among officers in the army. However, with the USA preoccupied with events in Vietnam at the time, there was no immediate reaction from the US government.

At this time, **Henry Kissinger** began to play an increasingly dominant role in American policy towards the Middle East, first as Nixon's security advisor and from 1973 as secretary of state. The lesson that the USA learnt in its costly and unsuccessful intervention in Southeast Asia resulted in a new direction in foreign policy, termed the 'Nixon Doctrine'. This meant that the United States would avoid direct military intervention, and rely instead on regional allies to protect its interests. In the Middle East, the US ally would be Israel. Kissinger worked towards advancing American interests and reducing Soviet influence in the region, even if it damaged continuing peace prospects. Historians such as Avi Shlaim believe that the USA was a greater obstacle to peace in the Middle East than the USSR.

169

Henry Kissinger (b. 1923)
Kissinger served as US secretary of state from 1973 to 1977. His achievements included helping to improve relations with the USSR and China, and negotiating the American withdrawal from Vietnam. He was probably best known for his role in trying to promote a settlement between Israel and the Arab states, through what was termed 'shuttle diplomacy'. This involved travelling frequently from country to country in the region, acting as a mediator between their governments.

SOURCE Q

Although the Soviet Union was allied to the Arab radical regimes, it never questioned Israel's right to exist and indeed offered to guarantee Israel within the pre-1967 borders. Like America, the Soviet Union took resolution 242 to mean an Israeli withdrawal to the old borders with only minor modifications. Unlike America, the Soviet Union strictly rationed the supply of arms to its allies in the region. In fact, the Soviet refusal to give Egypt a military option against Israel led Sadat to expel all Soviet advisers in 1972. All the available evidence suggests that following Sadat's rise to power there was opportunity for a negotiated settlement. The chance was missed not because of the Soviet stand but as a result of Israeli intransigence backed by global strategists in the White House.

Shlaim, A. 1995. War and Peace in the Middle East. *New York, USA. Penguin.* p. 47.

The causes of the 1973 War

By 1973, several factors had contributed to a build-up of tensions in the Middle East. Fatah raids into Israel were a principal cause, together with Israeli reprisal raids on Palestinian camps. The building of Jewish settlements in the West Bank and Sinai worsened this difficult situation. A failure to resolve the issues that arose as a result of the 1967 War was also fundamental to the ongoing conflict. This was aggravated by the increased militarisation of the area, the consequence of arms supplies to the region. Arab states received Soviet weapons, while Israel and moderate Arab governments, such as Jordan, had American military support.

At the same time, the Arab states were moving towards greater unity. In March 1971, Syria and Egypt established a form of alliance with Libya, although neither Assad nor Sadat fully supported the policies and actions of Libya's leader, **Muammar Gaddafi**. Egypt and Syria shared a common interest: to regain Sinai and the Golan Heights before Israel consolidated its occupation by building more settlements in the occupied territories. During 1973, the two countries secretly prepared for war.

By 1973, there was a degree of complacency in Israel about the possibility of an Arab attack. This was caused partly by the break between Egypt and the USSR, and also by confidence in American support for Israel and the flow of military aid. Following the massacre of Israeli athletes at the 1972 Munich Olympics (see page 142), there was also increased international sympathy for Israel. This meant that there was less pressure to give up the occupied territories. In speeches and interviews, the Israeli defence minister, Moshe Dayan, spoke openly about an Israeli state stretching from the Jordan River to the Suez Canal.

Sadat realised that Israel was not prepared to make any concessions regarding the occupied territories. It seemed to him that the only way of reaching a settlement was another war, which would force the United Nations and the superpowers to take more interest in the Arab situation.

Sadat also worked to establish a united Arab front. In January 1973, the armies of Egypt and Syria were placed under joint command. Libya was excluded from this, but contributed to the costs of military equipment. Sadat also made efforts to secure support from both conservative and radical governments in the Arab world. The conservative monarch King Feisal of Saudi Arabia said he would provide financial support. Feisal also agreed to restrict oil production as a means of international pressure, and to ensure that the Gulf oil-producing states did the same. Sadat also negotiated with President Boumedienne of Algeria, to ensure support from the more radical Arab states.

In May 1973, as a symbolic gesture of solidarity, Arab oil-producing countries stopped production for one hour on the day that Israel celebrated its 25th anniversary as a nation. The Arab states gained another diplomatic victory when most members of the Organisation of African Unity, meeting in Addis Ababa in May 1973, agreed to cut diplomatic ties with Israel. After a meeting between Sadat, Assad and Hussein, diplomatic relations between Jordan and Syria were restored, as the two nations settled their earlier differences over the PLO. Egypt's ally Syria obtained an assurance of Soviet support at the United Nations in the event of war. In these ways, Sadat had strengthened Egypt's diplomatic position ahead of the war that started in October 1973.

Muammar Gaddafi (1942–2011) Gaddafi trained as a military officer, and seized power in Libya in 1969 by overthrowing the government of King Idris in a bloodless coup. He published his revolutionary philosophy in a 'Green Book', and introduced a policy of 'Islamic socialism'. Gaddafi ruled Libya as a dictator of an extremely authoritarian regime. His support for international terrorism in the 1980s brought him into conflict with Western governments. His ruthless suppression of protests during the Arab Spring led to civil war in Libya, and ultimately his defeat and death at the hands of opposition fighters.

SOURCE R

Ritchie Ovendale analyses the situation facing Sadat by 1973.

The Egyptian economy was straining: there was the cost of the Aswan Dam; the war in the Yemen; industrial development; and most of all the $8-9 million it had cost to re-equip the defence forces between 1968 and 1973. Egyptians could not be expected to suffer austerity indefinitely. The army was showing the strains of almost five years of total mobilization and some of the conscripts had been in full-time service for the whole period. Egypt, particularly after Nasser's death, had enjoyed more international support for its cause, and some sympathizers felt that it was doing little to utilize it ...

The emerging détente between Russia and the United States could also mean that Egypt would not have another chance. The superpowers could accept the status quo or impose a humiliating settlement in their own interests. A war, even if it was only partly successful, could lead to the opening of the Suez Canal and a source of revenue for Egypt. It could also restore Egypt's flagging position in the Arab world.

Ovendale, R. 1984. The Origins of the Arab–Israeli Wars. London, UK. Longman. p. 191.

171

The events of the 1973 War

The Egyptian and Syrian military preparations, and the initial Arab attack that began on 6 October 1973, were carried out with secrecy. Some historians suggest that the attack was timed to coincide with the Jewish festival of Yom Kippur, the holiest day in the Jewish religious calendar. However, Ovendale states that the day was not selected for its religious significance at all, but because of favourable weather conditions and tides for crossing the Suez Canal. He also suggests that the timing actually helped the Israelis, as most reserve soldiers were either at home or in the synagogues, and the roads were not congested with normal working-day traffic. Religious considerations therefore do not seem to have played a part in the timing of the attack, which was also during the month of Ramadan – the Muslim fast – and therefore not ideal for the Arab armies.

A few hours before the attack, Israeli military intelligence warned Dayan that an attack was imminent. However, Israel did not launch any pre-emptive strike as it had done in 1967. Harms suggests that Israel did not want to risk losing American support. It also did not want to give the Arab states the opportunity to claim that they were acting in self-defence if Israel attacked first.

The Egyptian and Syrian attacks were well-planned, and they gained considerable initial success. Egyptian troops and tanks crossed the Suez Canal, destroyed 300 Israeli tanks, and recaptured half of Sinai. At the same time, the Syrians occupied key positions in the Golan Heights, forcing the Israelis to withdraw. The IDF was taken by surprise, and it was three days before it was fully mobilised and ready to retaliate. However, the Israelis soon took the initiative and staged successful counter-attacks, crossing the Suez Canal and cutting off some of the Egyptian forces. In a major tank battle in the Sinai desert, hundreds of Egyptian tanks were destroyed.

A temporary bridge across the Suez Canal allows Israeli troops to cross to the western side during the 1973 War

Watergate This was a political scandal in the USA, named after the building in which the Democratic Party had its headquarters during the 1972 presidential election campaign. Five men were caught breaking into the building with sophisticated electronic surveillance equipment. It later emerged that they were linked to the Republican campaign to re-elect Nixon, and that the White House was implicated in the break-in. Nixon resigned as president before he could be impeached for obstructing justice. To impeach means to charge a public official with improper conduct while in office.

OPEC The Organisation of Petroleum Exporting Countries (OPEC), formed in 1960, has a significant influence over the world supply of oil and the oil price. It has 12 member states – from the Middle East, Africa and Latin America – that between them control one-third of the world's oil production, and hold two-thirds of the world's oil reserves.

In the United States, Nixon was preoccupied with the domestic scandal of **Watergate**, but the situation in the Middle East had serious implications for the USA. Nixon and his advisors faced a dilemma. It was not in American interests for Israel to be defeated, but at the same time Nixon did not want to risk a possible oil embargo by alienating Egypt, Syria and other Arab countries. Nixon was also aware that the American public would not want their country to become involved in another Vietnam. Above all, he was concerned about how the Soviet Union would react to the crisis. When Israel appealed to the USA for more supplies, Kissinger hesitated at first. However, when the USSR supplied Egypt with more weapons, the USA responded with a massive airlift of arms to Israel. When the Soviets proposed a joint superpower-sponsored ceasefire resolution, Nixon initially rejected it.

The Arab states then used what proved to be a trump card – the 'oil weapon'. They were members of **OPEC** (the Organisation of Petroleum Exporting Countries), which controlled the world supply of oil. They announced a 25% reduction in oil production and a rise in oil prices until Israel withdrew from the occupied territories. When news of the American airlift of arms to Israel became known, Saudi Arabia cut off oil supplies to the USA altogether and raised the price of oil by 70%. This caused Western countries to reconsider their support for Israel. The embargo caused major fuel shortages in Western European countries, and a serious economic crisis. During 1973, the price of oil rose from $2 a barrel to $12 a barrel. The price of oil continued to rise throughout the 1970s, reaching $34 a barrel by 1980. This created a critical economic situation in many countries. The threat to the economies of the Western countries forced them to recognise how much they depended on good relations with the Arab countries, and to reassess their policy towards the Middle East. There was intense behind-the-scenes diplomacy to resolve the crisis so that oil supplies would be resumed.

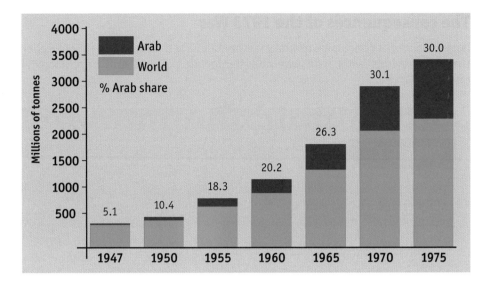

World oil production figures from 1947 to 1975, showing the increasing importance of the Middle East in this market

When the USSR proposed superpower intervention to separate the warring sides in the Middle East, the USA became suspicious. It put its forces on nuclear alert, the highest state of war readiness. For a tense few days there were fears of a world war, but both superpowers were anxious to avoid a confrontation. This was a period of **détente** during the Cold War, and the 1973 War in the Middle East threatened this relative stability. Both Nixon and the Soviet leader, **Leonid Brezhnev**, saw more advantage in co-operation, and so they supported the UN-sponsored ceasefire. On 22 October 1973, the UN Security Council unanimously adopted Resolution 338. Both superpowers put pressure on their Middle Eastern allies to accept it, and UN peacekeeping troops were once again sent to the region to oversee the ceasefire.

détente This was a period of better relations between East and West during the Cold War in the early 1970s.

173

Leonid Brezhnev (1906–82)
Brezhnev was general secretary of the Communist Party from 1964 to 1982, and president of the USSR from 1977 to 1982. Brezhnev supported conservative policies at home, and was intent on maintaining Soviet control in Eastern Europe. The 'Brezhnev Doctrine' (November 1968) was used to justify Soviet intervention in support of communist governments that were under threat.

SOURCE S

The Security Council

1. *Calls upon* all parties to the present fighting to cease all firing and terminate all military activity immediately, no later than 12 hours after the moment of the adoption of this decision, in the positions they now occupy;

2. *Calls upon* the parties concerned to start immediately after the cease-fire the implementation of Security Council resolution 242 (1967) in all of its parts;

3. *Decides* that, immediately and concurrently with the cease-fire, negotiations shall start between the parties concerned under appropriate auspices aimed at establishing a just and durable peace in the Middle East.

Extract from UN Security Council Resolution 338. 22 October 1973. United Nations Information System on the Question of Palestine (UNISPAL). http://unispal.un.org/unispal.nsf/d744b47860e5c97e85256c40005d01d6/7fb7c26fcbe 80a31852560c50065f878?OpenDocument

The consequences of the 1973 War

Israel had won a conclusive military victory but Israeli losses were much higher than in previous wars. The war had significant political and psychological effects in Israel.

SOURCE T

The 1973 Yom Kippur War wrought substantial change in Israel. The war stunned a population that had believed that the Arabs would not dare attack. Also, Israel had lionized its military: In the popular view, the IDF's capability for combat reached near legendary levels. Its intelligence services were regarded as among the finest in the world. At the same time, Arab military capabilities had been underestimated, and senior Israeli decision makers had talked about the absence of war in the Middle East for the next 10 to 15 years.

Israel's confident optimism was eroded by the war, and the subsequent reevaluation tended to breed a feeling of uncertainty. There was a mixture of anger and frustration engendered by political and military factors associated with the conduct of the war. Despite significant military accomplishments, Israel, under international pressure, was unable to achieve its desired goals. In purely tangible terms, the war had perhaps the most far-reaching effect of any of the conflicts to that date … The war shook morale and confidence.

Reich, B. 2005. *A Brief History of Israel (Second Edition). New York, USA. Checkmark Books. pp. 100–1.*

The 1973 War also had negative effects on the Israeli economy. The mobilisation of large numbers of the civilian reserve army caused problems for agriculture and industrial production. The cost of the war in terms of military expenditure, lost production and damage to installations was high, and this resulted in higher taxes. Ongoing economic problems included an extremely high rate of inflation (40%), and the need to continue to draft a large proportion of the young population into the army. To meet ongoing defence costs, the government introduced a tough austerity programme. It raised taxes, introduced a value-added tax, and reduced spending on services such as health, education, social security, housing and welfare.

The war also had internal political repercussions in Israel. Many people questioned the seeming failure of the government and military leaders to anticipate the attack. Right-wing leaders such as Menachem Begin criticised the government's handling of the whole crisis and its acceptance of the ceasefire. They argued that these actions would invite, rather than prevent, future Arab attacks. Begin called on Golda Meir and the defence minister, Moshe Dayan, to resign. In response to these criticisms, the government appointed a commission of enquiry – the Agranat Commission – to investigate the charges. As a result of its findings, a number of senior officials in the military and intelligence departments were dismissed, and in 1974 both Meir and Dayan announced their resignations.

After the 1973 War, there was a shift in the attitudes of many states towards the conflict in the Middle East. This was partly as a result of the oil embargo. Western countries began to put more pressure on Israel to resolve the Palestinian issue. In November 1973, the European Economic Community (later the European Union) called on Israel to withdraw from the occupied territories, and to recognise the rights of the Palestinians. Japan, which had until then adopted a more neutral stance, also called for the implementation of UN Resolution 242 and for Israel to withdraw from all Arab territories. There was increasing international resentment at the continuing tension in the Middle East, and a growing perception that Israel was at fault for not accepting a compromise solution. The new international mood was demonstrated in 1974 when the PLO was invited to attend the UN debate on the Palestinian issue, and Yasser Arafat was invited to address the General Assembly.

The Arab states had lost the war, but it had not been a demoralising defeat as it had been in 1967. They had co-operated successfully, achieved considerable initial success, and taken the IDF by surprise. In this way, the war destroyed the myth of Israeli invincibility, and helped to restore Arab dignity and self-respect. According to Gregory Harms, the Arab attack was 'co-ordinated, well-planned and focused: the Israelis had never seen such intense fighting'. Although the IDF fought back and won, it was an inconclusive victory. Sadat had broken the stalemate that existed before the war. He had forced a change in American policy, and the USA was more willing to put pressure on Israel to negotiate. Sources U and V analyse the implications of the war for Egypt and its leader, Anwar Sadat.

SOURCE U

Sadat emerged from the October War a world statesman, something Nasser had aspired to but never achieved. Relations were established between Washington and Cairo: Sadat perceived that only the United States could effectively persuade Israel to make concessions in the occupied territories. The calculation that the superpowers would prevent a victory by either side proved correct, as did the hope that another war would force the powers and the United Nations to take an interest in the Arab predicament. The October War secured serious Israeli security negotiations on the basis of resolution 242.

Ovendale, R. 1984. The Origins of the Arab–Israeli Wars. London, UK. Longman. p. 195.

> **Question**
>
> Why do historians consider the 1973 War to be a victory for Egypt in spite of its military defeat by Israel?

SOURCE V

Egypt … had scored a psychological and political victory. Sadat's plan to bring his territorial concerns to international attention had worked, and though this cost him a military defeat, he returned a sense of satisfaction to his country as well as adding a feather to his own cap. The US ended up the sole power-player in the region, having secured a newfound relationship with Egypt, Russia's primary client in the Middle East.

Harms, G. 2005. The Palestine–Israel Conflict: A Basic Introduction. London, UK. Pluto Press. p. 126.

The superpowers were more involved in the 1973 War than in any previous Arab–Israeli war. Their involvement was not direct, but they supplied arms and put pressure on their respective allies. After the war, the Middle East continued to be an area of rivalry in the Cold War. However, it was not an area of superpower confrontation in the same way that Korea, Cuba and Angola were.

Activities

1 Design a spider diagram to illustrate the consequences of the 1973 War for Israel, for the Arab states and for superpower relations.

2 Divide into two groups. One group should prepare an argument to support, and another to oppose, this statement:

'The underlying cause of both the 1967 and 1973 Wars in the Middle East was the desire of the Arab states for revenge.'

3 Copy this table, and summarise the significance of each of the listed people in the events surrounding the 1973 War.

	Position held in 1973	Significance of actions at the time of the 1973 War
Anwar Sadat		
Gold Meir		
Hafez al-Assad		
Moshe Dayan		
Richard Nixon		
Henry Kissinger		
Leonid Brezhnev		

4 Find out what you can about the 1973 oil crisis. Look for information on the effects it had on the economies of:

a industrialised nations
b developing countries
c your own country.

End of chapter activities

Summary

You should be able to explain the causes, events and consequences of the 1967 and 1973 Wars between Israel and the Arab states. You should also be able to clarify the role of the superpowers, and their influence on these events. You need to pay particular attention to the complex relations between the Middle Eastern countries and the superpowers, especially the USA, and the impact that this had. You should also examine the role played by Nasser and Sadat in the lead-up to the 1967 and 1973 Wars respectively. You should be able to compare the significance of the two wars for Israel, the Arab states and the Palestinians.

Summary activity

Copy the diagram below. Use the information in this chapter, and from other sources, to make brief notes under each heading.

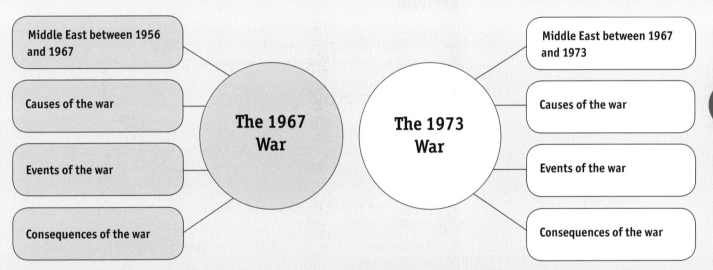

Paper 1 exam practice

Question

According to Source A, what ethical dilemmas did the 1967 War pose for many Israelis?
[3 marks]

Skill

Comprehension of the message of a source

SOURCE A

In the aftermath of the Israeli victory of 1967 many difficult questions were being asked: One of them was whether Jews could, or should, remain an occupying power, ruling over Arab people and land. Another was the question about the nature of a society which had fought three wars in less than twenty years.

Gilbert, M. 1998. Israel: A History. London, UK. Black Swan. pp. 400–1.

Student answer

Source A states that many people in Israel began to question whether it was right for the Jews to take control of land that had belonged to the Arabs and try to control it. They also questioned whether it was possible to rule over such lands effectively.

Examiner comments

The candidate has selected two relevant and explicit pieces of information from the source to explain two of the ethical dilemmas facing people – whether they should, and whether they could, be an occupying power ruling the Arabs. However, the answer fails to explain the ethical dilemma implied in the last sentence, and so fails to give the full message suggested by the source.

Activity

Look again at the source, and the student answer above. Now try to write a brief sentence to give an overall view of the message that the author is trying to get across, and so gain the full 3 marks available.

Paper 2 practice questions

1 Discuss the role of the superpowers in the 1967 and 1973 Arab–Israeli wars.

2 Analyse the foreign policy of Anwar Sadat in the period leading up to the 1973 War, to determine whether he was a more astute statesman than Nasser had been in the lead-up to the 1967 War.

3 Evaluate the extent to which the 1967 War can be considered a success for Israel.

4 Compare and contrast the results of the 1967 and 1973 Wars for stability in the Middle East.

5 Discuss the impact of the 1967 and 1973 Wars on the situation of the Palestinians.

8 Superpower involvement and the Camp David Accords

Introduction

The 1973 War was the last war fought between Israel and the Arab states. The period after the war was marked by intensive lobbying, especially by the USA, to promote a lasting peace agreement in the Middle East. This resulted in the 1978 Camp David Accords between Israel and Egypt, and a 1979 peace treaty between the two states. These agreements were significant because, for the first time, an Arab government recognised Israel as a legitimate state in the Middle East. They also resulted in a rift between Egypt and other Arab governments, which bitterly condemned Egypt's actions as a betrayal of Arab unity and of the Palestinian cause. The agreements did nothing to solve the issues of the Palestinian refugees or of the Israeli occupation of the West Bank and Gaza. After 1979, the Arab–Israeli conflict became in effect an Israeli–Palestinian conflict.

Key questions

- What was the situation in the Middle East after the 1973 War?
- What were the Camp David Accords and their significance?
- What role did the UN and the superpowers play between 1973 and 1979?

Overview

- After the 1973 War, the US secretary of state, Henry Kissinger, acted as mediator to promote peace in the Middle East. The Sinai Accords resulted in better relations between Israel and Egypt, but Israel's relations with other Arab states remained tense.
- The PLO received greater recognition internationally, but the hostility between Israel and PLO guerrillas continued. The economic situation of the Palestinians living under Israeli occupation deteriorated.
- In Israel, there were differing views about the building of settlements in the occupied territories. The election of a right-wing Likud government in 1977 was seen by many, both in Israel and internationally, as a further obstacle to peace.
- From 1977, newly elected American president Jimmy Carter put new efforts into promoting peace in the Middle East. These attempts were initially unsuccessful, due to disagreement over the representation of the Palestinians.

Timeline

1973 Dec: Geneva Peace Conference

1974 Jan: Sinai I Accord between Egypt and Israel

Apr: Golda Meir resigns and is replaced by Rabin

May: agreement between Syria and Israel

Nov: UN grants observer status to PLO

1975 Apr: outbreak of civil war in Lebanon

Sep: Geneva agreement: Sinai II Accord between Egypt and Israel

1976 Jun: Entebbe Raid

1977 May: Likud government comes to power in Israel

Oct: US–Soviet communiqué calling for renewal of peace talks

Nov: Sadat visits Jerusalem

Dec: Begin visits Egypt

1978 Mar: Israeli invasion of Lebanon

Apr: growing support for 'Peace Now' movement in Israel

Sep: Camp David Accords

Dec: Sadat and Begin win Nobel Peace Prize

1979 Feb: Iranian Revolution

Mar: peace treaty between Egypt and Israel signed in Washington, DC

Dec: Soviet invasion of Afghanistan

1981 Oct: assassination of Anwar Sadat

1982 Apr: Israeli withdrawal from Sinai complete

- The stalemate was broken dramatically when the Egyptian president, Anwar Sadat, made a historic visit to Jerusalem. He addressed the Israeli Knesset, urging a peaceful resolution of the differences between Israel and its Arab neighbours.

- To encourage further progress, Carter invited the Israeli and Egyptian leaders to a summit meeting in the USA, where they reached agreement in the Camp David Accords in September 1978.

- Reactions to the Camp David Accords were mixed. While much of the world hailed them as a breakthrough, they were condemned by most Arab governments as a betrayal of the Palestinians and of broader Arab unity. The accords were followed by a formal peace treaty between Egypt and Israel, signed in Washington in March 1979.

- The peace agreement between Israel and Egypt, the strongest Arab military power, brought to an end the conflict between Israel and the Arab states. However, it did not resolve the issue of the Palestinians or of the occupied territories. Conflict between Israel and the Palestinians escalated in the following decades.

- The 1970s were a period of détente during the Cold War, when the tensions between the superpowers were reduced. This had implications for the Middle East. This decade was also a time during which Soviet influence in the Middle East declined, and the US role became more dominant.

- After 1979, the Arab–Israeli conflict became instead an Israeli–Palestinian conflict. It was marked by sustained uprisings (*intifada*) by the Palestinians, and by a determined extension of Israeli settlements in the occupied territories.

Sadat, Carter and Begin after reaching the Camp David Accords, on 18 September, 1978; the agreement was made in the White House in Washington, DC

180

What was the situation in the Middle East after the 1973 War?

After the 1973 War, a United Nations peace conference – supported by both the USA and the USSR – was set up in Geneva in December 1973. However, it failed to make any progress. After such a round table conference proved unworkable, the US secretary of state, Henry Kissinger, stepped in to try to break the deadlock. Using **shuttle diplomacy** between Cairo, Jerusalem, Damascus, Amman and Riyadh (Saudi Arabia), Kissinger aimed to promote direct negotiations and agreements between the Middle Eastern governments. During 1974, he secured partial 'land-for-peace' deals: in the Sinai I Accord, Israel agreed to withdraw from the western side of the Suez Canal; in an agreement with Syria, it also agreed to withdraw from part of the Golan Heights. In return, Egypt and Syria undertook not to use force against Israel to solve future differences. However, the serious underlying issues – the situation and status of the Palestinian refugees, and the continued Israeli occupation of the West Bank, Gaza and much of Sinai and the Golan Heights – remained unresolved.

Egypt and the other Arab states after 1973

Anwar Sadat, who had emerged from the war with an improved reputation in the Arab world, developed a good working relationship with Kissinger. Sadat realised that American involvement was vital to secure Israeli co-operation for any peace deal. He continued to reduce Egyptian ties with the USSR, on which Egypt had depended for arms since 1956. The shift from the Soviet to the Western bloc brought economic benefits to Egypt. Sadat introduced an 'open-door' policy that encouraged and increased private investment in order to revive export industries and reduce Egypt's substantial foreign debts. The 1974 Investment Law gave concessions to foreign companies operating in Egypt. Sadat's reputation as a more democratic and pro-Western leader helped to revive Egypt's tourist trade. This in turn helped economic growth.

After the Israeli withdrawal from the Suez Canal in 1974, Egypt was able to clear the canal of mines and other war wreckage, and reopen it to shipping. Egypt was also able to rebuild the cities along the canal, which had been damaged by shelling during the War of Attrition. The revenues from the reopened canal helped to revive Egypt's economy, as did a growing oil trade.

The Sinai II Accord between Egypt and Israel was reached in Geneva in September 1975. According to its terms, Israel agreed to withdraw from a stretch of territory along the east bank of the Suez Canal, allowing Egypt to regain part of the Sinai Peninsula. However, Israel only agreed to this partial withdrawal after promises of substantial American arms supplies, and an undertaking by the USA not to recognise the PLO or enter into agreements with it. As a result of the Sinai Accords, tensions between Israel and Egypt were reduced. Many Israelis now believed that, without Egypt, any military threat posed by the Arabs was substantially reduced. Historian Bernard Reich believes that many Arabs also thought that in signing these agreements, 'Egypt had been effectively neutralised in the military conflict'.

Relations between Egypt and Syria were strained, as Syria was far less ready to co-operate with the United States. When other Arab states agreed to lift the oil embargo against the USA in March 1974, Syria – backed by Libya – refused to support this move. Syria criticised the separate negotiations between Egypt and Israel, at a time when large areas of Syrian and Jordanian territory remained under Israeli occupation. The Syrians also objected to the exclusion of the PLO from any peace negotiations. Syria subsequently drew closer to the USSR, which had not been part of the 1975 Geneva Agreement.

> **shuttle diplomacy** This term refers to diplomatic negotiations conducted by a mediator between governments which are reluctant to talk directly to each other. It involves frequent travel between the countries involved. Acting on behalf of the Nixon and Ford administrations, Henry Kissinger travelled around the Middle East between 1973 and 1975, in an effort to break the deadlock in negotiations between Israel and the Arab governments.

Since 1970, the uneasy peace between the Christian and Muslim communities in Lebanon had been threatened by the arrival of the large numbers of PLO guerrillas who had been expelled from Jordan. When civil war broke out in Lebanon in 1975, the PLO supported the Muslims and became involved in the bitter fighting. As the situation in Lebanon became more unstable, Syrian forces invaded in June 1976 to occupy the northern part, leaving the PLO to dominate the south. There were increasing tensions and border incidents along the southern border with Israel. This resulted in an Israeli invasion of Lebanon in March 1978, codenamed Operation Litani. Despite a UN ceasefire, an Israeli withdrawal and the presence of a UN peacekeeping force in Lebanon, clashes and attacks between Israel and the PLO continued along the Lebanese border.

The position of the Palestinians after 1973

Arafat speaks before the United Nations in New York, USA, in November 1974

After the 1973 War, the Arab states gave greater support to the PLO by recognising it as the legitimate representative of the Palestinian people. They agreed that the PLO should attend any future Middle East peace conference, and they sought greater international recognition for the organisation and its leader, Yasser Arafat. The Arab states proposed that Arafat should be invited to address the General Assembly of the United Nations in November 1974. This idea was overwhelmingly supported by UN members, despite opposition from Israel and the USA. You can read an extract from Yasser Arafat's speech to the UN on page 143. The General Assembly subsequently agreed that the PLO should have **observer status** at the UN. They also condemned Zionism as a form of racism.

observer status States and organisations with observer status have the right to attend and speak at meetings of the General Assembly, but they cannot vote on resolutions.

As a result of these developments, the Palestinian issue took on a greater urgency by the mid 1970s – both among the Arab states themselves, and in international forums such as the United Nations. Meanwhile, PLO guerrilla attacks and Israeli reprisals continued. In one incident in the northern Galilee town of Ma'alot in May 1974, PLO guerrillas occupied a school and took the pupils as hostages. When IDF commandos stormed the school, 22 children – as well as the guerrillas – were killed. Incidents such as these strengthened Israel's determination not to negotiate with the PLO. This view was later reinforced by the **Entebbe Raid**.

The Palestinians who had come under Israeli control during the 1967 War were affected both politically and economically by the ongoing occupation. In Source A, historian James Gelvin comments on the economic realities of their situation.

SOURCE A

Israeli policies transformed the economy of the territories. The Israelis found a captive market in the West Bank and Gaza Strip. They enjoyed exclusive rights to export manufactured goods to the territories and, because Israeli farmers had access to subsidies denied residents of the territories, were able to flood the Palestinian market with cheaper agricultural products. Land-use restrictions, production and marketing quotas, Jordanian import controls, and access to the Israeli labor market all served to change the orientation of the Palestinian workforce away from agriculture toward (usually unskilled) employment in Israel. Within four years of the 1967 War, about half of all workers from the occupied territories regularly commuted to jobs in Israel …

Overall, after the 1967 war, Israel integrated the economies of the West Bank and Gaza Strip with its own. This has made separation all the more difficult. And because this integration occurred under compulsion, and because the level of Israeli economic development had far outstripped that of the territories, the effect was to create a colonial-style dependent economy in those territories.

Gelvin, J. 2007. *The Israel–Palestine Conflict: One Hundred Years of War (Second Edition). New York, USA. Cambridge University Press. p. 185.*

Israel after 1973

The Israeli general election, which had been scheduled to take place in October 1973, was postponed until December because of the war. The Labour coalition lost some support to **Likud**, a newly formed right-wing opposition group. However, it was still re-elected, and Golda Meir remained prime minister. Meir resigned in April 1974, after a public outcry in response to the findings of the Agranat Commission. This commission investigated responsibility for Israel's lack of preparedness for war in 1973; it ultimately cleared the political leaders of responsibility, blaming the military leaders instead.

Entebbe Raid In June 1976, members of the Popular Front for the Liberation of Palestine (PFLP) hijacked an Air France plane on a flight from Tel Aviv to Paris, with 96 Israelis among its 250 passengers. They forced the plane to fly to Entebbe in Uganda. There, the hijackers demanded the release of 53 Palestinians held in Israeli and European jails, in return for the lives of the hostages. When negotiations for the release of the hostages reached a deadlock, Israeli commandos staged a daring raid on Entebbe. They rescued the hostages and killed the 13 hijackers. They also killed 53 Ugandan soldiers who tried to resist the raid. Only one Israeli commando was killed – Yonatan Netanyahu, whose brother Benjamin Netanyahu became prime minister of Israel 20 years later.

Question

In Source A, why does Gelvin refer to the economy of the occupied territories as a 'colonial-style' economy?

Likud This is a right-wing political party established by Menachem Begin in 1973. It supported a revival of Jewish culture, based on the ideas of revisionist Zionism. It also promoted the establishment of Jewish settlements in the occupied territories, and opposed the creation of a Palestinian state. Its victory in the 1977 election marked a major shift in Israeli politics. Since then, it has played a dominant role in the country. Four Likud leaders have served as Israel's prime minister: Menachem Begin (1977–83), Yitzhak Shamir (1983–84 and 1986–92), Ariel Sharon (2001–06) and Benjamin Netanyahu (1996–99 and 2009 to the present).

SOURCE B

Historian Avi Shlaim evaluates Golda Meir's term of leadership.

Golda Meir's premiership was marked by a stubborn refusal to reevaluate Israel's relations with the Arab world. She personally had no understanding of the Arabs, no empathy with them, and no faith in the possibility of peaceful coexistence with them. This bolstered a simplistic view of the world in which Israel could do no wrong and the Arabs no right. More than most Israeli leaders, she exhibited the siege mentality, the notion that Israel had to barricade itself behind an iron wall, the fatalistic belief that Israel was doomed forever to live by the sword. Meir was a formidable war leader, but her own policy of immobilism was largely responsible for the outbreak of the Yom Kippur War. In her five years as prime minister she made two monumental mistakes. First, she turned down Jarring's suggestion that Israel should trade Sinai for peace with Egypt, the very terms on which the Egyptian-Israeli peace treaty was to be based eight years later. Second, she turned down Sadat's proposal for an interim settlement, thus leaving him no option except to go to war in order to subvert an intolerable status quo. Few leaders talked more about peace and did less to give it a chance to develop.

Shlaim, A. 2000. The Iron Wall: Israel and the Arab World. London, UK. Penguin. pp. 323–24.

Theory of knowledge

History and perspective

Historians use primary sources to reach conclusions about leaders and events in history. What kind of primary sources would the writer of Source B have used to draw these critical conclusions about Golda Meir's attitude and actions? How might another historian argue against these views? What does this suggest about perspective in historical writing? Are perspective and bias the same thing?

Israeli Arabs march in the Land Day Protest on 30 March 1976, demonstrating against the Israeli government's confiscation of land in the Galilee area; six Israeli Arabs were killed, and around 100 were injured, in confrontations with the Israeli army and police during the protest

The government of Yitzhak Rabin, who succeeded Golda Meir as prime minister, faced several problems during his term of office (1974–75). High defence spending had a negative effect on the economy, and resulted in increased taxes, a higher cost of living and high levels of inflation. There was also the problem of a decrease in immigration and the implications of this for Israel: in 1975, emigration figures almost equalled those of new immigrants. Added to these problems was a growing politicisation of the Israeli Arab minority – those Arabs who were Israeli citizens, and had lived in Israel since 1948. In 1976, there were protests and riots when land belonging to Israeli Arabs was confiscated to use for Jewish settlements in Galilee. Six protesters were killed when Israeli troops opened fire.

During this period, several areas of disagreement between Israel and the United States began to emerge. In 1975, the USA refused to use its veto to block the participation of the PLO in a Security Council debate on the Middle East. It even voiced some criticism of Israeli policies during the UN debate. Israel was critical of the US supply of military equipment to several Arab states – especially military aid to Saudi Arabia, the sale of aircraft to Egypt and the training of Egyptian pilots in American military schools. Another issue on which the two governments disagreed was the building of Jewish settlements in the areas occupied by Israel in the 1967 War.

SOURCE C

The divergence of US and Israeli positions, despite the reiteration of American support during the presidential election campaigns and the continued flow of economic and military assistance, seemed to foreshadow a period of crucial decision. In the last analysis, the time of tranquility Israel enjoyed after Sinai II became only a brief respite from the forces and pressures unleashed by the Yom Kippur War.

Reich, B. 2005. A Brief History of Israel. (Second Edition). New York, USA. Checkmark Books. p. 113.

Activity

Explain the seeming inconsistencies in American policy towards Israel suggested in Source C. What were the 'forces and pressures' that were unleashed by the 1973 War?

The issue of Jewish settlements in the occupied territories caused great debate in Israel itself, and within the Labour Party coalition government. Those who opposed the settlements believed that they would intensify Arab opposition to Israel, and reduce the likelihood of a peaceful solution to the ongoing conflict. Those who supported the settlements did so for a variety of reasons. Some thought that the establishment of a limited number of settlements would be a useful line of defence, while others supported unlimited settlement for other reasons – nationalist, ideological, religious and economic.

The most prominent of the settler organisations, Gush Emunim, was founded in 1974. It viewed the establishment of Jewish settlements in all of *Eretz Israel* as a religious mission, and referred to the occupied West Bank by the biblical names of Judea and Samaria. In some cases, members of Gush Emunim simply built settlements, ignoring official orders. In 1975, they put such pressure on the government that it was forced to compromise by allowing a group of settlers to move 'temporarily' into a former army camp.

SOURCE D

In December 1975 the nature of Israel's position in the West Bank was changed, on a small scale, but irrevocably. For the past two years a fanatical extremist religious group calling itself Gush Emunim (Bloc of the Faithful) … pressed for the widest possible settlement of the whole West Bank. The aim of Gush Emunim was not merely to rebuild settlements where earlier ones had been destroyed – in 1929, 1936 and 1948. Gush Emunim was inspired by Rabbi Zvi Yehuda Kook … who had taught …'that the main purpose of the Jewish people is to attain both physical and spiritual redemption by living in and building up an integral Eretz Yisrael. The territory of Eretz Yisrael is assigned a sanctity which obligates its retention once liberated from foreign rule, as well as its settlement, even in defiance of government authority.'

For Gush Emunim, the Palestinian Arab presence in the West Bank, predating modern Zionism by several centuries, was 'foreign rule' … It saw every square mile of the unpopulated areas of the West Bank and Gaza Strip as areas of predestined and preordained settlement, however close they might be to Arab villages or centres of Arab population …

The impetus given to Gush Emunim by the government's compromise was enormous. Within ten years there were 40,000 Jewish settlers in several dozen such settlements throughout the West Bank. Twenty years later the number had risen to 140,000.

Gilbert, M. 1998. Israel: A History. London, UK. Black Swan. pp. 469–70.

SOURCE E

The right of the Jewish people to the land of Israel is eternal and indisputable and is linked with the right of security and peace; therefore, Judea and Samaria will not be handed to any foreign administration; between the sea and the Jordan there will only be Israeli sovereignty …

Settlement, both urban and rural, in all parts of the Land of Israel is the focal point of the Zionist effort to redeem the country, to maintain vital security areas and serves as a reservoir of strength and inspiration for the renewal of the pioneering spirit. The Likud government will call the younger generation in Israel and the dispersions [the diaspora] to settle and help every group and individual in the task of inhabiting and cultivating the wasteland, while taking care not to dispossess anyone.

Extract from Likud's election manifesto for 1977. Quoted in Laqueur, W. and Rubin, B. 1995. The Israel–Arab Reader: A Documentary History. New York, USA. Penguin. pp. 591–92.

Activity

Use the text and Sources D and E to explain the significance of the settlement issue in Israeli politics.

In other cases, Gush Emunim lobbied for support among political leaders and parties, and became increasingly powerful in the process. As the Labour Party coalition government was divided about whether to support, condone or restrict their actions, opposition leaders and parties seized the opportunity that the emotive issue offered. Notable among these leaders was Begin, leader of Likud – his party used the issue to gain support in the 1977 elections (see Source E).

Likud won the 1977 elections, partly as a result of the settlement issue. This meant that the Mapai/Labour Party was voted out of power for the first time since the establishment of Israel in 1948. Menachem Begin, the former Irgun leader, became prime minister of a right-wing coalition government.

Begin's uncompromising approach towards dealing with the Arab states was a factor that secured his election. He also benefited greatly from the support of the Mizrachi and Sephardic Jewish communities, who had become increasingly dissatisfied with their economic situation and blamed the Labour Party government.

Many people in Israel and abroad saw the election result as a setback for peace in the region. In a speech before the Knesset, Begin declared that he viewed the PLO as 'the Jewish people's most implacable enemy since the Nazis'.

SOURCE F

Ilan Pappe explains his view of the reasons for Begin's victory in the 1977 election.

A coalition of dissatisfied Israelis brought Begin to power: Mizrachi Jews suffering from years of discrimination, religious Jews feeling marginalized in the Jewish state, Labourites shocked by the 1973 Arab surprise attack, and expansionist Jews (both secular and religious) hoping Begin would impose Israeli rule over the occupied territories. The Mizrachi Jews brought Begin to power, but the disappointed Ashkenazi Jews toppled Labour. They did not vote for Begin, but they did not support Labour. Many abstained or voted for a different party.

Pappe, I. 2006. A History of Modern Palestine *(Second Edition)*. *Cambridge, UK. Cambridge University Press. p. 212.*

SOURCE G

Avi Shlaim explains the link between the Holocaust and Begin's political views.

Begin lost his parents and his brother in the Holocaust, and this searing experience haunted him for the rest of his life. As a result, he saw the world as a profoundly antisemitic, extremely hostile, and highly dangerous environment. He perceived Arab hostility as an extension of the antisemitism that had resulted in the annihilation of European Jewry. Throughout his political career Begin had demonstrated hostility towards the Arabs. The experience of the Holocaust intensified his mistrust of all non-Jews, including the Arabs. It seemed to prove that the Gentiles were out to destroy the Jewish people and that only Jewish military power could protect the Jews against this danger. It strengthened his activist instincts and deepened his commitment to the goal of Jewish control over Jewish destiny ... For him and his colleagues ... the lines of cause and effect between the Holocaust and the tenets of Israeli foreign policy were clearer, stronger, and more direct than for any other political group in Israel.

Shlaim, A. 2000. The Iron Wall: Israel and the Arab World. *London, UK. Penguin. pp. 353–54.*

Activity

Look at pages 80–84 in Chapter 4 at the explanation of the different groups within the Jewish population in Israel. With this in mind, discuss this view given in Source F of the 1977 election results.

187

Begin strongly believed that territories such as the West Bank were part of *Eretz Israel* and should be maintained at all cost. Under his government, the expansion of settlements in the occupied territories began in earnest. Within four years, the number of settlers on the West Bank had increased by 400%. Historian Colin Shindler suggests that the increased number of settlements, and their location in strategic places, was 'designed to disrupt Palestinian territorial contiguity and thereby avert the emergence of a future Palestinian state'.

The attitude of the Israeli government under Begin, and his successors, towards the dismantling of the settlements added to the complexities of the Arab–Israeli conflict, and to the difficulties of reaching a peaceful solution.

Construction workers build houses for Jewish settlers in the occupied West Bank, in September 1991

obstacle to peace This was a phrase used by the US government of President Ronald Reagan in the 1980s to refer to the settlements. It was a way to avoid describing them as illegal.

Activity

Explain why, from a Palestinian perspective, the settlements would be both a symbolic and tangible show of Israeli power.

SOURCE Ḥ

Whatever the arguments back and forth, Israeli settlements have certainly proved to be an 'obstacle to peace'. They have been a stumbling block in all negotiations between Israel, its neighbours, and the Palestinians since they were first built. They are a daily reminder to Palestinians and others of Israeli power and territorial claims. The settlements assert these claims both symbolically and tangibly. Those placed on hilltops in the West Bank are not built to blend in with the surrounding environment. To the contrary, they are built to stand out, like Crusader fortresses of old. In the Gaza Strip, where before the Israeli disengagement in 2005 settlers made up .5 percent of the population, settlements took up 40 percent of the land and siphoned off scarce water supplies to nourish the lawns and fill the swimming pools of settlers. Adding insult to injury, settlements are connected to each other and Israel through a network of 'access' and 'bypass roads' – 160 kilometres' worth in the West Bank – that cut through the Palestinian countryside and make the dream of a unified Palestinian state all the more elusive.

Gelvin, J. 2007. The Israel–Palestine Conflict: One Hundred Years of War (Second Edition). New York, USA. Cambridge University Press. pp. 193–94.

Activities

1. Design a spider diagram to summarise Egypt's relations with other governments and organisations between 1973 and 1977. The diagram should include:
   - the UN
   - the USA
   - Israel
   - the PLO
   - Syria.

2. Find out about the situation of the Palestinians living in the Middle East between 1973 and 1979. Compare the circumstances that these different groups faced:
   - Palestinians in Israel (the Israeli Arabs)
   - Palestinians under Israeli occupation in the West Bank and Gaza
   - Palestinians in Lebanon
   - Palestinians in Jordan and other Arab states.

3. Draw up a table to compare the policies of different Israeli governments on key issues. You may use a table such as this one, and fill in the key points in each box.

	Golda Meir (1969–74)	Yitzhak Rabin (1974–77)	Menachem Begin (1977–83)
Relations with the USA			
Policy towards Egypt			
Attitude towards settlements			
Attitude towards Palestinians			
Other			

4. Divide into two groups. One group should work out an argument to support, and the other to oppose, the following statement:

   'The expansion of Jewish settlements on the West Bank proved to be the biggest obstacle to a peaceful settlement of the Arab–Israeli conflict.'

What were the Camp David Accords and their significance?

After the round of shuttle diplomacy that resulted in the Sinai Accords of 1974 and 1975, no further progress was made until 1977. A change of administration in the USA brought a new sense of urgency to the search for a more lasting peace agreement in the Middle East. This resulted in a significant breakthrough – the Camp David Accords of 1978.

The background to the peace talks between Egypt and Israel

In January 1977, the Democratic Party candidate, **Jimmy Carter**, succeeded **Gerald Ford** as president of the USA. Carter saw peace in the Middle East as an important priority, and believed that a new approach was needed to resolve the conflict. He sent his secretary of state, Cyrus Vance, to visit the Middle Eastern capitals with a new proposal: in return for a phased withdrawal by Israel from the occupied territories, and self-determination for the Palestinians in a separate state or a federation with Jordan, the PLO would have to accept Israel's right to existence and to respect its sovereignty.

Jimmy Carter (b. 1924)
Carter was president from 1977 until his defeat in the 1980 presidential election by Ronald Reagan. After his term as president, he won international recognition for his work to promote peace and uphold human rights. He was awarded the 2002 Nobel Peace Prize.

Gerald Ford (1913–2006)
Ford was vice-president to Richard Nixon, and succeeded him as president in August 1974 after Nixon's resignation as a result of the Watergate scandal (see page 172). His pardon of Nixon a month later 'for any crimes he may have committed' provoked widespread criticism. Ford served as president until the end of 1976.

Carter was the first US president to support the concept of a Palestinian homeland. Under the Carter administration, the USA recognised the right of the PLO to represent the Palestinians in any negotiations.

With the support of the USSR, Carter sought to reconvene the Geneva Peace Conference and bring all the relevant parties to the negotiating table. The superpowers issued a joint statement in October 1977, announcing their support for a renewal of peace negotiations based on UN Resolution 242. However, arrangements broke down over disagreements about the form of Palestinian representation at such a conference. Israel refused to accept a separate PLO delegation, and the Arab governments rejected a proposal that the Palestinians should be represented in a joint Arab delegation, rather than by the PLO itself.

Talks about reconvening the Geneva Conference dragged on. Both sides in the conflict raised obstacles, mainly about the representation of the Palestinians at these talks. By November 1977, the new peace initiative seemed to have reached a stalemate. However, this was broken dramatically by President Anwar Sadat. To the surprise of most Israelis – and indeed the world – and to the anger of many Arab leaders, Sadat made an unexpected gesture. He announced in the Egyptian National Assembly (with Yasser Arafat as an invited guest in the audience) that he was willing to go to Israel to discuss peace talks. This was a bold move, as until then no Arab leader had been prepared to recognise Israel's right to exist. Before he went, Sadat made it clear that he saw the Geneva Conference as the means by which to secure the recognition of the rights of the Palestinians and the restoration of their lands. Nevertheless, other Arab states condemned the move, as they believed it could undermine Arab unity. President Assad of Syria warned Sadat that there would be a hostile Arab reaction to the visit.

Historians suggest different motives for Sadat's decision to visit Israel. Bernard Reich believes that Sadat realised that the cost of trying to beat Israel by force was too high, and that he was trying to bridge the gap between the two sides by making a single dramatic gesture. Other historians suggest that a powerful incentive was the economic benefits to Egypt that would result from reduced defence spending and regaining control of Sinai.

Although Begin was suspicious, the Israeli government could not risk alienating the USA, and so responded favourably to the offer. Israel invited Sadat to visit Jerusalem and address the Israeli parliament, the Knesset.

SOURCE 1

Historian Colin Shindler explains how Carter brought new energy and a new perspective to the American standpoint on the Middle East conflict.

Jimmy Carter combined a Biblical sympathy for Israel with a deep belief in using American power to further human rights. He was also the first American President to recognize that the Palestinians had legitimate rights that could not be airbrushed from the political canvas. He vehemently opposed the construction of new settlements and complained about Israeli incursions into Lebanon using military equipment which had been sold to them by the United States. Carter had spoken of the need for a 'Palestinian homeland' in March 1977, but clearly was unaware then of the complexities of the conflict. President Carter was therefore surprised when Begin told him that he passionately opposed the idea of 'a Palestinian entity' because it would inevitably lead to a state. Begin also refused to contemplate a freeze on settlements …

In January 1978, Carter joined Sadat in the Aswan declaration in arguing that the Palestinians had 'legitimate rights' and that Israel should withdraw to the 1967 borders. Begin's refusal to give way on the question of both Palestinian nationalism and the increasing number of Jewish settlements led to a stalemate with Egypt and a virtual breakdown of the dialogue throughout 1978. The Americans were increasingly critical of new settlements by stealth – official recognition for previously unauthorized ones; military encampments turned over to civilian control; unauthorized outposts being designated archaeological sites.

Shindler, C. 2008. A History of Modern Israel. *Cambridge, UK. Cambridge University Press. pp. 156 and 160.*

In his speech to the Knesset a week later, Sadat emphasised the common spiritual heritage shared by Arabs and Jews, rather than focusing on their current political differences. At the same time, he also spoke forcefully about Israeli policies.

SOURCE J

Today I come to you with firm steps, to build a new life and to establish peace. We all on this earth, Moslems, Christians and Jews alike, worship God and nobody but Him …

I did not come to you to conclude a separate peace between Egypt and Israel, for this has no place in Egyptian policy. The problem does not concern Egypt and Israel alone. Hence any peace between Egypt and Israel or between any of the front-line states and Israel is bound to fall short of establishing a durable and just peace in the entire area. Furthermore, it would not be possible to achieve that just and durable peace so pressingly advocated by the entire world in the absence of a just solution to the Palestinian problem …

I came here to you to build together a durable and just peace and to prevent any Arab or Israeli bloodshed. For this reason I declared that I was ready to go to the end of the world …

[P]eace cannot be real unless it rests on justice and not on the occupation of the land of others. It is not right that you should demand for yourselves what you deny to others. In all frankness, and in the spirit that impelled me to come to you today, I say to you: You should give up for once and for all the dreams of conquest, and the belief that force is the best way to deal with the Arabs.

Extract from President Anwar Sadat's speech to the Israeli Knesset, 20 November 1977. http://sadat.umd. edu/archives/speeches/AADI%20adat%20 Speech%20to%20Knesset%2011.20.77.pdf

Questions

What aspects of Sadat's speech in Source J may have alarmed or angered members of the Israeli parliament? What aspects of his visit and his speech would they have welcomed?

Question

How do you think that ordinary Israelis reacted when they heard Begin's response to Sadat's peace initiative?

According to some accounts, Begin's reaction to Sadat's initiative was not encouraging (see Source K).

As a direct result of Sadat's visit to Israel, a gulf developed between Egypt and the other Arab states. This was apparent almost immediately: when Sadat called a conference in Cairo in December 1977, only Israel, the USA and the UN sent representatives. The other Arab states and the USSR refused to attend. Instead, the Arab states met in Tripoli in Libya, where the presidents of Syria, Algeria, South Yemen and Libya issued a statement accusing Sadat of treason.

SOURCE K

Begin spoke after Sadat. It was clear that he was unable to rise to the historic occasion. His tone was hectoring and his reply notable for its harshness and lack of generosity. He delved into the past, ancient and recent, and compiled a long list of Israel's grievances against the Arabs. He did not move beyond Israel's well-recognised positions and made no promises. The president of Egypt, he said, knew before coming to Jerusalem that Israel's views on permanent boundaries differed from those of Egypt. What he proposed to Sadat was negotiations without any preconditions. Begin ignored the Palestinian issue completely and implied that Israel had no intention of giving up control of Jerusalem. His speech contained nothing to encourage optimism.

Shlaim, A. 2000. The Iron Wall: Israel and the Arab World. London, UK. Penguin. p. 361.

Menachem Begin subsequently made a return visit to Egypt, and peace talks between the two countries began. In January 1978, they formed joint committees to keep the momentum of negotiations going, but these broke down in March after the Israeli invasion of Lebanon. The UN was quick to respond to the invasion, and within days passed US-sponsored resolutions calling for an immediate Israeli withdrawal. The UN also established a United Nations Interim Force in Lebanon (UNIFIL) to confirm the Israeli withdrawal, restore peace and assist the Lebanese government in reinstating its authority in southern Lebanon.

Relations between Israel and the United States grew strained during this period, especially over the sale of American military aircraft to Egypt and Saudi Arabia. This went ahead despite the efforts of Israel and its supporters in the USA to get the American government to cancel the sale. According to Bernard Reich, Israel 'perceived this sale as another indication of the Carter administration's tilt toward the Arabs and away from Israel'. During 1978, the US government became increasingly concerned about the attitude and actions of Begin's government. It was particularly worried by Israel's announcement of plans to create 31 new settlements in the occupied territories, and by Begin's assertion that, in his view, UN Resolution 242 did not apply to the West Bank at all.

Begin's actions caused concern in Israel as well. In April 1978, the **Peace Now** movement staged a large rally in Tel Aviv in support of a more flexible approach to negotiations with the Arabs. A petition in support of Peace Now was signed by 350 Israeli academics and intellectuals. Over the next few years, the Peace Now movement held mass demonstrations and rallies to urge the government to pursue the peace option, and pressed for negotiations with the Palestinians. It supported the return of the occupied territories and the establishment of a separate Palestinian state as a necessary requirement for peace in the region. In September 1978, about 100,000 people attended a Peace Now rally in Tel Aviv, the largest mass rally in Israel's history.

Since its creation in 1978, Peace Now has aimed to promote Israeli–Palestinian peace; in 1988, Peace Now led a demonstration of more than 100,000 people, calling for immediate peaceful negotiations between Israeli and Palestinian leaders

Peace Now This is a human rights and non-governmental organisation formed in Israel in 1977, following Sadat's visit to Jerusalem. Its initial aim was to raise public support for the peace process. It condemned the Israeli invasion of Lebanon in 1982. It has continued to oppose the building of settlements, and to support negotiations with the Palestinians and the establishment of a Palestinian state.

Theory of knowledge

History and generalisations
What does a movement such as Peace Now teach us about making generalised assumptions about societies or nations? What is the link between generalisation and stereotyping? Why are they dangerous? How can a historian avoid making generalisations?

By this time, the negotiations between Israel and Egypt had reached a deadlock and relations between the two countries were strained. It took a considerable effort by the Carter administration to get the momentum going again.

The Camp David Accords

In September 1978, in an effort to get the two sides to restart peace talks, Carter offered to act as mediator and invited the leaders of Egypt and Israel to the presidential retreat at Camp David in Maryland, USA. Intense talks between the three leaders and their advisors took place in isolation. The world was kept informed of the progress of the talks in brief communiqués released to the media. The talks lasted for 13 days, after which the leaders signed the Camp David Accords at the White House. There were two agreements: 'A Framework for Peace in the Middle East', which provided the framework for a comprehensive settlement of the broader Arab–Israeli conflict; and a more specific 'Framework for a Peace Treaty between Egypt and Israel', which provided the framework for a **bilateral** peace treaty between the two countries.

bilateral This term means between two states, governments or parties.

In the first Camp David Accord, Egypt and Israel agreed to start talks about the future of the West Bank and Gaza, and about some form of self-government for the Palestinians. The wording was vague and spoke about a 'resolution of the Palestinian problem in all its aspects'. It also mentioned the establishment of a self-governing authority to oversee administration during a five-year transitional period before determining the 'final status' of these territories. However, the two governments were not required to give a firm commitment to implementing this plan within a specified timeframe.

The second Camp David Accord was more precise. The two governments agreed to negotiate and sign a formal peace treaty within three months. Israel agreed to withdraw from the Sinai Peninsula and return it to Egypt within three years. In return, Egypt agreed to recognise Israel officially, and to allow Israeli shipping to use the Suez Canal and Straits of Tiran. The two countries also agreed to establish diplomatic relations.

The fact that there were two separate agreements effectively separated the issue of the future of the Palestinians from a peace treaty between Israel and Egypt. As Colin Shindler comments, 'the linkage between a peace with Egypt and a just solution for the Palestinians had been broken'.

Reactions to the Camp David Accords

The Camp David Accords were hailed internationally as a major breakthrough, and Sadat and Begin were jointly awarded the 1978 Nobel Peace Prize. The accords were generally welcomed in Israel and Egypt, although with a degree of caution. However, both leaders faced hostility from critics in their own countries.

Begin had to persuade the Knesset to support the withdrawal of Israeli troops and settlers from Sinai, and there was enormous opposition from within the governing coalition and from members of his own Likud party. Some of his critics – who had previously been committed supporters of his policies – compared the Camp David Accords to the Munich Agreement of 1938, when the British prime minister Neville Chamberlain had given in to pressure from Hitler. However, when the vote was taken, two-thirds of the members of the Knesset supported the plan, although many members of the right-wing coalition voted against it. Colin Shindler describes the significance of this in Israeli politics: 'The price of Camp David was the fragmentation of the grand coalition of the Right that Begin had been constructing since 1949.'

SOURCE L

Bernard Reich examines the opposing views of Sadat and Begin to the linking of the two accords.

Generally, Egypt sought to achieve the maximum connection between the bilateral Egypt peace process and the overall, comprehensive peace process. Israel sought to reach agreement with Egypt on bilateral questions while reducing the connection between that agreement and the overall settlement of the Arab–Israeli conflict. For Sadat, movement towards Palestinian autonomy was crucial, for it would serve to reduce Arab criticism that he had made a separate peace with Israel. For Begin, any movement towards Palestinian autonomy on the West Bank and Gaza would draw additional opposition from right-wing elements of his party and the religious parties, which were important elements of support for his government. Israel also feared that if the peace treaty were linked to a timetable for Palestinian autonomy, it could give the Palestinians an effective veto over an Egypt-Israel peace treaty merely by refusing to participate in any autonomy discussions and arrangements, thereby preventing the timetable from being met. The Egyptian demand for linkage between the two Camp David Accords, including a detailed timetable for Israel's relinquishing of its military rule over the West Bank and Gaza and a fixed date for the election of a Palestinian parliamentary council, was rejected by the Israeli cabinet.

Reich, B. 2005. A Brief History of Israel (Second Edition). New York, USA. Checkmark Books. p. 126.

Questions

Read Sources J (page 191), L and M. Based on the evidence in these sources, is it fair to accuse Sadat of abandoning the interests of the Palestinians? What other sources would you need to consult to reach a balanced conclusion on this issue?

SOURCE M

Ilan Pappe examines the implications of Sadat's actions for the Palestinians.

Sadat came to Jerusalem, disappointed with previous international efforts to solve the conflict, such as an attempt to convene an international peace conference, which had ended in failure. Incidentally, this last peace effort could have helped the PLO, as the Soviet Union had insisted that its status, the problem of refugees and the occupied parts of Palestine, were to be central aspects of the negotiations. Jimmy Carter, the first American president to locate the Palestine question at the centre of the 'peace process', had fully endorsed this prioritization. It was forestalled by the Sadat initiative, which had been pre-arranged by senior Israeli and Egyptian politicians long before Sadat's historic visit. The Egyptian president knew he would receive the whole of the Sinai Peninsula in return for normalization of his country's relations with Israel …

The Egyptian president had promised the Palestinians that he would link the bilateral agreement to a settlement of the Palestine question, but he never succeeded in doing so. Likud returned the Sinai so that the West Bank and the Gaza Strip would be sidelined in the peace agenda. Both sides concurred on a new term, 'autonomy', as a strategic goal for settling the problem of the occupied territories, which in essence meant the status quo in those areas.

Pappe, I. 2006. A History of Modern Palestine. (Second Edition). Cambridge, UK. Cambridge University Press. pp. 213–14.

Many Egyptians welcomed the Camp David Accords as an opportunity for Egypt to restore its economy and focus on domestic issues. However, others thought that Sadat had betrayed Egyptian and Arab interests. They compared him unfavourably with Nasser, who had stood up to Israel and the West. After Camp David, many Egyptians resented Egypt's exclusion from the wider Arab world, and the country's closer links with the West. This especially worried Islamic activists, who opposed Sadat's willingness to negotiate with Israel and what they perceived to be his submissiveness in the face of American pressure.

This cartoon, published in the Guardian in November 1977, comments on Sadat's role in the Camp David Accords; it shows Sadat walking alone through a parted Red Sea, a reference to the biblical account of Moses leading the Israelites out of Egypt

The reaction to the Camp David Accords in other parts of the Arab world was hostile. Many Arabs felt they were a selfish action on Egypt's part, designed to satisfy its ambition to regain Sinai. They believed that in doing this, Egypt had abandoned its allies, significantly weakened the Arab position and undermined Arab unity in its aim of destroying Israel. They also believed that Sadat had betrayed Palestinian interests by not insisting on a clear commitment from Israel over the position of the Palestinians, and the future of the West Bank, Gaza and Jerusalem. They considered the wording of the accords on these issues to be too vague, in using terminology such as 'self-determination' and 'transitional period' that was open to interpretation and debate. The Camp David Accords were condemned by Arab governments such as Syria, Libya, Iraq and Algeria. Of the 22 countries in the Arab League, only Morocco, Sudan and Oman supported Sadat's move. Jordan and Saudi Arabia expressed their concern, but refused to either condemn or support it. The Arab League and the PLO broke off diplomatic relations with Egypt, and the Arab League imposed a boycott of Egyptian goods.

Although the Camp David Accords proposed that a peace treaty between Israel and Egypt should be finalised within three months, it took twice as long as this. This was partly due to opposing views about the linking of the two accords, and also to strains placed on the negotiations by the expansion of Israeli settlements on the West Bank. Reich comments that these Israeli actions placed Sadat and the United States in an 'awkward position', and raised doubts about Israel's sincerity regarding negotiations over Palestinian autonomy. The Israeli government in turn felt that the USA was favouring Egypt in the negotiations, and being unjust in its criticism of Israel. As a result of the ongoing suspicions, both sides adopted a harder line in the negotiations. Eventually Carter himself flew to the Middle East on a round of shuttle diplomacy between Cairo and Jerusalem, and persuaded both sides to make concessions.

The peace treaty was eventually finalised and signed in Washington, DC in March 1979. On the day it was signed, Palestinians in the occupied territories held a general strike in protest.

SOURCE N

I have come from the Land of Israel, the land of Zion and Jerusalem, and here I stand in humility and with pride, as a son of the Jewish people, as one of the generation of the Holocaust and Redemption …

It is a great day in the annals of two ancient nations, Egypt and Israel, whose sons met in our generation five times on the battlefield, fighting and falling. Let us turn our hearts to our heroes and pay tribute to their eternal memory; it is thanks to them that we could have reached this day…

It is, of course, a great day in your life, Mr President of the Arab Republic of Egypt … But now is the time, for all of us, to show civil courage in order to proclaim to our peoples, and to others: no more war, no more bloodshed, no more bereavement – peace unto you, Shalom, Salaam – forever.

Extract from Menachem Begin's address delivered at the signing of the peace treaty between Israel and Egypt, 26 March 1979. Reich, B. 2005. A Brief History of Israel (Second Edition). New York, USA. Checkmark Books. pp. 130–31.

The significance of the Camp David Accords

Peace between Israel and Egypt

The Camp David Accords and the subsequent peace treaty ended the state of war between Israel and Egypt, and were a significant step towards a resolution of the Arab–Israeli conflict. It was the first peace treaty between Israel and an Arab country, and brought to an end over 30 years of intermittent war between Israel and the Arab states. It was also the first time that an Arab government had accepted Israel as a legitimate state in the Middle East. The two countries set about normalising relations: they established embassies in Cairo and Tel Aviv, exchanged ambassadors, formed trade links, and set up direct communications links by telephone and post.

Most Israelis felt more secure now that the largest Arab country had signed a peace treaty and recognised its right to existence. Now that Egypt was no longer an opponent, Syria alone did not present a significant military threat to Israel. This reduced the prospect of Israel fighting a war on two fronts. Many Israelis considered the accords and the peace treaty to be a triumph for Begin. He had managed to secure peace with the strongest Arab state without committing Israel to withdrawing from the West Bank, or to recognising the Palestinians' right to self-government.

The return of Sinai to Egypt

Despite strong opposition from the settlers themselves, the Israeli government went ahead with its undertaking to withdraw from the settlements in Sinai, which had been built for security reasons in the early 1970s. One of the settlements was the town of Yamit, which had been built as a deep-water port. The government also had to overcome fierce opposition from right-wing Israelis who were against giving up any territory at all. It used the army to evict people from the settlements in Sinai – in April 1982, the last settlers and squatters were removed.

Although the Egyptian government had offered to buy Yamit and other settlements, Begin refused. They were instead destroyed when the Israelis withdrew. Shindler states that this decision was made for both 'psychological reasons and matters of security'. It is significant that the hardline and right-wing Begin, who had always opposed the return of the occupied territories, had agreed to return Sinai to Egypt. However, Sinai was outside the borders of what had been the mandate of Palestine, and Begin had never considered it to be part of *Eretz Israel*.

Egypt's relations with other Arab states

As a result of the peace agreement, Egypt gained the return of Sinai and a chance to rebuild and modernise its economy. However, Sadat had risked a great deal with his bold initiative. He faced the hostility of most Arab governments, and the hatred of extremists who saw him as a traitor to the Arab cause. Sadat had hoped that the PLO and other Arab states would accept the realities of the situation and continue the peace process. However, the attitude of the 'Rejectionists', led by Colonel Muammar Gaddafi of Libya, made this impossible.

Gaddafi assumed leadership of the pan-Arab movement, and Egypt was no longer considered to be the leader of the Arab world. Some Arabs were also angered by Sadat's opposition to Islamic fundamentalism, both inside and outside Egypt. This opposition was evident in his condemnation of the **1979 Iranian Revolution**, and the fact that he gave sanctuary and a state funeral to the exiled shah of Iran. (You will read more about the Iranian Revolution on page 201). In 1981, Sadat was assassinated by Islamic extremists in the Egyptian army, while at a military parade to mark the anniversary of the 1973 War.

The consequences of the Camp David talks

The outcome of the Camp David talks was seen as a triumph for Jimmy Carter, and as evidence of the success of US policy in the Middle East. As a result of the peace treaty, both Israel and Egypt received more economic and military aid from the USA.

1979 Iranian Revolution This started as a popular pro-democracy movement against the autocratic government of the shah. However, it resulted in the establishment of a fundamentalist Islamic republic.

Fact
The importance of Egypt as a US ally was demonstrated by the fact that three former American presidents – Nixon, Ford and Carter – attended Sadat's funeral in Cairo on 10 October 1981. Sadat was succeeded by the vice president, Hosni Mubarak, who declared martial law in the aftermath of the assassination. Egypt continued to receive massive American economic and military aid, despite the autocratic nature of the Mubarak regime. Mubarak was forced to step down in a democratic revolution in Egypt in February 2011. He was put on trial on charges of using violence to kill protestors, and of abusing state power to accumulate wealth.

Some believe that the Camp David Accords and the subsequent peace treaty ended the Arab–Israeli conflict: without Egypt, the other Arab states could not wage an effective war against Israel, and so there were no further wars between the two sides. However, the peace treaty did not end Israeli occupation of the West Bank, Gaza and the Golan Heights, and did nothing to resolve the situation of the Palestinians. Therefore it did not bring peace to the Middle East, or end the conflict between Israel and the Palestinians. Without effective backing from the Arab states, the Palestinians realised that they had to depend on their own initiative. The Palestinian conflict against Israel in fact intensified in the following decades, as you will read in the next chapter.

Activities

1 Divide into two groups to discuss the contributions of Anwar Sadat and Menachem Begin to the peace process in the Middle East. Each group should prepare an argument for a class debate. One group should support the view that Sadat and Begin deserved to be joint winners of the 1978 Nobel Peace Prize. The other group should argue that Sadat, as the leader who initiated direct contact between the two governments and showed a greater willingness to compromise, was a more worthy winner of the award.

2 Write an argument to support or challenge the view that the Camp David Accords were a triumph for President Carter and American foreign policy.

3 Write two short newspaper editorials commenting on the Camp David Accords from the perspectives of two of the countries listed below. The articles should reflect an understanding of the significance or implications for the country concerned, and show the appropriate bias.

   • the USSR
   • Jordan
   • Britain
   • Libya

4 Read the report about the assassination of Anwar Sadat on this website: http://news.bbc.co.uk/onthisday/hi/dates/stories/october/6/newsid _2515000/2515841.stm

   Imagine that you were a journalist working in Cairo in 1981, who interviewed Sadat shortly before his assassination. Draw up a list of questions that you would have liked to ask him, and draft the responses that you think he may have given.

What role did the UN and the superpowers play between 1973 and 1979?

The role of the UN in promoting peace in the region

After 1973, the United Nations continued to play a role in promoting peace in the Middle East. It convened the Geneva Peace Conference in December 1973, at which the Sinai I Accord was signed. After the accord was signed, UN troops were once more sent to act as a buffer between Egyptian and Israeli forces along the Suez Canal. However, the USA bypassed the UN – and deliberately excluded the USSR – in subsequent peace negotiations. Up until this time, the process had been viewed as a joint peacemaking exercise. The shuttle diplomacy of Henry Kissinger and the Camp David negotiations were American rather than UN initiatives.

198

During the 1970s, the UN General Assembly focused more directly on the position of the Palestinians. Shortly after Yasser Arafat was invited to address the General Assembly in November 1974, the UN passed resolutions recognising the rights of the Palestinians – to self-determination, to a return to Palestine, and to observer status for the PLO at the UN. The United Nations also passed a controversial resolution that condemned Zionism as a form of racism.

The UN was drawn into the Middle East once again after the Israeli invasion of Lebanon in March 1978. The purpose of UNIFIL (the UN Interim Force in Lebanon) was to ensure an Israeli withdrawal by June 1978, and to hand back effective government in the southern part of Lebanon to the Lebanese government. It also aimed to prevent the area from being used for hostile operations – such as PLO raids into Israel or Israeli reprisals into Lebanon.

A truck belonging to the United Nations peacekeeping troops moves into Lebanon in 1978, watched by a Palestinian guerrilla standing guard on the outskirts of a southern city

SOURCE O

Ilan Pappe explains how a change in the profile of UN membership by the 1970s contributed to the change in attitude towards the Palestinian issue.

After 1975, with the legitimization of the PLO in the UN, the organization's Middle Eastern resolutions all focused on the refugee question and were much more pro-Palestinian. This was mainly the result of the increase in the number of African and Asian countries in the organization, although the progress in this regard was hampered by repeated American vetoes in the Security Council.

Pappe, I. 2006. A History of Modern Palestine (Second Edition). Cambridge, UK. Cambridge University Press. p. 208.

Question

Why did the Palestinian issue have a greater chance of succeeding in the General Assembly than in the Security Council?

The role of the superpowers

After 1973 the influence of the USSR in the Middle East began to decline, while that of the USA became more dominant. In 1974 there was a rift between Egypt and the USSR, when Sadat expelled the remaining Soviet advisors. Two years later, Sadat withdrew facilities for Soviet warships at the port of Alexandria. After this, Egypt became increasingly dependent on the USA for arms and aid, and Soviet influence was limited to the more radical regimes in Syria, Iraq, Yemen and Libya.

In the immediate aftermath of the 1973 War, however, both superpowers worked together to secure a peace settlement in the Middle East. Both nations were also involved in trying to get the Geneva talks on track. At this time, the US administration was focused on the domestic scandal (see page 172) and the final American withdrawal from Vietnam. As a result, US negotiations in the Middle East were left largely in the hands of Henry Kissinger, secretary of state to both Nixon and Ford. Kissinger played a significant role during 1974 and 1975.

SOURCE P

The American government's immediate reaction to the Sadat visit was surprise, bewilderment, and even apprehension that Israel and Egypt might cut a deal and leave American interests stranded. Secretary of State Cyrus Vance made a rapid visit to both Jerusalem and Cairo, where he was given assurances that close American participation in the process would be welcomed.

Gilbert, M. 1998. Israel: A History. London, UK. Black Swan. p. 489.

At first, he worked jointly with the Soviet Union to promote peace talks in Geneva, and then he acted alone using shuttle diplomacy, effectively excluding the USSR from the process. American policy during this period was affected by two conflicting realities. On one hand was the realisation, after the 1973 OPEC oil embargo, of the importance of maintaining good relations with the Arab states. This meant accepting for the first time that the Palestinians had to be party to any peace settlement. On the other hand, however, American policy makers had to take into account the attitude of the American electorate, which was largely pro-Israel, and the existence of the powerful Jewish lobby in American politics. This affected the extent to which US policy could put pressure on Israel.

Activity

From your knowledge of the Arab–Israeli conflict, suggest examples to support the view that the superpowers 'played a significant role in driving and sustaining the conflict', as James Gelvin states in Source Q.

SOURCE Q

Historian James Gelvin provides an overview of the links between the Arab–Israeli conflict and the Cold War.

It was no coincidence that the Arab–Israeli phase of the conflict began at the dawn of the Cold War and ended soon after American president George H. W. Bush and Soviet president Mikhail Gorbachev pronounced the Cold War over. Although the Arab–Israeli conflict certainly played itself out according to its own internal logic, just as certainly the Cold War rivalry between the two superpowers played a significant role in driving and sustaining the conflict.

Beginning in 1948, when both the United States and the Soviet Union weighed the Cold War costs and benefits before granting recognition to Israel, the two superpowers never for a moment forgot the global implications of their policies in the region. For forty years, American policy makers approached or justified their intervention in the conflict in terms of containing the Soviet Union or rolling back its influence in the region. Thus, Henry Kissinger designed his shuttle diplomacy to marginalize the role of the Soviet Union and make the United States indispensible to all parties in the conflict, and President Reagan pronounced Israel a strategic asset in the struggle against international communism. For forty years, the Soviet Union exploited the conflict in an effort to break containment and gain a regional advantage over its antagonist, hoping that it might translate a regional advantage into a global one. Hence, for example, the Soviet Union deliberately escalated tensions on the eve of the 1967 war to energize an anti-Israel, pro-Soviet Arab alliance, and it restocked the arsenals of its allies in the aftermath of the war. Then, abruptly, the Soviet Union imploded, leaving statesmen and politicians to deal with an entirely new problem: how to define the post Cold War world order.

Gelvin, J. 2005. The Israel–Palestine Conflict: One Hundred Years of War. New York, USA. Cambridge University Press. pp. 229–30.

When Jimmy Carter became president in 1977, he tried to adopt a more even-handed approach to the conflict. His administration believed that the attitude of Begin's government was an obstacle to peace, and openly criticised the building of Israeli settlements as a barrier to negotiations. When the USA announced that it planned to sell military aircraft to Egypt and Saudi Arabia as well as to Israel, Israel condemned Saudi Arabia as a threat to its own security. Israel and its supporters in the USA pressurised the American government to cancel the sale to Saudi Arabia. However, the US Senate upheld the decision to sell planes to all three countries, leading to strained relations between Israel and the USA.

In October 1977, the superpowers co-operated again and issued a joint US–Soviet communiqué to lay the groundwork for peace. It was based on UN Resolution 242, which meant an Israeli withdrawal from the occupied territories and recognition of Israel by the Arab states. The communiqué caused an outcry from the Israeli government and the influential pro-Israeli lobby in America, and the USA retracted from its position. This effectively ended the joint superpower collaboration to reopen the Geneva peace talks. The American government later revived its more direct unilateral approach to resolving the issues. However, it was Sadat's sudden announcement of his willingness to visit Israel that started the peace process again.

After the exchange of visits between Sadat and Begin, the peace negotiations between Egypt and Israel began to struggle. The USA stepped in promptly to maintain the momentum by inviting both leaders to meet with President Carter at Camp David. The American role in the Camp David Accords, and the subsequent peace treaty signed in Washington, was therefore substantial.

It is important to remember that the attitudes and policies of the superpowers towards the Arab–Israeli conflict were part of the wider context of the Cold War. It was one of the regions in the world where the USA and the USSR competed for power and influence. The 1970s were a period of détente when the superpowers tried to improve relations. However, the underlying tensions between them remained, and American peacemaking efforts need to be understood in this context.

Events in the Middle East, and their effects on relations between the superpowers, became more complex during 1979. In February 1979, the shah of Iran – **Mohammed Reza Pahlevi** – was overthrown and replaced by the **Ayatollah Khomeini**, bringing a fundamentalist Islamic regime to power. Pahlevi had been a key US ally in the Middle East, but the hostility of the new regime towards the USA was soon demonstrated. On 4 November 1979, the American embassy in the Iranian capital of Tehran was seized by a radical group. Sixty-eight Americans were taken hostage, and held for over a year before being released. An unsuccessful US attempt to launch a rescue mission was one of the factors that resulted in a loss of support for Carter. In the presidential election of 1980, Carter was conclusively defeated by the Republican candidate, Ronald Reagan. As US president, Reagan adopted a more uncompromising attitude towards the USSR.

Another factor that contributed to the end of détente, and the start of a new phase in the Cold War, was the Soviet invasion of Afghanistan in 1979. The USSR acted to support the communist Afghan regime against an uprising by Islamic militants. The USA responded by increasing its secret support for the militants, the *Mujaheddin*, in their fight against the Soviet invasion. Other Muslim countries also condemned the offensive by the USSR, and this affected Soviet relations with its Arab allies.

Mohammad Reza Pahlavi (1919–80) Pahlavi, the shah of Iran, ruled from 1941 until he was forced into exile in 1979. His modernisation policies and his support for a secular state provoked opposition from Islamic clerics. Pahlavi's regime was known for its brutal suppression of opposition by a ruthless secret police, the SAVAK. After his departure, the monarchy was abolished.

Ayatollah Khomeini (1900–89) Khomeini was an Iranian Shi'ite Muslim cleric. He was exiled from Iran in 1964 because of his opposition to the shah's secular and modernisation policies. He returned to Iran in 1979 and transformed the country into an Islamic republic. Khomeini was appointed Iran's political and religious leader for life. His rule was marked by the suppression of opposition within Iran, and a ten-year war against Iraq.

Mujaheddin The *Mujaheddin* were anti-communist Islamic militants who were backed by the USA and Pakistan in their fight against the communist government and the Soviet occupation of Afghanistan. One of the *Mujaheddin* leaders who received American aid was Osama Bin Laden – who later, as the leader of Al Qaeda, masterminded the destruction of the Twin Towers of the World Trade Center in New York on 11 September 2001.

Activities

1 Make a table to summarise UN actions during and after key points in the Arab–Israeli conflict. Include the major resolutions that were passed, and other significant decisions and actions. You may use a table such as this one, in which some of the details have been filled in.

Key event in conflict	UN resolutions and actions
1947–48 establishment of Israel	UN Partition Plan; Bernadotte's peace mission to Palestine; UN-sponsored armistice agreements
1948–49 first Arab–Israeli war	
1956 Suez Crisis and Sinai War	
1967 War (Six Day War)	Resolution 242
1973 War (October War or Yom Kippur War)	
1975–78 Lebanon	
1973–79 peace talks	

2 Design a spider diagram to illustrate the relationship between the following countries and organisation between 1973 and 1979:

- Israel
- Egypt
- USA
- USSR
- UN.

3 Make a table, such as the one below, to summarise US policies towards Israel and the Arab states under different administrations. In your table, include key points of any policy or action, and short notes of their significance.

President in office	Key events	US policy and actions	Significance
Truman 1945–52	establishment of Israel; 1948–49 War		
Eisenhower 1953–60	1956 Suez Crisis		
Kennedy 1961–63			
Johnson 1963–68	establishment of PLO; 1967 War		
Nixon 1969–74	War of Attrition, 1969–70; 1973 War		
Ford 1974–76			
Carter 1977–80	peace agreement between Israel and Egypt		

4 At the website address below, read the account of the return of the Ayatollah Khomeini to Iran. Find more information on the Iranian Revolution from other sources.

http://news.bbc.co.uk/onthisday/hi/dates/stories/february/1/newsid_2521000/2521003.stm

Write a report, from the perspective of a Western journalist in Iran at the time of the 1979 revolution. Explain the impact that you think the Iranian Revolution may have on the rest of the Middle East.

End of chapter activities

Summary

You should now be able to explain the situation in the Middle East after the 1973 War, and the changes in Israel and Egypt that led to the historic peace agreement between the two countries. You should understand the role played by leaders such as Anwar Sadat, Menachem Begin, Henry Kissinger and Jimmy Carter in the peace process. You need to be able to comment on the significance of the peace process, and the reactions that it provoked. You must also be able to examine critically the role played by the UN and the superpowers, especially the USA, in the Middle East at this time.

Summary activity

Copy the diagram opposite. Use the information in this chapter, and from other sources, to make brief notes under each heading.

Paper 1 exam practice

Question

Compare and contrast the attitudes reflected in Sources A and B towards Anwar Sadat and his visit to Jerusalem in November 1977. [6 marks]

Skill

Cross-referencing

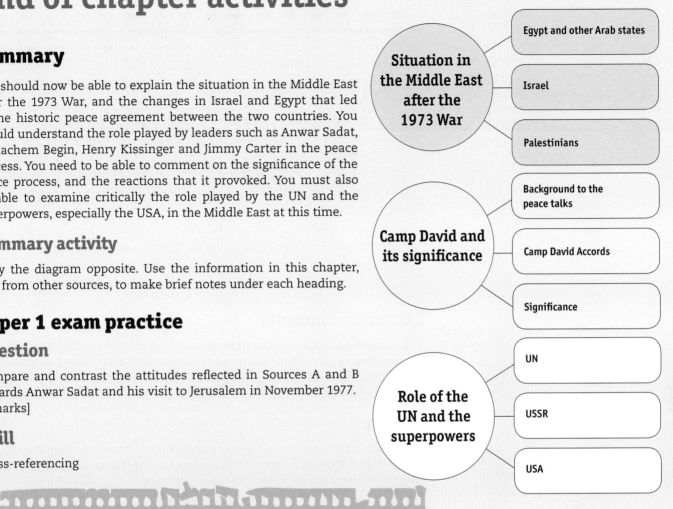

Situation in the Middle East after the 1973 War
- Egypt and other Arab states
- Israel
- Palestinians

Camp David and its significance
- Background to the peace talks
- Camp David Accords
- Significance

Role of the UN and the superpowers
- UN
- USSR
- USA

203

SOURCE A

Anwar Sadat, the man responsible for the October War, arrived in an Egyptian civilian aircraft and landed at Israel's international airport as the guest of the Israeli government. Sadat coined the slogan 'No more war,' and this simple message had a powerful emotional impact on the Israeli public. One of Sadat's aims in embarking on his dramatic trip to Jerusalem was to break down the psychological barrier that in his view made up a large part of the Arab–Israeli conflict, and in this way he was brilliantly successful.

Shlaim, A. 2000. The Iron Wall: Israel and the Arab World. London, UK. Penguin. p. 360.

SOURCE B

It was domestic circumstances that induced President Anwar al-Sadat, who succeeded Nasser as president of Egypt in 1970, to make peace. Anwar al-Sadat never enjoyed the popularity of his predecessor and had to find something he could use to shore up his weak base of support at home. If he could regain the Sinai, which Nasser had lost, if he could sweeten the deal by getting buckets of American aid, if he could divert resources destined for defense to strengthen the civilian economy, he believed he just might be able to win the devotion of his people.

Gelvin, J. 2005. The Israel–Palestine Conflict: One Hundred Years of War. Cambridge, UK. Cambridge University Press. pp. 178–79.

Student answer

Source A has a positive attitude towards Sadat, and praises his efforts to break the deadlock in negotiations. It states that his visit succeeded in breaking down the psychological barrier that had separated Israel and Egypt, because it made a 'powerful emotional impact' on Israelis. The source concludes by saying that Sadat was 'brilliantly successful'.

Source B is more sceptical of Sadat's motives, and suggests that his visit was prompted by self-interest. It states that he went to Israel in order to win support at home by getting Sinai back, as well as obtaining American approval and aid. It suggests that Sadat wanted to win popularity by improving the Egyptian economy through decreased military spending, which would be possible if there was peace with Israel.

Examiner comments

This answer shows a good understanding of each of the sources, but it does not link them at all. It treats each source separately, and there is no attempt to show similarities and differences between them. The candidate has therefore only done enough to get into Band 3, and be awarded 3 of the 6 marks available.

Activity

Look again at the two sources, the simplified markscheme, and the student answer above. Now try to rewrite the answer, linking the two sources by pointing out the similarities and differences between them.

Paper 2 practice questions

1 Analyse internal developments in Israel and Egypt after the 1973 War to explain why it was Egypt, rather than Israel, that was more willing to negotiate a peaceful solution to the conflict between them.

2 To what extent is it true to say that the Camp David Accords achieved only one of their objectives?

3 Evaluate the view that the Camp David Accords were a triumph for Menachem Begin but a tragedy for Anwar Sadat.

4 Discuss the role of the USA in relations between Israel and the Arab states between 1973 and 1979.

5 Assess the impact of the involvement of the superpowers on relations between Israel and the Arab states between 1973 and 1979.

Introduction

Developments in Arab–Israeli relations after 1979 are not part of the IB curriculum. However, in order to understand fully the complexities of the Arab–Israeli conflict, it is important to have a broad overview of this period. This chapter gives an outline of the key developments in the three decades since the peace treaty between Israel and Egypt in 1979.

The 1980s: a decade of ongoing conflict and violence

Mourners at the funeral on July 13, 2005, of two Israeli teenage girls killed in a Palestinian suicide bombing attack in Netanya, Israel

Timeline

1982 Jun: Israeli invasion of Lebanon

1987 Dec: start of first *intifada*

1991 Jan: start of Gulf War

1992 Jun: Rabin becomes Israel's prime minister

1993 Sep: Oslo Accord signed in Washington, DC

1995 Nov: assassination of Rabin

1996 Jan: establishment of Palestinian Authority with Yasser Arafat as leader

Jun: Netanyahu becomes prime minister of a right-wing Israeli government

2000 Jul: unsuccessful peace talks at Camp David

Sep: start of second *intifada*

2001 Mar: Ariel Sharon becomes prime minister of Israel

2002 Apr: Operation Defensive Shield

2003 Apr: 'Road Map' to peace

2004 Nov: death of Yasser Arafat; Arafat succeeded by Mahmoud Abbas

2005 Feb: ceasefire agreement between Abbas and Sharon

Aug–Sep: Israeli withdrawal from Gaza

2006 Jan: Hamas victory in Palestinian elections

Jul: Hezbollah raids into Israel; Israeli invasion of Lebanon

2007 Jun: Hamas seizes control in Gaza

2008 Dec: Israeli invasion of Gaza

2009 Jan: withdrawal of Israeli forces from Gaza

2011 Sep: Palestinian campaign for statehood at the UN

205

The Israeli invasion of Lebanon in 1982

In Lebanon, there was a fragile balance between Christian and Muslim groups. This situation remained tense and unstable, despite the withdrawal of Israeli forces in 1978 as part of the UN-sponsored peace deal. By the early 1980s, there were more than 400,000 Palestinians in the refugee camps in Lebanon. These camps had become the main centre for PLO operations against Israel. In June 1982, Israeli forces again invaded Lebanon, in an operation codenamed Operation Peace for Galilee. The reason given for this incursion was the attempted murder of the Israeli ambassador in London by a faction within the PLO. The UN peacekeeping force in Lebanon was unable to stop the powerful invasion force, which included 170,000 troops, 600 planes and 3500 tanks. Israel's declared aims were to destroy the PLO bases and to establish a security zone of 40 km (25 miles) in southern Lebanon. This zone would supposedly act as a buffer to prevent further *fedayeen* raids into Israel.

However, the Israeli armed forces soon exceeded these aims. They advanced north to the Lebanese capital, Beirut, and besieged the city in an attempt to destroy the PLO bases located there. Beirut was bombarded daily from land, sea and air for two months. Crowded civilian neighbourhoods were reduced to rubble. In this 'Battle for Beirut', more than 20,000 people were killed, most of them civilians. Thousands more were wounded. The once prosperous city of Beirut was virtually destroyed. The USA stepped in to persuade Israel to stop the attacks, in return for an agreement that the PLO would withdraw from Lebanon. American, French and Italian troops were sent to oversee the evacuation of 14,000 Palestinian fighters, and the PLO headquarters, from Lebanon to Tunisia. Arafat was assured of the safety of the Palestinian refugees who remained in Beirut. After the removal of the PLO to Tunisia, the Israelis withdrew their troops from Beirut. However, they continued to occupy the southern part of Lebanon.

A month after the withdrawal of the PLO, the newly elected Christian president of Lebanon – Bachir Gemayal – was assassinated. His supporters sought revenge, and invaded the Palestinian refugee camps of Sabra and Shatila in Beirut. They killed between 1000 and 2000 men, women and children in the worst massacre of the prolonged civil war in Lebanon. Israeli troops allowed Christian militia to enter the camps, and stood by while the massacres went on for two days. Some observers claimed that the IDF shot flares into the air to provide light for the militia to seek out their victims.

News and images of the massacres raised an international outcry. In Israel, there were mass protests about the actions of their armed forces. An Israeli government enquiry placed the responsibility on the defence minister, Ariel Sharon. Sharon was forced to resign, although he later became prime minister of Israel in 2001. Israeli actions further angered Muslims in Lebanon, many of whom joined a radical new organisation called **Hezbollah**. One of Hezbollah's aims was to force the IDF to withdraw completely from Lebanon.

The first *intifada*

By the 1980s, many of the Palestinians in the occupied territories – who numbered over 2 million – were still living in camps built by the United Nations after 1948. Conditions were crowded, amenities were limited, and rates of poverty and unemployment were high. Israel had not formally annexed the West Bank and Gaza, and so the Palestinians living there did not become Israeli citizens. Instead they were under the control of the IDF, which imposed strict military rule in order to prevent resistance.

Hezbollah This is an Islamist political and paramilitary organisation, formed in Lebanon in 1982. Its ideas are based on the teachings of the Iranian Shi'ite Muslim cleric, the Ayatollah Khomeini. Hezbollah's original aim was to force Israel to withdraw its forces from Lebanon. However, it has since grown into a significant political, religious and military force in Lebanon. It is labelled by the West as a terrorist organisation, because of its support for violence and its call for the total destruction of Israel.

The movements of the Palestinians were strictly monitored and controlled by curfews and roadblocks. Thousands were imprisoned without trial. Some Palestinians were deported from the West Bank, mainly to Jordan, their property was destroyed and their land was confiscated for the building of new Jewish settlements. By the middle of the 1980s, 55% of the land on the West Bank and 30% of the land in Gaza was under Israeli control. Tensions in the occupied territories remained high, and were aggravated by the Israeli military presence and the extension of Jewish settlements. The situation was especially tense in Gaza – a strip of territory only 45 km (28 miles) long, and 8 km (5 miles) wide in places, with a population of more than half a million refugees.

In December 1987, matters in Gaza reached a breaking point when an Israeli military vehicle crashed into a truck carrying Palestinian workers from Jabaliya refugee camp, killing four of them. Unrest spread to other villages in Gaza, and to the West Bank. Crowds of Palestinians, mainly young people, threw stones and home-made petrol bombs at Israeli troops. They also erected barricades, often made of burning tyres, in the streets. This was the start of the first *intifada*, or uprising, of the Palestinian people against Israeli occupation. It started off as a largely spontaneous movement, but it developed into a deliberate and sustained uprising that lasted for six years. The uprising was accompanied by strikes and a boycott of Israeli goods.

SOURCE A

Stewart Ross describes the start of the intifada.

In the end, unloved, ignored and downtrodden, the Palestinians of the Occupied Territories spontaneously decided they would take no more. Spectacularly taking matters into their own hands, they rose up against their perceived persecutors. There had always been acts of violence against the forces of occupation, averaging 350 recorded incidents a year between 1968 and 1976. This had risen to 700 a year over the next seven years, then to around 3000 a year in the early 1980s. These figures were nothing compared with what happened next. In the first six months of 1987, the IDF reported no less than 42 355 cases of active hostility towards it. The rebellion had begun.

Ross, S. 2010. The Israeli–Palestinian Conflict. *London, UK. Hodder Education.* p. 192.

The IDF responded with heavy-handed tactics, using tear gas, rubber bullets, water cannons, and also live ammunition. In addition, they were responsible for mass arrests and imprisonments without trial, and beatings by soldiers armed with clubs. The photographs and newsreels of the Israeli repression of the *intifada* brought international condemnation. People were appalled by the violent methods of suppression against mostly unarmed protesters, many of them children. The uprising focused world attention once more on the Palestinian issue. Images of Israeli soldiers firing at children reinforced perceptions of Israel as the perpetrator, and of Palestinians as the victims of aggression.

In January 1988, the Palestinians formed a Unified National Command throughout the occupied territories. Later, there was a split in this Unified Command, with the emergence of a group calling itself the Islamic Resistance Movement – or **Hamas**. This group viewed the *intifada* as an Islamic struggle, rather than simply a fight for freedom from Israeli occupation. Hamas was also resolutely opposed to any compromise agreement with Israel. As Hamas competed with the PLO to gain support, there were street battles between supporters of the two groups in Gaza. The situation in the occupied territories became even more tense when the Israeli authorities closed off access into Israel, thereby preventing Palestinian workers from getting to their jobs.

Hamas This group was established in 1988 by Sheik Ahmed Yassin. Unlike the PLO, it refused to recognise the state of Israel and was opposed to any negotiations with it. Hamas later supported extremist measures, including the use of suicide bombers to target civilian sites inside Israel. In March 2004, during the second *intifada*, Yassin was killed by a missile as he left a mosque near his home in Gaza. He was the subject of a targeted assassination by the IDF.

According to Be'tselem, an Israeli human rights organisation, nearly 1000 Palestinians were killed by Israeli security forces during the six-year uprising. Almost 500 were killed by their fellow Palestinians, on suspicion of collaborating with the Israeli authorities. Around 40,000 Palestinians were imprisoned in Israeli jails. In the same period, 78 Israeli civilians were killed by Palestinians. The *intifada* did not succeed in driving the Israelis out of the occupied territories. However, at the same time, the IDF struggled to end the violent uprising. It made both sides realise the need for negotiations to seek an end to the conflict.

The 1990s: changing attitudes and hopes for peace

Changing attitudes in the early 1990s

By the early 1990s, events and changes – some of them outside the Middle East – had a significant effect on the countries involved in the conflict. The possibility of a negotiated settlement became more likely than at any time in the past. The most important change was a fundamental shift in the balance of world power, in favour of the USA. This was caused by the collapse of the communist governments of Eastern Europe in 1989, the end of the Cold War in 1990, and the collapse of the USSR in 1991.

The United States

With the end of the Cold War, the USA was no longer in competition with the USSR. This meant that American foreign policy was no longer as strongly influenced by a need to keep Israel as a dependable Western ally in the Middle East. Public sympathy and support for Israel was also affected by images of the harsh suppression of protests during the *intifada*. As a result, American politicians were less impressed by the pro-Israel lobby in Washington. During the **Gulf War** against Iraq, Arab states such as Saudi Arabia, Egypt and Syria supported the American-led invasion to liberate Kuwait. The US government was therefore eager to retain the support of Arab governments, and so was willing to put more pressure on Israel. This meant that from 1991 there was a change in US policy: the USA had previously been unhesitating in its support for Israel, but it now called on Israel to stop building further settlements – or else risk losing loans and aid.

The Arab states

The collapse of the USSR also affected the Arab states. They could no longer depend on Soviet military backing, and so it would be even less likely that they could match Israel in any future military confrontation. As a result, the Arab states were more prepared to negotiate, and they put pressure on the Palestinians to do so as well.

The Palestinians

In 1988, the PLO had announced its support for a 'two state solution', meaning the existence of a Palestinian state alongside the state of Israel. This was significant because it was the first time that the PLO had recognised Israel's right to exist. The situation of the PLO also changed radically in 1990. In that year, Saddam Hussein – the leader of Iraq – invaded independent Kuwait, an important source of funding for the PLO. Yasser Arafat's support for Saddam Hussein cost the PLO the support of other Arab states – Saudi Arabia, Egypt, Syria, Morocco, Qatar, Oman and the United Arab Emirates – which were opposed to the Iraqi invasion. Saudi Arabia and Kuwait had supported the PLO financially up until this time, but now cut off aid.

Fact

The Cold War came to an end after a series of successful popular protests overturned the communist governments in Eastern Europe. Their collapse was symbolised by the fall of the Berlin Wall in November 1989. The USSR broke up into 15 smaller and weaker states, which could not rival the power of the USA. The collapse of the world's leading communist state ended the global ideological conflict, and left the USA as the only superpower in a new world order.

Gulf War In 1990, Iraqi forces invaded the small, oil-rich kingdom of Kuwait. This invasion followed disputes over a shared oilfield and the price of oil. In January 1991, a coalition of 28 countries – led by the USA – sent a large army to liberate Kuwait. The war created 2–3 million refugees. It also caused severe ecological damage, as a result of burning oil wells and bombing and missile attacks. During the war, Iraq fired missiles at the Israeli cities of Tel Aviv and Haifa. In doing this, it hoped to bring Israel into the war, and break up the alliance between the Arab states and the other coalition forces.

PLO deposits in Kuwaiti banks were frozen. The Gulf States, such as the UAE, Bahrain and Qatar, also expelled about 400,000 Palestinians who worked there. Some historians estimate that the PLO lost donations worth about US$10 million between 1991 and 1993. This loss of funding meant that the PLO had to cut back on the provision of educational, health, welfare and social services to the Palestinian refugees. The weakened position of the PLO made it difficult for the group to resist pressures to negotiate.

Israel

The Israelis were also under pressure because of the ongoing *intifada*, their inability to crush this uprising, and the negative image that their actions had generated. The changing mood in the USA was also a matter of concern to Israel. The Israeli economy had been weakened by the military costs, the frequent army call-ups, and the closure of borders to Palestinian workers. Many Israelis were beginning to view the occupied territories as a liability, rather than as essential to Israel's security. In the 1992 election, the right-wing Likud Party – which had been in power since 1977 – was defeated. A new government was formed by the Labour Party, which had previously dominated Israeli politics from 1948 to 1977. Yitzhak Rabin, a former IDF chief of staff, defence minister and prime minister, returned to power. The Labour government was more amenable to reaching an agreement with the Palestinians about some form of self-government in the occupied territories.

The Oslo Accords

As a result of these changing attitudes, both sides were more willing to negotiate. The first peace talks started in Madrid in October 1991. The Madrid talks were the first time that the Israeli government had met directly with a Palestinian delegation. Previously, although some Israeli leaders had been prepared to negotiate with Arab governments, they had refused to recognise the Palestinians as an entity with a separate identity. Delegations from the USA, the European Union, Egypt, Jordan, Syria and Lebanon also attended the talks.

The Madrid talks were followed by a series of secret meetings (14 in all) between Israeli government advisors and representatives of the PLO. These were held in hotels and other venues in Oslo, Norway, between January and August 1993.

Rabin, US president Bill Clinton, Arafat and US secretary of state Warren Christopher pose together after signing the Oslo Accord on 13 September 1993

They were sponsored by the Norwegian minister of foreign affairs, Johan Jørgen Holst. Finally, in August 1993, the Oslo Accord was agreed upon. In the following month, the agreement was formally signed at the White House in Washington, DC. The two sides agreed that:

- a temporary Palestinian Authority would be set up for five years, after which a permanent agreement based on UN Resolutions 242 and 338 would be implemented.
- Israeli troops would withdraw from Gaza and parts of the West Bank, and be replaced by a Palestinian police force.
- Israel would hand over responsibility for education, welfare and social services to the Palestinians, but would retain control of defence and foreign affairs.
- within three years, talks would start on the issues of Jerusalem, the Palestinian refugees, Jewish settlements in the occupied territories, and security issues.

Although it was not a final settlement, the world welcomed the Oslo Accord. Yasser Arafat, Yitzhak Rabin and the Israeli foreign minister, Shimon Peres, were jointly awarded the Nobel Peace Prize. Prospects for future stability improved even more in 1994, when Jordan signed a peace treaty with Israel. It became the second Arab state (after Egypt) to do so. In 1995 a second Oslo Accord was signed, in which Israel agreed to further concessions. Over the next few years, the Israelis withdrew forces from Gaza and from several West Bank towns and cities. However, Israel retained control of 60% of the West Bank and 40% of Gaza, and controlled land, security and water supplies.

Not all Israelis supported Rabin's peace initiatives, especially extreme right-wingers who were opposed to any compromise with the Palestinians. In November 1995, Rabin was assassinated by a right-wing fanatic, **Yigal Amir**. After Rabin's assassination, little progress was made in advancing the issues that had not been resolved in the Oslo Accords. In 1996, however, elections were held for the Palestinian Authority, and Arafat won a clear victory. Nevertheless, many Palestinians were frustrated by the slow pace of change, and they switched their support to the more radical Hamas.

Also in 1996, a right-wing government was elected in Israel. The new prime minister, **Benjamin Netanyahu**, announced plans to build a ring of new Jewish settlements around East Jerusalem. This would effectively cut the area off from the rest of the West Bank. The accelerated Israeli building programme, as well as a terror campaign of suicide bombings and other extremist tactics by Hamas, hardened attitudes on the Israeli and Palestinian sides. Little progress was made in implementing the other provisions of the Oslo Accords.

2000 and beyond: deeper divisions and elusive prospects for peace

In 2000, the American government tried to get the peace process going again by inviting delegations from both sides for talks at Camp David. However, the attempt to bring about a new Camp David agreement failed. Tensions between Israel and Palestine remained, and soon erupted into even greater violence.

The second *intifada*

By 2000, the occupied territories were run by the Palestinian Authority, but Israel still had military control. Since the Oslo Accords, little progress had been made on the four fundamental problems: the creation of a Palestinian state, the status of Jerusalem, Jewish settlements, and the right of Palestinian refugees to return to their homes in what had been the mandate of Palestine.

Yigal Amir (b. 1970) At his trial, Amir claimed that Rabin was a traitor to the Jewish people because he had signed away parts of *Eretz Israel* and wanted to 'give our land to the Arabs'. He said that his aim in shooting Rabin was to stop the Middle East peace process. Amir was sentenced to life imprisonment for his crime. Extremist right-wing groups have since organised campaigns calling for his release, which the Israeli government has rejected.

Benjamin Netanyahu (b. 1949) Netanyahu, the leader of the Likud Party, served as Israel's prime minister from 1996 to 1999. He was then re-elected in 2009. He has supported a hardline policy towards negotiations with the Palestinians and the expansion of Jewish settlements in the occupied territories.

Israel had continued to build more settlements, and between 1993 and 2000 there was a 77% increase in the number of Jewish settlers living in the occupied territories. Israel also controlled the water and electricity supplies, as well as much of the land and the main roads. It also restricted the movement of Palestinians by imposing curfews and setting up checkpoints and roadblocks. All of these measures created a growing sense of frustration, bitterness and anger towards Israel among the Palestinians.

In this tense situation, right-wing opposition leader – **Ariel Sharon** – made a provocative move. In September 2000, accompanied by hundreds of armed police, he visited the Temple Mount area of Jerusalem. This was a place of religious significance to Muslims as well as Jews, as it was the site of the Al-Aqsa mosque – the third most holy site in Islam. Sharon's action triggered the second *intifada*, sometimes called the Al Aqsa Intifada. Soon there were demonstrations and riots throughout the occupied territories. There were also protests from Israeli Arabs, the Palestinians living in Israel itself. Historians have debated the reasons for Sharon's controversial move. Some think that he was deliberately trying to provoke the Palestinians, while others suggest that it was a demonstration of Israeli power and authority. Other historians believe that Sharon was trying to score points against his political opponents in Israel. Whatever his motivation, the result was bloodshed on a huge scale. The fighting was bitter and intense, with atrocities committed by both sides.

The Palestinians now had guns, hand grenades and Qassam rockets (home-made missiles), and so were better armed than they had been in the first *intifada*. They attacked Israeli settlements as well as the army. Extremist groups sent suicide bombers into Israel, on missions that were designed to cause panic and fear. These attackers exploded their bombs in crowded streets, markets, buses, discos and restaurants, causing death and injury to civilians. The IDF responded with a massive show of force, using tanks, aircraft and gunship helicopters to crush the uprising. Hundreds of Palestinian protesters were killed, including many children. A new Israeli tactic was to seek out radical leaders whom they believed were behind the uprising, and to assassinate them. In particular, the leaders of militant groups such as Hamas, **Islamic Jihad** and the **Al-Aqsa Martyrs Brigades** became targets for assassination. These organisations were behind the suicide-bombing missions into Israel that caused such fear and outrage amongst Israeli civilians.

In March 2001, Sharon became prime minister of Israel. Many Israelis believed that his hardline tactics were the best way of coping with the *intifada*. However, not all Israelis supported Sharon or his methods, and there were protests. In 2002, Sharon launched a military operation, which he called Operation Defensive Shield to crush the Palestinian uprising. It included plans for a 'security barrier' to seal off the West Bank. This barrier was 350 km (280 miles) long. In some places, it was a barbed wire fence; in others, it was a huge concrete wall standing 8 m (26 ft) high. The official aim of the wall was to protect Israelis against further attack by keeping the Palestinians out of the area.

In the process, 36 Palestinian villages lost land, and another 32 towns and villages were cut off from other West Bank communities. The crossing points were heavily guarded by Israeli security forces. The wall increased resentment and bitterness among the Palestinians, and many critics of Israel referred to it as the 'Wall of Shame'. It failed to stop the uprising, and by the middle of 2003 more than 2000 Palestinians and 800 Israelis had been killed since the *intifada* began.

Ariel Sharon (b. 1928) Sharon fought in all four Arab–Israeli wars, and developed a reputation for using unorthodox and ruthless tactics. He went into politics and helped to form Likud. As minister of defence at the time of Israel's invasion of Lebanon in 1982, Sharon was held responsible for the massacres at the Shatila and Sabra refugee camps, and lost his position as a result. He was also held responsible causing the second *intifada*. He became prime minister in 2001, and surprised many with his willingness to negotiate with the Palestinians and his decision to withdraw from Gaza. He was disabled by a stroke in 2006.

Islamic Jihad This was an Islamist group that was inspired by the teachings of the Ayatollah Khomeini in Iran. Its campaign was a holy war (*jihad*) against all pro-Western governments, especially Israel. It rejected any form of negotiation, and claimed responsibility for many acts of extreme violence during the two *intifadas*.

Al Aqsa Martyrs Brigades This group emerged shortly after the start of the second *intifada*. Some people believed them to be an extremist armed branch of Fatah, but Arafat denied this. This group was secular rather than Islamist in outlook, and their suicide attacks were not motivated by religion.

Thousands of Palestinians and left-wing Israelis demonstrate on the Palestinian side of the 'security barrier' in 2004, demanding that the barrier be taken down

Another peace initiative: the 'Road Map'

In 2003, the USA made another attempt to encourage a peaceful settlement, by promoting a 'Road Map' for peace in the Middle East. This had the backing of the UN, the European Union and Russia. The 'Road Map' was essentially a timetable for the establishment of a Palestinian state in three stages:

- Firstly, the Palestinians should put a stop to suicide bombings and other violence, while Israel should stop building settlements – and abandon any built since 2000.
- The second stage would be the establishment of an independent and democratic Palestinian state.
- The final stage would permanently define the frontiers of this Palestinian state, decide the status of Jerusalem, and determine the right of Palestinian refugees to return.

At first, the proposal failed to stop the violence. However, later that year the Israeli government announced that it was prepared to withdraw from Gaza.

In November 2004, Yasser Arafat died. He was replaced as leader of the PLO and president of the Palestinian Authority by **Mahmoud Abbas**. Abbas met Sharon, together with the leaders of Jordan and Egypt, at Sharm el-Sheikh. Here, they agreed to a ceasefire. This was followed by an Israeli withdrawal from Gaza. However, both Sharon and Abbas were criticised by extremists on their own sides. Hamas remained opposed to any dealings with Israel, and criticised Abbas for his willingness to negotiate. In addition, the issue of Jewish settlements on the West Bank was not resolved – it remained a fundamental problem that separated the two sides.

Mahmoud Abbas (b. 1935)

Abbas was born in Palestine, and fled with his family to Syria at the time of the 1948–49 War. He was educated in Damascus, Egypt and Moscow, and joined Fatah in the 1950s. Abbas became a key member of the PLO under Arafat. He signed the agreement following the Oslo Accord on behalf of the PLO. Abbas gained a reputation as a moderate, and succeeded Arafat as leader of the PLO and of the Palestinian Authority. He was criticised by Hamas for his willingness to negotiate with Israel, and was accused by his critics of being authoritarian and unwilling to relinquish control.

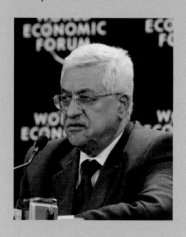

SOURCE B

Nevertheless, the issue of Jewish settlements on the West Bank remained the greatest obstacle to peace. For the peace process to succeed, trust between the two sides was necessary. Although Palestinian violence undoubtedly contributed to the breakdown of trust, the fundamental reason was the Israeli policy of expanding settlements on the West Bank. This policy was carried on under both hardline and more moderate Israeli governments and it prevented the emergence of a viable Palestinian state without which there could be no end to the conflict.

Scott-Baumann, M. 2009. *Crisis in the Middle East: Israel and the Arab States 1945–2007. London, UK. Hodder Education. p. 105.*

Fact

In 2006, former US president Jimmy Carter, the man responsible for the Camp David Accords of 1978, published a book entitled *Palestine: Peace not Apartheid*. In it, he criticised Israel for building what he called an 'imprisonment wall' through the West Bank. He also condemned Israel's 'continued control and colonisation of Palestinian land', which he described as the main obstacle to peace in the region. Carter also accused the US government of intensifying global anti-American terrorism by condoning Israel's actions.

The growth of Hamas and Hezbollah

The conditions of everyday life for Palestinians in the occupied territories continued to deteriorate, and there seemed to be no prospect of a political settlement. Many Palestinians blamed the PLO for its inability to solve these issues. Abbas lacked the popular support that Arafat had inspired for much of his life. Many Palestinians accused the PLO leadership of corruption and incompetence. Tensions between Hamas and the PLO became increasingly bitter. When elections were held for the Palestinian parliament in 2006, Hamas won a majority of seats. However, Abbas remained as the president of the Palestinian Authority. Israel, the USA and many other countries refused to deal with Hamas because of its support for violence, and its refusal to recognise Israel. The 2006 election result therefore made peace seem increasingly unlikely.

Hezbollah fighters based in the south of Lebanon had continued to launch guerrilla raids across the border into Israel. In response to one such raid in July 2006, Israeli forces once again invaded Lebanon. They attacked Hezbollah bases in the south and in Beirut itself, resulting in heavy civilian casualties. Hezbollah hit back with missile attacks on Israeli towns in the north of the country, killing over 100 Israeli civilians. The UN arranged a ceasefire, and once again a UN peacekeeping force was sent to Lebanon. The IDF had failed to destroy Hezbollah, and the potential for future clashes along the border with Lebanon remained high.

Meanwhile, clashes between Hamas and Fatah supporters in Gaza escalated. This conflict ended with a Hamas victory and the expulsion of the Fatah leadership to the West Bank. With Gaza now under the control of the more extreme Hamas, Israel sealed off Gaza's land, sea and air borders. Israel's main intention was to cut off arms supplies to the area, but in the process it also stopped food and medical supplies. With most of the population unemployed, life for the people of Gaza became even worse. The UN and international aid agencies warned of an impending humanitarian crisis in the territory. In December 2008, in response to rocket attacks from Gaza, the Israeli army invaded in an attempt to crush all resistance. By the time the Israeli army withdrew in January 2009, about 700 people had been killed, many of them children. A UN investigation into the actions of the IDF in Gaza found that both sides were guilty of war crimes.

213

The Palestinian campaign for statehood

There had been an attempt to get peace talks going again at the US Naval Academy at Annapolis, Maryland, in November 2007. Although the Palestinian and Israeli leaders both attended the talks, as well as representatives from the Arab states and European Union, this effort was not productive. The same obstacles to peace remained.

In 2009, the Likud leader, Benjamin Netanyahu, became prime minister of Israel once again. By this time, a new American president – Barack Obama – had stated that restarting the peace process was a priority of his foreign policy. However, little progress was made over the next two years. There were serious obstructions on both sides: on the Palestinian side, Hamas refused to enter into any negotiations with Israel; on the Israeli side, new settlements continued to be constructed on the West Bank.

SOURCE C

Settlement activities embody the core of the policy of colonial military occupation of the land of the Palestinian people and all of the brutality of aggression and racial discrimination against our people that this policy entails. This policy, which constitutes a breach of international humanitarian law and United Nations resolutions, is the primary cause for the failure of the peace process, the collapse of dozens of opportunities, and the burial of the great hopes that arose from the signing of the Declaration of Principles in 1993 [the Oslo Accords] between the Palestine Liberation Organization and Israel to achieve a just peace that would begin a new era for our region …

I am here to say on behalf of the Palestinian people and the Palestine Liberation Organization: We extend our hands to the Israeli government and the Israeli people for peace-making. I say to them: Let us urgently build together a future for our children where they can enjoy freedom, security and prosperity. Let us build the bridges of dialogue instead of checkpoints and walls of separation, and build cooperative relations based on parity and equity between two neighbouring States – Palestine and Israel – instead of policies of occupation, settlement, war and eliminating the other.

Extract from a speech by Palestinian leader Mahmoud Abbas to the United Nations General Assembly in New York on 23 September 2011. Quoted in the Egyptian newspaper Ahram. *http://english.ahram.org. eg/NewsContent/2/8/22286/World/ Region/-Mahmoud-Abbas-speech-at-the-UN--The-full-official.aspx*

SOURCE D

The truth is that Israel wants peace. The truth is that I want peace. The truth is that in the Middle East at all times, but especially during these turbulent days, peace must be anchored in security. The truth is that we cannot achieve peace through UN resolutions, but only through direct negotiations between the parties. The truth is that so far the Palestinians have refused to negotiate. The truth is that Israel wants peace with a Palestinian state, but the Palestinians want a state without peace. And the truth is you shouldn't let that happen …

President Abbas just stood here, and he said that the core of the Israeli-Palestinian conflict is the settlements. Well, that's odd. Our conflict has been raging for – was raging for nearly half a century before there was a single Israeli settlement in the West Bank … The core of the conflict is not the settlements. The settlements are a result of the conflict.

The settlements [are] an issue that has to be addressed and resolved in the course of negotiations. But the core of the conflict has always been and unfortunately remains the refusal of the Palestinians to recognize a Jewish state in any border.

Extract from a speech by Israeli prime minister Benjamin Netanyahu to the United Nations General Assembly in New York on 23 September 2011. Quoted in the Israeli newspaper Haaretz. *http://www.haaretz.com/news/diplomacy-defense/full-transcript-of-netanyahu-speech-at-un-general-assembly-1.386464*

In September 2011, the Palestinians made an attempt to further their pursuit of statehood. Mahmoud Abbas made a formal request to the UN, asking for the admission of Palestine as a full member. He received a standing ovation when he addressed the UN General Assembly in New York. His speech received wide publicity and support on the West Bank. However, in Gaza, Hamas rejected it. The group said that the Palestinians should not beg for a state from the UN, but should liberate it themselves. Later the same day, the Israeli prime minister, Benjamin Netanyahu, responded in a speech to the UN General Assembly (see Sources C and D on page 214).

Although the Palestinians received broad support in the 193-member General Assembly, the decision to grant full membership rested with the Security Council. US president Barack Obama made it clear that the United States backed the Israeli position – that the issue should be resolved by direct negotiations between the countries involved, rather than by the UN. Because of this, Obama stated that the USA would exercise its veto in the Security Council to turn down the Palestinian request.

American support for Israel was demonstrated once again in October 2011, when the USA, Israel and 12 other countries voted against Palestine's admission as a member of a UN agency, **UNESCO**. Despite this opposition, Palestine was admitted as a member by an overwhelming majority. To indicate its disapproval of the move, the United States announced that it would withhold American funding to UNESCO. This funding was worth about $80 million annually (about 22% of UNESCO's budget). The USA claimed that Palestine's admission as a member of international organisations would not lead to a peaceful resolution of the issue of Palestinian statehood.

> **UNESCO** The UN Educational, Scientific and Cultural Organisation has its headquarters in Paris. It aims to use education, science and culture to promote international co-operation, peace, justice and human rights. Its activities include programmes to promote literacy and gender equality, and to recognise and save World Heritage Sites.

Developments after 1979 have therefore further demonstrated some of the enormous complexities in solving the Arab–Israeli conflict. These include the opposing and seemingly irreconcilable viewpoints of the Israeli government and the Palestinians, disunity among the Palestinians themselves, and, above all, the critical role that the USA has in the success of any future peace agreement.

Young Palestinians throw stones at Israeli border police and soldiers during a 2011 protest against Jewish settlement in the occupied West Bank

Introduction

You have now completed your study of the main issues and events of the Arab–Israeli conflict between 1945 and 1979. In the previous chapters, you have had practice at answering some of the types of source-based questions that you will deal with in Paper 1. In this chapter, you will gain experience of tackling:

- the longer Paper 1 question, which requires you to use both sources and your own knowledge to write a mini-essay
- the essay questions you will meet in Paper 2.

Exam skills needed for IB History

This book is designed primarily to prepare both Standard and Higher Level students for the Paper 1 Arab–Israeli conflict topic (Prescribed Subject 1), by providing the necessary historical knowledge and understanding, as well as an awareness of the key historical debates. However, it will also help you prepare for Paper 2, by giving you the chance to practise writing essays. The skills you need for answering both Paper 1 and Paper 2 exam questions are explained in the following pages.

Paper 1 skills

This section of the book is designed to give you the skills and understanding to tackle Paper 1 questions. These are based on the comprehension, critical analysis and evaluation of different types of historical sources as evidence, along with the use of appropriate historical contextual knowledge.

For example, you will need to test sources for value and limitations (i.e. their reliability and utility, especially in view of their origins and purpose) – a skill essential for historians. A range of sources has been provided, including extracts from official documents, tables of statistics, memoirs and speeches, as well as visual sources such as photographs and cartoons.

In order to analyse and evaluate sources as historical evidence, you will need to ask the following **'W' questions** of historical sources:

- **Who** produced it? Were they in a position to know?
- **What** type of source is it? What is its nature – is it a primary or secondary source?
- **Where** and **when** was it produced? What was happening at the time?
- **Why** was it produced? Was its purpose to inform or to persuade? Is it an accurate attempt to record facts, or is it an example of propaganda?
- **Who** was the intended audience – decision-makers, or the general public?

You should then consider how the answers to these questions affect a source's value.

The example below shows you how to find the information, related to the 'W' questions, that you will need in order to evaluate sources for their value and limitations.

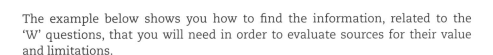

SOURCE A

The Canal was dug by Egypt's sons and 120,000 of them died while working. The Suez Canal Company in Paris is an imposter company ... Egypt ... announces that it will fight to the last drop of its blood ... for the sake of Egypt. We shall not let warmongers, imperialists, or those who trade in human beings dominate us. We shall depend on our hands and on our blood ... We shall build a strong and dignified Egypt, the Arab Egypt. Today, citizens, the Suez Canal Company has been nationalised ... Today our wealth has been restored to us.

An extract from a speech made by Gamal Abdel Nasser on 26 July 1956, announcing the nationalisation of the Suez Canal to a large crowd of his supporters in Alexandria.

speech WHAT? (type of source)
Gamal Abdel Nasser WHO? (produced it)
26 July 1956 WHEN? (date/time of production)
announcing the nationalisation of the Suez Canal WHY? (possible purpose)
large crowd of his supporters in Alexandria WHO?/ WHERE? (intended audience)

This approach will help you become familiar with interpreting, understanding, analysing and evaluating different types of historical sources. It will also aid you in synthesising critical analysis of sources with historical knowledge when constructing an explanation or analysis of some aspect or development of the past.

Remember – for Paper 1, as for Paper 2, you need to acquire, select and use relevant historical knowledge to explain causes and consequences, continuity and change. You also need to develop and show (where relevant) an awareness of historical debates and different interpretations.

Paper 1 contains four types of question:
1 Comprehension/understanding of a source (2 or 3 marks)
2 Cross-referencing/comparing or contrasting two sources (6 marks)
3 Assessing the value and limitations of two sources (6 marks)
4 Using and evaluating sources and knowledge to reach a judgement (8 marks)

Comprehension/understanding of a source

Comprehension questions require you to understand a source, and extract two or three relevant points that relate to the particular question.

Examiner's tips

Read the source and highlight/underline key points.

Write a concise answer. Just a couple of brief sentences are needed, giving the information necessary to show that you have understood the message of the source – but make sure you make three clear points for a 3-mark question and two clear points for a 2-mark question. If relevant, also try to make some brief overall comment about the source. Make it as easy as possible for the examiner to give you the marks by clearly distinguishing between the points.

Timing
For a 3-mark question, you should not spend more than about seven minutes. For a 2-mark question, you should take no more than about five minutes. Don't spend too long on these questions or you will run out of time!

217

Common mistakes

- Make sure you don't comment on the wrong source! Mistakes like this are made every year. Remember – every mark is important for your final grade.
- Don't just copy the source. Summarise the key points in your own words.

Simplified markscheme

For **each item of relevant/correct information** identified, award 1 mark – up to a **maximum of 2 or 3 marks**.

Cross-referencing/comparing or contrasting two sources

Cross-referencing questions require you to compare **and** contrast the information/content/nature of **two** sources, relating to a particular issue.

Examiner's tips

For cross-referencing questions, you need to provide an integrated comparison, rather than dealing with each source separately.

Step 1 – Read the sources and highlight/underline key points.

Step 2 – Draw a rough chart or diagram to show the **similarities** and the **differences** between the two sources. That way, you should ensure that you address both elements of the question.

Step 3 – Write your answer, making sure that you write an integrated comparison. For example, you should comment on how the two sources deal with one aspect, then go on to compare and contrast the sources on another aspect. Avoid simply describing/paraphrasing each source in turn – you need to make **clear and explicit** comparisons and contrasts, using precise details from the sources.

Common mistakes

- Don't just comment on **one** of the sources! Such an oversight happens every year – and will lose you 4 of the 6 marks available.
- Make sure you comment on the sources identified in the question – don't select one (or two) incorrect sources!
- Be careful to make **explicit** comparisons – do not fall into the trap of writing about the two sources separately, and leaving the similarities/differences implicit.

Simplified markscheme

Band		Marks
1	**Both** sources **linked**, with **detailed references** to the two sources, identifying **both** similarities **and** differences.	6
2	**Both** sources **linked**, with **detailed references** to the two sources, identifying **either** similarities **or** differences.	4–5
3	Comments on both sources, **but** treating each one **separately**.	3
4	Discusses/comments on just **one** source.	0–2

Examples of comprehension questions can be found at the end of Chapter 2, (see page 37), Chapter 3 (see page 64) and Chapter 7 (see page 177).

Examples of cross-referencing questions can be found at the end of chapters 4 and 8.

Assessing the value and limitations of two sources

Value and limitations (utility/reliability) questions require you to assess **two** sources over a range of possible issues/aspects – and to comment on their value to historians studying a particular event or period of history.

Examiner's tips

The main areas you need to consider in relation to the sources and the information/view they provide are:

- **origin** and **purpose**
- value and limitations

These areas need to be linked in your answer, showing how the value and limitations of each source to historians relates to the source's origin and purpose.

For example, a source might be useful because it is primary – the event depicted was witnessed by the person that produced the source. But was the person in a position to know? Is the view an untypical view of the event? What is its nature? Is it a private diary entry (therefore possibly more likely to be true), or is it a speech or piece of propaganda intended to persuade?

The value of a source may be limited by some aspects, but that doesn't mean it has no value at all. For example, it may be valuable as evidence of the types of propaganda put out at the time. Similarly, a secondary – or even a tertiary – source can have more value than some primary sources: for instance, because the author might be writing at a time when new evidence has become available.

For these questions, it is best to deal with each source separately, as you are not being asked to decide which source is more important/useful.

Step 1 – Read the sources and highlight/underline key points.

Step 2 – For **each source**, draw a rough chart or spider diagram to show the origin/purpose of the source, and how it links to that source's value/limitation.

Step 3 – Write your answer, remembering to deal with **all** the aspects required: **origins, purpose, value and limitations**. To do this, you will need to make **explicit** links between a source's origins/purpose **and** its value/limitations to an historian.

Common mistakes

- Don't just comment on **one** of the two sources! As with cross-referencing questions, every year a few students make this mistake, and lose up to 4 of the 6 marks available.
- Don't just comment on content and ignore the nature, origins and purpose of the sources.
- Don't say 'a source is/isn't useful because it's primary/secondary'.

origin The 'who, what, when and where?' questions.
purpose This means 'reasons, what the writer/creator was trying to achieve, who the intended audience was'.

Remember that a source doesn't have to be primary to be useful. Remember, too, that content isn't the only aspect to have possible value. The context, the person who produced it, and so on, can be important in offering an insight.

Simplified markscheme

Band		Marks
1	**Both** sources assessed, with **explicit consideration** of **BOTH** origins and purpose **AND** value and limitations.	5–6
2	**Both** sources assessed, but without consideration of **BOTH** origins and purpose **AND** value and limitations. **OR explicit consideration** of **BOTH** origins and purpose **AND** value and limitations – **BUT** only for **one** source.	3–4
3	**Limited** consideration/comments on origins and purpose **OR** value and limitations. Possibly only one/the wrong source(s) addressed.	0–2

Examples of value and limitations questions can be found at the end of Chapter 5 (see page 118) and Chapter 6 (see page 147).

Using and evaluating sources and knowledge to reach a judgement

The fourth type of Paper 1 is a judgement question. Judgement questions are a *synthesis of source evaluation and own knowledge*.

Examiner's tips

- This fourth type of Paper 1 question requires you to produce a mini-essay – with a clear/relevant argument – to address the question/statement given in the question. You should try to develop and present an argument and/or come to a balanced judgement by analysing and using these **five** sources **and** your own knowledge.

- Before you write your answer to this kind of question, you may find it useful to draw a rough chart to note what the sources show in relation to the question. This will also make sure you refer to all or at least most of the sources. Note, however, that some sources may hint at more than one factor/result. When using your own knowledge, make sure it is relevant to the question.

- Look carefully at the simplified markscheme opposite – this will help you focus on what you need to do to reach the top bands and so score the higher marks.

Common mistake

- Don't just deal with sources **or** your own knowledge! Every year, some candidates do this, and so limit themselves to – at best – only 5 out of the 8 marks available.

Simplified markscheme

Band		Marks
1	**Developed and balanced** analysis and comments using **BOTH** sources **AND** own knowledge. References to sources are precise; sources and detailed own knowledge are used together; where relevant, a judgement is made.	8
2	**Developed** analysis/comments using **BOTH** sources **AND** some detailed own knowledge; some clear references to sources. But sources and own knowledge not always **combined**.	6–7
3	**Some developed** analysis/comments, using the sources **OR** some relevant own knowledge.	4–5
4	**Limited/general** comments using sources **OR** own knowledge.	0–3

Student answers

The student answers below have brief examiner's comments in the margins, as well as a longer overall comment at the end. Those parts of the answers that make use of the sources are highlighted in green. Those parts that show the use of relevant own knowledge are **highlighted in red**. In this way, you should find it easier to follow why particular bands and marks were – or were not – awarded.

Question 1

Using Sources A, B, C, D and E on pages 221–22, **and** your own knowledge, analyse the view that the 1967 War aggravated the conflict between Israel and the Arab states.

[8 marks]

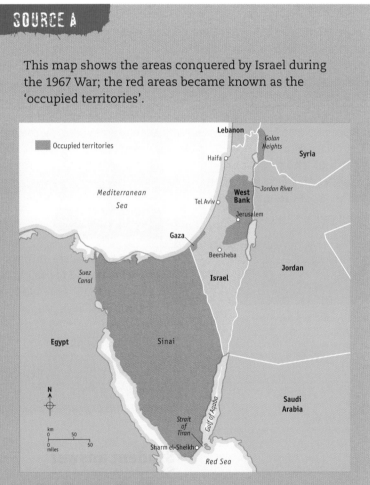

SOURCE A

This map shows the areas conquered by Israel during the 1967 War; the red areas became known as the 'occupied territories'.

SOURCE B

Israel had conquered 42,000 square miles [nearly 109,000 square km] and was now three and a half times its original size. Exceedingly vulnerable before the war, its major cities all within range of Arab guns, the Jewish state now threatened Damascus, Cairo, and Amman. Its own capital, Jerusalem, was united. Though ties had been severed with the Soviet Union and permanent strains left in its relations with France … Israel had earned the solid respect of the United States …

Moribund before the war, Israel's economy suddenly flourished as tourists and donations flooded the country, and oil was extracted from Sinai wells. Emigration all but ceased, and thousands of new immigrants hastened to partake of the glory.

Israel indeed basked in that glory as its press for weeks afterward praised the army's audacity, its ingenuity and power.

Oren, M. 2002. *Six Days of War: June 1967 and the Making of the Modern Middle East*. *New York, USA. Ballantyne Books. pp. 307–9.*

SOURCE C

The Arab heads of state have agreed to unite their political efforts on the international and diplomatic level to eliminate the effects of the aggression and to ensure the withdrawal of the aggressive Israeli forces from the Arab lands which have been occupied since the 5 June aggression. This will be done within the framework of the main principle to which the Arab states adhere, namely: no peace with Israel, no recognition of Israel, no negotiations with it, and adherence to the rights of the Palestinian people in their country.

Extract from the Khartoum Arab Summit Communiqué, 1 September 1967.

SOURCE D

In the immediate aftermath of the Six Day War, the Palestinian population behaved as if in a state of shock. It seemed amenable and cooperative to its new rulers, and there was a general feeling among Israelis that theirs was indeed an enlightened and benign occupation …

Whether occupiers could ever be respected, whether occupation could ever be benign, was a question seldom asked in Israel during the early days of occupation. But even in those early days there were those who asked it, and who were worried at the effect of occupation, both on the anger of the ruled, and the arrogance of the rulers.

Gilbert, M. 1998. Israel: A History. London, UK. Black Swan. pp. 397–98.

SOURCE E

Religious Zionists, impassioned nationalists and security specialists now all argued for a Greater Israel. All of a sudden, a besieged state now experienced the freedom of space, but the price was a fragmentation of its unity. Holding the territories now became the status quo. A stunning military victory had laid the foundations for the advance of the Israeli Right after decades in the political wilderness.

Shindler, C. 2008. A History of Modern Israel. Cambridge, UK. Cambridge University Press. p. 125.

Student answer

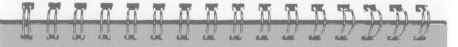

The 1967 War definitely made the conflict between Israel and the Arab states very much worse. Israel's occupation of so much Arab territory antagonised the Arab states, created anger among the Palestinians who were now under Israeli occupation, and encouraged religious Zionists and Israeli nationalists to demand the extension of settlements, which resulted in a greater potential for conflict.

Examiner's comment

This is a well-focused introduction. It shows clearly the line of argument that the student intends to follow in the answer.

During the 1967 War (also called the Six Day War), Israel defeated Egypt, Jordan and Syria. In the process, it took over large parts of Arab land, as Source A shows – Gaza and Sinai from Egypt, the West Bank from Jordan and the Golan Heights from Syria. This meant that Israel was very much larger than it had been before the war. It also meant that more than a million additional Palestinians were now under Israel's control.

Source B explains the significance of what is shown on the map. It is clear that the three Arab capitals were all much closer to the new borders of Israel, and that Israel was considerably larger than it had been. Source B also focuses on some of the positive results of the war for Israel, such as greater security, a booming economy, and more immigrants. However, the source does not comment on whether or not the war aggravated the conflict between Israel and the Arab states.

Examiner's comment
The student has missed an opportunity here to demonstrate an understanding of the issues that caused the conflict to intensify after the 1967 War – for example, the impact of Israel's overwhelming victory on the morale of the Arab states, and the existence of the Palestinians in the newly acquired territories.

223

After the war, the members of the Arab League met in Khartoum and condemned Israel for its continued occupation of the land it had occupied. They agreed that they would unite to oppose Israel's 'aggression' (Source C). They agreed that there would be no peace, no recognition of Israel and no negotiations with it, until Israel withdrew from these lands. They also declared their support for the rights of the Palestinian people. The Khartoum Declaration shows clearly that the attitude of the Arab states towards Israel hardened after the 1967 War.

Source D describes the Palestinians now under Israeli occupation as being initially 'amenable and cooperative' and in a 'state of shock'. However, the source also suggests that the long-term effect of the occupation would be anger. When it later became clear that Israel was not going to withdraw from the occupied territories, this anger spilled over into violence and uprisings against Israeli occupation.

Examiner's comment
Although there is some useful own knowledge here, the student has missed the opportunity to link these two sources and explain how the anger of the Palestinians (Source D) would aggravate the conflict between Israel and the Arab states (Source C).

A factor that definitely aggravated the conflict was the expansion of Israeli settlements into the newly occupied territory. *Source E explains that there were different reasons why many Israelis supported this expansion.* Some were religious Zionists who saw the occupied territories as part of the biblical kingdom of Judea and Samaria, some were nationalists who wanted a larger and stronger Israeli state, and some wanted secure borders against future attacks. *The source also states that the issue caused disunity in Israel, and that the right wing became more dominant after this.* This development helped to aggravate the conflict with the Arab states because the Israeli right wing did not want to hand back the occupied territories, or to negotiate with the Arab states, and they supported the building of settlements.

Examiner's comment
The student demonstrates a good understanding of the domestic significance of the shifts in Israeli politics.

It is clear from the information in these sources that the 1967 War aggravated the conflict. Israel's convincing victory made the Arab states more determined to fight back. The Palestinians in the occupied territories did not want to accept Israeli rule. The continued occupation of these territories, and the building of Jewish settlements there, added to the tensions.

Overall examiner's comments

There is a clear argument in the introduction, and the answer uses all the sources. There is some useful own knowledge. However, the student misses opportunities to link the sources. For example, Sj87ource B refers to the army's 'audacity, ingenuity and power' and Source E to the 'stunning military victory', and the political implications of this. In turn, a really good answer would question whether there is a link between both of these and the 'arrogance' referred to in Source D. In addition, a good answer would point out that none of these sources mentions one issue that aggravated the conflict after 1967: the radicalisation of Palestinian politics. Hence this answer fails to get into Band 1 – but this is a reasonably good Band 2 answer, and so probably scores 6 marks out of the 8 available.

Activity

Look again at the all sources, the simplified markscheme, and the student answer above. Now try to write a few paragraphs to push the answer up into Band 1, and so obtain the full 8 marks. As well as using all/most of the sources, and some precise own knowledge, try to link the sources rather than dealing with them separately.

Question 2

Using Sources A, B, C, D and E on pages 225–26 **and** your own knowledge, explain the impact of the competition between the superpowers during the Cold War on the Arab–Israeli conflict.

SOURCE A

After 1945, the Middle East became of vital concern to the super-powers because of its strategic position, its oil resources and the threat of the Arab–Israeli conflict to peace. Russia, with common frontiers with Turkey and Iran, renewed her traditional pressure on them and the USA replied with the Truman Doctrine, offering aid against the threat of Communist aggression. So the region became a theatre in the Cold War, yet without the clear-cut East-West division of the European scene; for the Arab states saw Israel as the greatest threat to their security and found little to choose between the USA and the USSR, both of whom had given immediate recognition to the new Jewish state.

Moreover, recent experience of British and French imperialism, which Britain vainly tried to continue through the Arab League, hardly encouraged newly independent Arab states to commit themselves to the neo-colonialism of the West. On the other hand, the atheistic Communism of the East did not attract Muslims.

Kohler, J. and Taylor, J. 1985. Africa and the Middle East. London, UK. Edward Arnold. p. 127.

SOURCE B

This cartoon is from the English satirical magazine, *Punch*, and appeared on 26 May 1948. Its title is 'The Adopted Child'. It shows Truman and Stalin with the baby Israel, shortly after the establishment of the new state in 1948.

THE ADOPTED CHILD

SOURCE C

The [Suez] crisis affirmed the [United States'] new status as the global superpower, challenged only by the Soviet Union. Suez was also to be the last incident in which America was to take strong action against Israel. As Eisenhower had feared, the Russians moved into the Middle East to fill the gap left by the disorderly retreat of the British, so the Americans felt compelled to get in as well. Thus the cold war spread to north Africa and Egypt (the Russians duly stepped in to finance the Aswan dam, and much else), and Israel became ever more closely tied to the United States.

'The Suez crisis: An affair to remember'. The Economist. 27 July 2006.

SOURCE D

Michael Oren examines the motives for the Soviet warning to Egypt in May 1967 that Israel was planning an attack on Syria.

The reasons for the Russians' warning would remain obscure, leaving room for a gamut of theories as to why they had tendered it at that particular juncture and what they sought to gain …

Lost in this conjecturing is the fact that there was little new in this Soviet warning to Sadat, that reports of intended Israeli aggression against Syria had been issued repeatedly over the past year. These admonitions, it was noted, reflected deep rifts in the Kremlin leadership and differing perceptions of Soviet interests in the Middle East – a middle road between avoiding all clashes in the region and plunging it into war. Fully expecting an Israeli retaliation against Syria, the Soviets were keen to prevent a battle that was liable to result in Arab defeat and superpower confrontation. Yet, at the same time, they wanted to maintain a heightened level of tension in the area, a reminder of the Arabs' need for Soviet aid.

Oren, M. 2002. Six Days of War: June 1967 and the Making of the Modern Middle East. New York, USA. Ballantyne Books. pp. 54–55.

SOURCE E

It was no coincidence that the Arab–Israeli phase of the conflict began at the dawn of the Cold War and ended soon after American president George H. W. Bush and Soviet president Mikhail Gorbachev pronounced the Cold War over. Although the Arab–Israeli conflict certainly played itself out according to its own internal logic, just as certainly the Cold War rivalry between the two superpowers played a significant role in driving and sustaining the conflict.

Beginning in 1948, when both the United States and the Soviet Union weighed the Cold War costs and benefits before granting recognition to Israel, the two superpowers never for a moment forgot the global implications of their policies in the region. For forty years, American policy makers approached or justified their intervention in the conflict in terms of containing the Soviet Union or rolling back its influence in the region …

For forty years, the Soviet Union exploited the conflict in an effort to break containment and gain a regional advantage over its antagonist, hoping that it might translate a regional advantage into a global one. Hence, for example, the Soviet Union deliberately escalated tensions on the eve of the 1967 war to energize an anti-Israel, pro-Soviet Arab alliance, and it restocked the arsenals of its allies in the aftermath of the war.

Gelvin, J. 2005. The Israel–Palestine Conflict: One Hundred Years of War. New York, USA. Cambridge University Press. pp. 229–30.

Student answer

There were several reasons for the competition between the superpowers in the Middle East. One was the region's strategic position, and another was its oil reserves. During the Cold War, the superpowers wanted to make sure that the other did not dominate the region, and so they both became involved by supplying weapons to their allies.

Examiner's comment

This introduction does not focus directly on the actual question, which is about the impact of the competition between the superpowers rather than the reasons for this competition.

According to Source A, the Middle East became a 'theatre in the Cold War' because the USA was concerned about the 'threat of communist aggression' in the region. So both superpowers wanted to extend their influence in the Middle East. However, the Arab states did not trust the West because of 'imperialism' and 'neocolonialism', and they did not trust the USSR because of its 'atheistic communism'. They were also suspicious because both superpowers had 'given immediate recognition' to the new state of Israel, which they saw as 'the greatest threat to their security'. The cartoon (Source B) shows the superpowers competing to impress the new state of Israel – the baby in the pram. Truman and Stalin were the leaders of the USA and USSR at the time.

Examiner's comment
The answer refers to Sources A and B and shows a link between them, which is good. However, the student needs to use some own knowledge to explain the context of concepts, such as 'imperialism', to which the source refers. The answer does not explain the cartoon fully – for example, it does not comment on its title, 'The Adopted Child'.

After the Suez Crisis, both superpowers became more fully involved in the Middle East, according to Source C. The USSR seized the opportunity to do so when Britain was forced to withdraw its forces after its ill-advised plotting with Israel and invasion of Egypt. The USSR provided aid to Egypt to complete the building of the Aswan Dam. It also provided weapons and military advisers. After the Suez Crisis, Israel became *'more closely tied'* to the USA, which supplied arms to Israel. In this way, the competition between the superpowers led to an arms race between Israel and the Arab states, and so had a negative impact on the Arab–Israeli conflict.

The Soviet warning to Egypt in May 1967 (referred to in Source D), that Israel was planning an attack on Syria, created more tension between Israel and the Arab states. *The USSR wanted to build up the tension in the region so that the Arab states would remember that they needed military aid from the USSR.* In this way, the competition between the superpowers definitely had a negative impact, as the increased tension was one of the reasons for the outbreak of the 1967 War.

Examiner's comment
The student uses Sources C and D, and shows an understanding of the Suez Crisis by supplying some useful own knowledge. However, there is room for some clearer explanation of the significance of the Soviet warning to Egypt – for example, by explaining the effect it had on Nasser, and how this in turn led to the crisis in June 1967.

As Source E explains, the competition between the superpowers played a big part in *'driving and sustaining'* the Arab–Israeli conflict. Throughout the Cold War, the USA justified getting involved in the Middle East by saying that it was *'containing'* Soviet influence. The USSR used the conflict to try to gain advantages for itself, and it *supplied weapons to the Arab states* after their defeat in the 1967 War.

Examiner's comment
The student has missed an opportunity here to link Source E to Source D, by explaining how the USSR 'deliberately escalated tensions' before the 1967 War.

227

Overall examiner's comments

The student has used information from the sources, including references and useful quotations. However, the answer lacks a clear argument throughout, and the sources are dealt with individually without reference to the obvious links between them. The answer does not include enough of the student's own knowledge to provide a clear and logical answer to the question, or to demonstrate a good understanding of the sources. The answer also lacks a concluding paragraph. For these reasons, the answer fails to get beyond Band 3, and would probably score 4 of the 8 marks available.

Activity

Look again at all the sources, the simplified markscheme, and the student answer above. Now try to write a few paragraphs to push the answer up into Band 1, and so obtain the full 8 marks. As well as using all/most of the sources, and some precise own knowledge, try to integrate the sources with your own knowledge and develop an argument that focuses on the question.

Question 3

Using Sources A, B, C, D and E, and your own knowledge, explain the reasons for the emergence of a radical form of nationalism among Palestinians in the diaspora.
[8 marks]

SOURCE A

The failure to achieve peace with the Arab world in 1949 left the refugees in a limbo between an Israel which did not want to readmit them and Arab states which did not wish to absorb them ... The stalemate left the refugees in an unenviable, parlous [dangerous] situation. Neither Israel nor the Arab states recognised the Palestinians as a national entity ... The refugees were marooned in a political no-man's land defined by the seemingly insurmountable hostility between Israel and the Arab states. ... In this political stand-off where neither return nor integration was offered, the Palestinians began to define themselves as a nation and not merely as part of a wider Arab world.

Shindler, C. 2008. A History of Modern Israel. Cambridge, UK. Cambridge University Press. pp. 51–53.

SOURCE B

Over time, the Palestine refugee camps everywhere acquired more permanent features, and came to resemble small Middle Eastern towns, each with its own market-place in the centre, coffee-houses and shops. And yet, as mini-cities, they were very small and severely overcrowded ... The camps lacked basic infrastructure in water, sewerage, housing, electricity or roads, and were the poorest dwellings in the entire Arab world. By the late 1950s, violence and despair were channelled into guerrilla activity, which recruited boys, and some girls, from an early age.

This process was part of the re-emergence of the Palestinian national movement. Two aspects need to be highlighted: one was highly political and active, in fact hyper-active; the other was social and cultural, a less visible but more measured process of at first disintegration and then cohesion. Main participants in the first were the members of the various Palestinian national organizations who, from sunrise to sunset, were busy inventing a new 'tradition' – the Palestinian guerrilla movement.

Pappe, I. 2006. A History of Modern Palestine (Second Edition). Cambridge, UK. Cambridge University Press. pp. 146–47.

A stamp from the United Arab Republic commemorating Palestine Day

SOURCE D

This new generation of Palestinian activists was rooted in a major change in the social basis of political power, which deeply influenced the politics of the subsequent decades. The entire stratum of leaders drawn from the notable [élite] class who had dominated Palestinian politics until 1948 had been swept away by the tidal wave of the nakba that had engulfed Palestinian society ... it meant the eclipse of the old political class and the rise of an entirely new generation of activists from new social strata, and with a different worldview, and entirely different solutions to the problems of Palestine and the Palestinian people ... This new generation operated in the condition of extreme dispersion and fragmentation that characterized Palestinian society after 1948 ...

It was the Palestinians of this new diaspora, in Cairo, Beirut, and Kuwait, who in the subsequent decades were to revive Palestinian identity and a Palestinian national movement on a new basis ... In time, they came up against the constraints placed on Palestinian activism by the Arab regimes, and had to decide how they related to the Arab governments that, since their first intervention in Palestinian politics in 1936, had played an ambiguous role at best, and often a negative one as far as the Palestinians were concerned.

Khalidi, R. 2006. The Iron Cage: The Story of the Palestinian Struggle for Statehood. *Oxford, UK. Oneworld Publications.* pp. 136–38.

SOURCE E

After the establishment of Israel ... most politically minded Palestinians had looked to Pan-Arabism as their most likely saviour, arguing that there was no way Israel would be able to resist the demands of a single mighty Arab state. Consequently, the majority had given Pan-Arabism priority over their own, Palestinian activism. The collapse of the Egypt-Syria-Iraq unification talks in 1963 shook this standpoint severely and the heavy Arab defeat in the Six Day War would finish it off completely ...

The 1967 War had helped the Palestinian cause by bringing together around 1 million Israeli, Gaza, Golan and West Bank Palestinians under the same administration ... the ironic consequence of Israeli military success was a greater sense of Palestinian cohesion and unity. This was fostered by Arafat's Fatah and the PLO which soon came to dominate. The war had finally revealed Pan-Arabism to be no more than a chimera [an illusion] born of a romantic reading of history. In its place Palestinians espoused Arafat's new, uncompromisingly aggressive and nationalistic leadership.

Ross, S. 2010. The Israeli-Palestinian Conflict. *London, UK. Hodder Education.* pp. 110 and 123.

Student answer

There were several reasons for the emergence of a radical form of nationalism among the Palestinians who went into exile in 1948. As Source A explains, a sense of national identity began to emerge among them when they were caught in a 'political no-man's land', because the Arab states did not assimilate them into their own populations and Israel would not allow them to return to their homes in what had been Palestine. Neither side recognised them as a 'national entity'. The ongoing state of hostility between Israel and the Arab states put them in a dangerous situation.

Examiner's comment

This is a clear introduction, but the student needs to use more own knowledge to explain the context and focus on the question before using the information in the sources.

Examiner's comment

There is no specific reference to Source B here, and the student does not use all the information available in the source. There is no focus on the question.

They ended up living in refugee camps in the surrounding Arab states, where conditions were very bad. As a result, many of them – especially young people – became bitter and desperate, and joined guerrilla movements.

The stamp (Source C) shows a Palestinian woman and child in a refugee camp, symbolised by the barbed wire. The woman's face shows a mixture of anger and determination. This links to the 'violence and despair' described in Source B. The map at the bottom of the stamp shows the whole of Palestine.

Examiner's comment

There is a good link demonstrated here between Sources C and B, but the answer should suggest what the map of Palestine is meant to symbolise.

Examiner's comment

Once again, the answer does not explain the context. The student has missed the opportunity to refer to the establishment of Fatah and the PLO.

Source D links to previous sources by referring to the dispersal of the Palestinian population in the Nakba (which is shown in the picture on the stamp). It also refers to the fact that Arab governments had often played a 'negative role' in Palestinian politics and had placed 'constraints on Palestinian activism'.

Examiner's comment

Here too the student has not shown the links between sources – in this case, Sources D and E – and their references to Arab governments and pan-Arabism, as opposed to Palestinian nationalism.

Source E refers to the impact of the 1967 War on the Palestinians, when Israel occupied vast areas such as the West Bank and Gaza. It explains that after this war, the Palestinians realised that the Arab governments were not going to help them, and instead they turned to their own organisations and leaders, such as Yasser Arafat.

It is clear from the information in these sources that the reasons for the emergence of a radical form of Palestinian nationalism were: the dispersal of the Palestinian refugees in 1948; the conditions in the refugee camps in which they found themselves, and the feeling of bitterness that this caused; the emergence of a sense of identity among them; their disillusion with Arab governments, and their decision to instead form their own nationalist organisations.

Examiner's comment
This is a good concluding paragraph that sums up the student's argument.

Overall examiner's comment

Although there is good use of information from some of the sources, there is too little evidence of the student's own knowledge. The answer lacks detail and depth, and tends to be superficial as well as too brief. There is a wealth of information in these sources which the student has not used. The student has also missed opportunities to link the sources. Above all, the answer does not develop an argument that focuses on the emergence of radical Palestinian nationalism. The answer would therefore gain 3–4 marks at most.

Activity

Look again at the all sources, the simplified markscheme, and the student answer above. Now try to add sufficient information to push the answer up into Band 1, and so gain the full 8 marks. Try to develop an answer to the question by using all/most of the information in the sources, and some precise own knowledge, and try to link the sources rather than paraphrasing each one.

231

Paper 2 skills and questions

For Paper 2, you have to answer two essay questions from two of the five different topics offered. Very often, you will be asked to comment on two states from two *different* IB regions of the world. Although each question has a specific markscheme, you can refer to the general 'generic' markscheme (see page 233) to get a good general idea of what examiners are looking for in order to be able to put answers into the higher bands.

You will need to acquire reasonably precise historical knowledge in order to address issues such as cause and effect, or change and continuity, and to learn how to explain historical developments in a clear, coherent, well-supported and relevant way. You will also need to understand, and be able to refer to, aspects relating to historical debates and interpretations.

Make sure you read the questions carefully, and select your questions wisely. It is important to produce a rough essay plan for each of your essays before you start to write an answer. You may find it helpful to plan both your essays **before** you begin to write. That way, you will soon know whether you have enough own knowledge to answer them adequately.

Remember to keep your answers relevant and focused on the question. For example, don't go outside the dates mentioned in the question, or answer on individuals/states different from the ones identified in the question. Don't just describe the events or developments – sometimes, students just focus on one key word or individual, and then write down all they know about it. Instead, select your own knowledge carefully, and pin the relevant information to the key features raised by the question. Also, if the question asks for 'reasons' and 'results', or two different countries/leaders, make sure you deal with **all** the parts of the question. Otherwise, you will limit yourself to half marks at best.

Examiner's tips

For Paper 2 answers, examiners are looking for clear/precise analysis, a balanced argument linked to the question, and the use of good, precise and relevant own knowledge. In order to obtain the highest marks, you should be able to refer – where appropriate – to historical debate and/or different historical interpretations or historians' knowledge, making sure it is relevant to the question.

Common mistakes

- When answering Paper 2 questions, try to avoid simply describing what happened. A detailed narrative, with no explicit attempts to link the knowledge to the question, will only get you half marks at most.
- If the question asks you to select examples from **two** different regions, make sure you don't chose two states from the **same** region. Every year, some candidates do this, and so limit themselves to – at best – only 12 out of the 20 marks available.

Simplified markscheme

Band		Marks
1	Clear analysis/argument, with very specific and relevant own knowledge, consistently and explicitly linked to the question. A balanced answer, with references to historical debate/historians, where appropriate.	17–20
2	Relevant analysis/argument, mainly clearly focused on the question, and with relevant supporting own knowledge. Factors identified and explained, but not all aspects of the question fully developed or addressed.	11–16
3	**EITHER** shows reasonable relevant own knowledge, identifying some factors, with limited focus/explanation – but **mainly narrative** in approach, with question only implicitly addressed **OR** coherent analysis/argument, but limited relevant/precise supporting own.	8–10
4	**Some limited/relevant** own knowledge, but **not linked effectively** to the question.	6–7
5	**Short/general** answer, but with very **little accurate/relevant knowledge and limited understanding** of the question.	0–5

Student answers

Those parts of the student answer which follow will have brief examiner's comments in the margins, as well as a longer overall comment at the end. Those parts that are particularly strong and well-focused will be highlighted in red. Errors/confusions/loss of focus will be highlighted in blue. In this way, you should find it easier to follow why marks were – or were not – awarded.

Question

Explain the circumstances surrounding the flight of refugees from Palestine/Israel between 1947 and 1949, and critically examine the different views developed by historians to explain it.
[20 marks]

Skill

Analysis/argument/assessment

Examiner's tip

Look carefully at the wording of this question, which asks for two things – an explanation of the **circumstances** and an examination of the different **explanations** for it. Make sure that you address both issues.

Student answer

Between 1947 and 1949, about three quarters of a million Palestinians left their homes in Palestine/Israel and fled to surrounding Arab countries. This Nakba, or catastrophe, as they called it, started before and continued during the first Arab–Israeli war. There are different and conflicting views for the mass flight of Palestinian Arabs at this time.

Examiner's comment
This is a short, focused introduction that addresses both parts of the question.

The flight of refugees happened in stages. It started in 1947 when Palestine was still a British mandate. Many wealthier Palestinians who could afford to do so left to escape the violence between Arabs, Jews and British troops. They intended to return once the violence had ended. Then, when a full-scale civil war broke out in the last two months of the mandate, many more Palestinian Arabs began to flee. This happened when the Jewish army, the Haganah, attacked and occupied many Arab villages, especially those near Jerusalem. They also attacked and occupied the Arab areas of coastal cities such as Haifa, and the Arab parts of West Jerusalem. Hundreds of thousands of Arabs fled.

When the state of Israel was declared in May 1948, Arab armies invaded Israel and the first Arab–Israeli war began. During this war, the Israeli army gained control of about 78% of Palestine. Most of the Palestinians living there fled, leaving their homes and possessions. There were several reasons why the Israelis won the war. Their forces were better organised and they were very determined to win. The Arab armies were not united and their leaders did not co-operate with each other properly. During the war, many Arab villages were abandoned and destroyed. By the end of the war over 750,000 Palestinians had become refugees. Even after the war ended in 1949, the mass departure of refugees continued. They ended up living in camps run by the United Nations in countries such as Jordan, Lebanon and Egypt.

Examiner's comment
The answer explains clearly that the mass departure of refugees happened in distinct phases, which is good. However, the reasons for the Israeli victory in the war are not relevant.

234

As well as the conflicting explanations from the traditional Israeli and Arab points of view, other explanations have been suggested by a group of revisionist Israeli historians. They used new evidence from documents that were released by the Israeli government in the 1980s. These revisionist or 'new' historians challenged the views of traditional Zionist historians. One of the issues that they focused on in their research was to try to establish why the Palestinian refugees fled.

One of the first revisionist historians to write about this was Benny Morris. He claimed that the Zionists themselves were partly to blame, because they used violence to clear Arab villages. However, he concluded that there were several reasons for the mass flight, and that Israel was partly to blame but not fully responsible. Other revisionist historians, however, claimed that there was evidence of a deliberate policy of ethnic cleansing to get rid of the Palestinians. As evidence for this, they referred to 'Plan D'. This was a plan for the Haganah to secure the area that was the proposed Jewish state before the British forces left Palestine. Some revisionist historians state that in implementing Plan D, the Haganah expelled as many Palestinians as possible from the proposed Jewish state. Other historians claim that the aim of Plan D was really to protect the Jewish areas from attack by invading Arab armies, and not to drive the Palestinians out.

Examiner's comment
The student has explained the emergence of the revisionist Israeli historians well, but needs to mention more than one of them by name.

Some revisionist historians emphasise incidents like the massacre at the village at Deir Yassin as the reason for the Arabs' flight. They claim that incidents like this caused panic among the Arab population, especially when the Jewish forces broadcast information about it to terrorise the rest of the Arab population. Other Israeli historians are very critical of the new historians. They claim that they are painting a negative picture of Zionism by blaming it for the Palestinian refugee problem.

Examiner's comment
The statements in this paragraph are too vague. The student needs to explain these views more fully and clearly.

It is evident that there are many differing viewpoints about the circumstances surrounding the flight of the refugees and what exactly caused it. The issue of the Palestinian refugees is at the heart of the ongoing Arab–Israeli conflict, and so it is not surprising that it is a subject of controversy and fierce debate.

Examiner's comment
This conclusion is clear and to the point. However, as the essay question specifically refers to 'the views developed by different historians', the conclusion should include a short reference to these viewpoints.

Overall examiner's comments

This answer makes a clear attempt to answer both parts of the question – the circumstances surrounding the mass departure of the refugees, and the differing views about the reasons for it. The structure of the essay is sound. The student has also included a good explanation of the background to the emergence of new historical interpretations. However, to get into the top band the answer needs to be more precise about specific historians, and explain their views more clearly. The answer would probably get around 15–16 marks.

Activity

Look again at the simplified markscheme on page 233, and the student answer above. Now try to write a few extra paragraphs to push the answer up into Band 1, and so obtain the full 20 marks.

Further information

Sources and quotations in this book have been taken from the following publications.

Arnold, Guy. 2006. *Africa: A Modern History*. London, UK. Atlantic Books.

Begin, Menachem. 1979. *The Revolt*. London, UK. W. H. Allen.

Bickerton, Ian. and Klausner, Clara. 2001. *A Concise History of the Arab–Israeli Conflict*. (Fourth Edition). New Jersey, USA. Prentice Hall.

Browne, Harry. 1971. *Flashpoints: Suez and Sinai*. London, UK. Longman.

Gelvin, James A. 2007. *The Israel–Palestine Conflict: One Hundred Years of War*. (Second Edition). New York, USA. Cambridge University Press.

Gilbert, Martin. 1998. *Israel: A History*. London, UK. Black Swan.

Goldman, Nahum. 1969. *The Autobiography of Nahum Goldman: Sixty Years of a Jewish Life*. New York, USA. Holt, Rinehart and Winston.

Harms, Gregory. 2005. *The Palestine–Israel Conflict: A Basic Introduction*. London, UK. Pluto Press.

Hourani, Albert. 1991. *A History of the Arab Peoples*. London, UK. Faber and Faber.

Kallaway, Peter. (ed.). *History Alive*. Pietermaritzburg, South Africa. Shuter and Shooter.

Karsh, Efraim. 2000. *Fabricating Israeli History: The 'New Historians'*. (Second Revised Edition). London, UK. Frank Cass.

Keay, John. 2003. *Sowing the Wind: The Mismanagement of the Middle East 1900– 1960*. London, UK. John Murray.

Khalidi, Rashid. 2006. *The Iron Cage: The Story of the Palestinian Struggle for Statehood*. Oxford, UK. Oneworld.

Kohler, J. A. and Taylor, J. K. G. 1985. *Africa and the Middle East*. London, UK. Edward Arnold.

Laqueur, Walter and Rubin, Barry. 1995. *The Israel–Arab Reader*. New York, USA. Penguin.

Mazrui, Ali. (ed.). 2003. *General History of Africa: Volume 8: Africa since 1935*. Cape Town, South Africa. New Africa Education/ UNESCO.

Meredith, Martin. 2005. *The State of Africa: A History of Fifty Years of Independence*. Johannesburg, South Africa. Jonathan Ball Publishers.

Morris, Benny. 1988. *The Birth of the Palestinian Refugee Problem, 1947–1949*. Cambridge, UK. Cambridge University Press.

Morris, Benny. 1993. *Israel's Border Wars 1949–1956: Arab Infiltration, Israeli Retaliation, and the Countdown to the Suez War*. Oxford, UK. Clarendon Press.

Morris, Benny. 2001. *Righteous Victims: A History of the Zionist–Arab Conflict, 1881–2001*. New York, USA. Vintage Books.

Oren, Michael B. 2002. *Six Days of War: June 1967 and the Making of the Modern Middle East*. New York, USA. Ballantyne Books.

Ovendale, Ritchie. 1984. *The Origins of the Arab–Israeli Wars*. London, UK. Longman.

Pappe, Ilan. 2006. *The Ethnic Cleansing of Palestine*. Oxford, UK. Oneworld.

Pappe, Ilan. 2006. *A History of Modern Palestine*. (Second Edition). Cambridge, UK. Cambridge University Press.

Peoples Press Palestine Book Project. 1981. *Our Roots are Still Alive: The Story of the Palestinian People*. New York, USA. Institute for Independent Social Journalism.

Rea, Tony. and Wright, John. 1997. *The Arab–Israeli Conflict*. Oxford, UK. Oxford University Press.

Reich, Bernard. 2005. *A Brief History of Israel*. (Second Edition). New York, USA. Checkmark Books.

Rodinson, Maxime. 1973. *Israel: A Colonial-Settler State?* New York, USA. Monad Press.

Rose, Norman. 2009. *'A Senseless, Squalid War': Voices form Palestine 1945–1948*. London, UK. The Bodley Head.

Ross, Stewart. 2010. *The Israeli–Palestinian Conflict*. London, UK. Hodder Education.

Scott-Baumann, Michael. 2009. *Crisis in the Middle East: Israel and the Arab States 1945-2007*. London, UK. Hodder Education.

Schools Council History 13–16 Project. 1977. *Arab–Israeli Conflict*. Edinburgh, UK. Holmes McDougall.

Shlaim, Avi. 2000. *The Iron Wall: Israel and the Arab World*. London, UK. Penguin.

Shindler, Colin. 2007. *What Do Zionists Believe?* London, UK. Granta Books.

Shindler, Colin. 2008. *A History of Modern Israel*. Cambridge, UK. Cambridge University Press.

Tessler, Mark. 1994. *A History of the Israeli–Palestinian Conflict*. Bloomington, USA. Indiana University Press.

Turki, Fawaz. 1972. *The Disinherited: Journal of a Palestinian Exile*. New York, USA. Monthly Review Press.

Index

Index

Acknowledgements

The volume editor and publishers acknowledge the following sources of copyright material and are grateful for the permissions granted. While every effort has been made, it has not always been possible to identify the sources of all the material used, or to trace all copyright holders. If any omissions are brought to our notice we will be happy to include the appropriate acknowledgement on reprinting.

p115 and p225 © The Economist Newspaper Limited, London (23/04/2012); p118 Copyright Guardian News & Media Ltd 1956.

Picture Credits

Cover © Ricki Rosen/Corbis; p. 5 Topfoto / AP; p. 17 Getty Images; © Press Association Images; p. 22 Wikimedia; p. 23 Wikimedia; p. 26 Wikimedia; p. 27 Wikimedia; p. 29 Wikimedia/Cohen Fritz; p. 30 Library of Congress/American Colony (Jerusalem); p. 33 ©Press Association Images; p. 34 DoD Media; p. 39 © TopFoto; p.41 Library of Congress/Edmonston Studio; p. 42 Time & Life Pictures/Getty Images; p. 47 Topham / AP; p. 51 © Punch Limited/Leslie Illingworth; p. 52 (t) Library of Congress/Matson Photo Service; p. 52 (b) Wikimedia; p. 53 ©TopFoto; p. 66 © Bettmann/CORBIS; p. 71 © Hulton-Deutsch Collection/CORBIS; p. 72 DoD Media/Helene C. Stikkel; p. 77 © Hulton-Deutsch Collection/CORBIS; p. 80 Getty Images; p. 87 The Central Zionist Archives, Jerusalem; p. 94 Getty Images; p. 95 Library of Congress/ Road Shehata; p. 96 Wikimedia; p. 101 © Press Association Images; p. 103 Mary Evans/The National Archives, London. England; p. 105 National Archives/Richard Little; p. 107 Getty Images; p. 110 Mary Evans/Interfoto; p. 113 UN/DPI; p. 114 51 © Punch Limited/Leslie Illingworth; p. 125 Getty Images; p. 129 © Press Association Images; p. 133 Getty Images; p. 135 Wikimedia; p. 136 © Press Association Images; p. 138 World Economic Forum/Remy Steinegger; p. 139 © Bettmann/CORBIS; p. 142 © Bettmann/CORBIS; p. 142 (margin box) PFLP; p. 150 © Press Association Images; p. 154 LBJ Library/Yoichi R. Okamoto; p. 155 © TopFoto; p.156 (t) DoD Media/Msgt Denham; p. 156 (b) US Air Force/Sgt Robert G. Clambus; p. 160 © 2007 - 2012 Zapiro (All Rights Reserved); p. 160 (margin box) Wikimedia/Bengt Oberger; p. 164 Library of Congress; p. 165 John Lowe at Golowe›s Collector Stamps; p. 167 Library of Congress/Marion S. Trikosko; p. 168 Getty Images; p. 170 US Navy/ Jesse B. Awalt; p. 172 Gamma-Keystone via Getty Images; p. 173 Bundesarchiv/Ulrich Kohls; p. 180 Getty Images; p. 182 AFP/Getty Images; p. 184 © David Rubinger/CORBIS; p. 188 Topham/AP; p. 189 (t) DoD Media; p. 189 (b) Wikimedia; p. 192 Time & Life Pictures/Getty Images; p. 195 Copyright Guardian News & Media Ltd 1977; p. 199 © Bettmann/CORBIS; p. 201 Wikimedia; p. 205 Getty Images Europe; p. 209 Getty Images; p. 211 DoD Media/Helene C. Stikkel; p. 212 Getty Images; p. 212 (margin box) World Economic Forum; p. 215 © epa european pressphoto agency b.v./Alamy; p. 225 © Punch Limited/E H Shepard; p. 229 John Lowe at Golowe›s Collector Stamps.

Produced for Cambridge University Press by

 White-Thomson Publishing
+44 (0)843 208 7460
www.wtpub.co.uk

Series editor: Allan Todd
Development editor: Margaret Haynes
Reviewer: Ros Davis
Project editor: Alice Harman
Lead editor: Sonya Newland
Designer: Clare Nicholas
Picture researcher: Alice Harman
Illustrator: Stefan Chabluk